Attitudes Toward Handicapped Students:
Professional, Peer and Parent Reactions

SCHOOL PSYCHOLOGY

ATTITUDES TOWARD HANDICAPPED STUDENTS:
Professional, Peer and Parent Reactions

MARCIA D. HORNE
University of Oklahoma

LEA LAWRENCE ERLBAUM ASSOCIATES, PUBLISHERS
1985 Hillsdale, New Jersey   London

Lawrence Erlbaum Associates, Inc., Publishers
365 Broadway
Hillsdale, New Jersey 07642

Library of Congress Cataloging in Publication Data

Horne, Marcia D.
    Attitudes toward handicapped students.

    Includes bibliographies and indexes.
    1. Handicapped children—Education—United States—
Public opinion.   2. Public opinion—United States.
3. Mainstreaming in education—United States—Public
opinion.   4. Teachers—United States—Attitudes.
5. Students—United States—Attitudes.   6. Attitudes
change.   I. Title.   [DNLM: 1. Attitude.   2. Education,
Special.   3. Handicapped—psychology.   4. Interpersonal
Relations.   WS 105.5.H2 H815a]
LC4031.H66   1985   371.9′0973   85–6780
ISBN 0–89859–584–3

Printed in the United States of America
10   9   8   7   6   5   4   3   2

Contents

Preface

Many handicapped children are now being educated in regular classrooms in our public schools. Therefore, it is important that professionals not only be knowledgeable about prevailing attitudes of societal members toward handicapped students, but also that they become aware of procedures that may be used to measure and change attitudes. There is also a need to learn more about the development, measurement, and modification of attitudes. In line with these needs the major purposes of this book are to:

1. Summarize and interpret research and theory on professional, peer, and parental attitudes toward handicapped students; and,
2. to suggest topics for future research.

The first of eight chapters is a discussion of the concept of attitude, the attitude-behavior relationship, and representative theories of attitude. Chapter 2 considers the importance of attitudes, especially in regard to the effect of student-student interaction on the intellectual, social, and emotional development of the individual. Chapter 3 is a review of the assessment procedures used to measure the attitudes of professionals and peers that are described in Chapter 4. In Chapter 5 the factors that may influence the development and maintenance of attitudes toward handicapped students are considered and in Chapter 6 procedures which have been, or could be, used to modify professional and peer attitudes are described. In the next Chapter research related to parental and sibling attitudes is described as is the effect on the family constellation of having a handicapped child. Suggestions for future research and a discussion of mainstreaming appear in the final Chapter.

This text was written for teachers, administrators, psychologists, social workers, researchers and others who need information about attitudes toward the handicapped. Although it can serve as a professional reference, this book should be especially useful in courses which prepare professionals to work with handicapped people.

ACKNOWLEDGMENTS

A number of people have been helpful and supportive in the preparation of this manuscript. Special thanks go to Drs. Richard Wisniewski and Jack Parker (few Deans would be as understanding or encouraging), to my parents Marshall and Marianne and to Maggie Ryan for her assistance in typing and general preparation of the final draft.

For Marshall and Marianne

Attitudes Toward Handicapped Students:
Professional, Peer and Parent Reactions

1 The Concept of Attitude: Definition and Theory

The purpose of this chapter is to review the concept of attitude. After presenting some introductory information about the concept of attitude, the chapter overviews representative theories.

There are many theories of attitude; the ones included in this chapter were chosen because they were considered to have significantly impacted upon contemporary attitude theory and at the same time are representative of different theoretical perspectives.

INTRODUCTION TO ATTITUDES

This section opens with a presentation of different definitions of the concept of attitude which have been presented in the literature. This is followed by a discussion of components of an attitude, the relationships between attitudes and behavior, and the possible functions attitudes may serve.

Definition of Attitude

Many researchers have offered definitions of attitude. A sample of these illustrates similarities and differences in conceptualizations.

> An attitude is a mental and neural state of readiness, organized through experience, exerting a directive or dynamic influence upon the individual's response to all objects and situations with which it is related (Allport, 1935).
>
> A social attitude . . . may be defined as a set of evaluative categorizations formed toward an object or class of objects as the individual learns, in interaction

with others, about his environment including evaluations of other persons. Through attitude formation, the individual relates himself, psychologically, to these objects. His attitudes become constituent parts of his self (ego) system. By definition, therefore, attitudes have emotional and motivational aspects inseparably intertwined with cognitive content (Sherif, Sherif & Nebergall, 1965, p. 20).

An attitude is a tendency to act toward or against some environmental factor which becomes thereby a positive or negative value (Bogardus, 1931, p. 52).

An attitude is an idea charged with emotion which predisposes a class of actions to a particular class of social situations (Triandis, 1971, p. 2).

An attitude is:

1. an implicit response
2. which is both (a) anticipatory and (b) mediating in reference to patterns of overt responses,
3. which is evoked (a) by a variety of stimulus patterns (b) as a result of previous learning or of gradients of generalization and discrimination,
4. which is itself cue- and drive-producing,
5. and which is considered socially significant in the individual's society (Doob, 1967, p. 43).

The first two definitions refer to a readiness to respond to a situation; the second incorporates the notion that attitudes are a learned response with enduring qualities. The next two point out that an attitude results in positive or negative behavior. The final definition illustrates a behavioral definition of attitudes.

There are many other definitions in the literature because, ''. . . social psychologists have tried to make their definition of attitude both a definition and theory of the concept'' (Kiesler, Collins, & Miller, 1969,　p. 4). Each definition is tailored to the psychologist's theoretical construct. Despite these differences most researchers would agree that an attitude can be described as, ''. . . a learned predisposition to respond in a consistently favorable or unfavorable manner with respect to a given object'' (Fishbein & Ajzen, 1975, p. 6).

The Components of Attitude

Theorists (and implicitly their definitions) have consistently suggested that there are three components of attitudes: affect, cognition, and conation. The affective component has to do with feelings of liking or disliking about the attitude object. This component is most directly measured using physiological measures such as the galvanic skin response, pupil dilation, or heart rate; although attitude scales such as the Guttman Scales may also be employed (McGuire, 1969). Cognition refers to the knowledge or beliefs a person has about the attitude object. It is the ''stereotype'' a person has, for example, about the handicapped which would be reflected on an adjective checklist. Conation refers to the behavioral intentions or actions of a person toward an attitude object. According to McGuire, this component may be the most measureable of the three. Conation is usually measured with a paper and pencil test (a social distance scale) in which the person reports how he would behave (e.g., would marry, would live next door to). There is, however, a low correlation between what a person says he would do and his actual behavior.

All three components are highly related, and it has been argued that some attitudes consist primarily of only one or two of these. McGuire concluded that:

> . . . given the less than perfect state of our measuring procedures, the three components have proven to be so highly intercorrelated that theorists who insist on distinguishing them should bear the burden of proving that the distinction is worthwhile (p. 157).

Attitudes and Behavior

Allport (1935) was among the early theorists who assumed that attitudes predict overt behaviors, an assumption that has been a long-standing issue in the attitudinal literature (Ajzen & Fishbein, 1970, 1982; Calder & Ross, 1973; Wicker, 1969). But after carefully reviewing the literature, Cooper and Croyle (1984) suggested that this debate is over. The relationship has been substantiated: attitudes can be used to predict behavior. The research thrust is now directed toward answering "how" and "when" questions. How an attitude is formed (the process) may be an important variable. For instance, Regan and Fazio (1977) found that attitudes formed as a result of direct behavioral experiences are more likely to be maintained and are more predictive of subsequent behavior than are those based on indirect experiences. Prior exposure to an attitude object, as well as personal experience also may influence the relationship (Fazio, Powell, & Herr, 1983). Furthermore, personality factors, such as self-monitoring[1] may intervene in the attitude-behavior relationship (Snyder & Kendzierski, 1982). Low self-monitoring persons make behavioral choices based on knowledge about themselves; high self-monitors make choices based on situational information. Low self-monitors may evidence greater attitude-behavior consistency than may high self-monitors because of the basis upon which their choices are made. High self-monitors' behaviors are more likely to vary because their choices may change with the situation (Zanna, Olson, & Fazio, 1980). Situational variables may also influence the relationship between attitudes and behavior.

Functions of Attitudes

According to Triandis (1971), people develop attitudes because attitudes: (1) "help them understand the world around them, by organizing and simplifying

---

[1]See Snyder (1974, 1979) for a discussion of the self monitoring construct.

input"; (2) "protect self-esteem by making it possible for them to avoid unpleasant truths about themselves"; (3) "help them adjust in a complex world by making it more likely that they will react so as to maximize their rewards from the environment"; and (4) "allow them to express their fundamental values" (p. 4).

McGuire identified four possible functions of attitudes: (1) utilitarian (adaptive) functions; (2) economy (knowledge) functions; (3) expressive (self-realizing) functions; and, (4) the ego-defensive function. Attitudes may be utilitarian in that they may help a person achieve a future goal, but the attitude may also have social-adjustment value. Attitudes with social-adjustment value facilitate social relationships. McGuire reported an example of persons who professed hostile attitudes toward Jews because it helped them to be accepted into an anti-Semitic social environment. Such utilitarian attitudes can be modified by changing a person's relationships with important others, or by changing a person's perception about where others stand on an issue.

The economy or knowledge function of attitudes refers to giving:

> . . . a simplified and practical manual of appropriate behavior toward specific objects. In life, as in science, the raw phenomena are too rich to be grasped in all their individuality. We tend to group them into convenient categories and tease out useful generalities about relationships among these abstract categories. Such are the stereotypes and beliefs that constitute our attitudinal world. By their simplification and their relatively univocal implications for action in the face of an otherwise overpoweringly complex social universe, attitudes give us a needed feeling of competence to deal with present and future experiences (McGuire, 1969, p. 158).

From the perspective of the economy function, attitudes are based on environmental experiences and observations. McGuire pointed out that attitudes based on this function should be changeable as a result of providing new information to the subject but that attitudes "are not all that sensitive to new information" (p. 159).

Expressive or self-realizing functions involve emotional functions such as, ". . . an opportunity for a cathartic acting-out of inner tensions," (p. 159). A person may also adopt an attitude to justify his behavior. In the former case, attitudes might be changed by giving a person another way to express himself, or substituting other issues about which to hold attitudes. Where attitudes are used to justify behavior, attitudes may be changed by requiring a person to conform overtly with new norms. "The result is that the person's attitude is modified to justify the new overt behavior; the person thus internalizes the new norm" (pp. 159–160).

Ego-defensive functions of attitudes are those that ". . . help us deal with our inner conflicts." McGuire cites Adorno et al.'s (1950) report of the anti-Semite who is negative not because of any experience with Jews, ". . . but as a defense mechanism to facilitate the person's repression of his oedipal hostility to his father'' (p. 160). Attitudes that are the result of a person's inner needs ''. . . are likely to be impervious to change by conventional informational approaches'' but may be changed by ''. . . self-insight, catharsis or cognitive reorganization'' (p. 160).

McGuire pointed out that there may be more than his four functions of attitude, that his four may overlap, and that an attitude may serve multiple functions. Furthermore he stated that:

> It would be surprising if psychological predispositions so pervasive as are many of our attitudes did not come, in time, to subserve many functions in our psychological economy. Any program to change such many-functioned attitudes offers formidable problems. The difficulty of changing a person's basic beliefs, even through so elaborate and intense a procedure as psychotherapy, becomes understandable, as does the fact that procedures that are effective in changing some attitudes have little effect on others (p. 160).

THEORIES OF ATTITUDE FORMATION AND CHANGE

Many theories have been proposed to explain how attitudes are formed and changed (for summaries see Fishbein & Ajzen, 1975; Greenwald, Brock & Ostrom, 1968; Insko, 1967; and Kiesler, Collins and Miller, 1969). This section of the chapter presents an overview of selected theoretical positions.

Behavioral Theories

Many theories of attitude change represent the application of learning theories to the attitude domain. In essence, behavioral theorists consider attitudes a response to environmental stimuli. There are, however, differences in behavioral theories of attitude; for example, in terms of the way the process of learning an attitude is conceptualized and the conditions which are specified as being necessary for learning to occur. Some behavioral theories are based on principles of operant learning, but others apply the principles of classical conditioning (see theories developed by Bem, 1965; Doob, 1947; Lott & Lott, 1960; Staats & Staats, 1958; Weiss, 1962). It has been pointed out (Kiesler, Collins, & Miller, 1969) that behavioral theories are limited in terms of their contribution to the study of attitudes for three reasons:

> First, they employ a somewhat more restricted definition of attitude than other theories of attitude change. Second, their experiments are usually more contrived and further removed from the propaganda situations of real life than other theories

reviewed. Finally, the theory has been relatively unsuccessful in stimulating theory-testing experiments (p. 103).

The Yale Perspective. Hovland, Janis, & Kelley (1953) worked in the Yale Communication Research Program, and are often identified in attitudinal texts as the "Yale group." Their approach (the authors clearly state that they were not attempting to present a systematic theory) merits some discussion since the theory has its roots in Hull's (1943) learning theory and is illustrative of a behavioral approach to attitudes; furthermore, the approach has been described as " . . . one of the major forces shaping contemporary research and theory on attitude change (Kiesler, Collins, & Miller, 1969, p. 103).

According to Hovland et al. opinions are learned as a result of exposure to communications which elicit an "answer response."

> When exposed to the recommended opinion, a member of the audience is assumed to react with at least two distinct responses. He thinks of his own answer to the question, and also the answer suggested by the communicator. The first response results from the previously established verbal habit constituting the individual's original opinion; the second response is assumed to result from a general aspect of verbal behavior, namely, the acquired tendency to repeat to oneself communications to which one is attending. Hence, a major effect lies in stimulating the individual to think both of his original opinions and the new opinion recommended in the communication (p. 11).

Whether or not a person changes his opinion depends on the incentive offered in the communication; a person will change his/her opinion if it is in some way personally rewarding or if he/she thinks the conclusion is "rational" or "logical."

The degree to which a person is persuaded to change his opinion depends on his: (1) attending to the communication; (2) understanding the content; (3) accepting the message; (4) retaining the new opinion; and (5) acting in accordance with the new opinion. Hovland et al. stressed the importance of motivational factors that influence accepting the message. They indicated that several variables may influence whether or not a person develops a new attitudinal response: (1) the source of the communication (e.g. the degree of creditability); (2) the setting in which the person receives the communication, including, for example, the response of other listeners of the communication; and (3) the nature of the content of the communication such as its strength or appeal. Factors about individuals may also influence their acceptance of the message. These include their personality factors, initial attitudes, and amount of ego involvement in the topic.

According to Kiesler, Collins, and Miller (1969), Hovland et al.'s approach to the study of attitudes, "probably stimulated more good research on attitude change than any other orientation. . . . But the lack of a more dominant theoretical orientation has, for some psychologists, left the work bereft of elegance'' (p. 118).

Consistency Theories

Consistency theories, which emerged in the 1950s, were proposed under different names such as balance theory, congruity theory, or symmetry theory. The theories differed in the way they defined consistency, the assumptions made and in the behavioral realms to which predictions were applied. But as McGuire (1966) pointed out, the theories:

> . . . had in common the notion that the person tends to behave in ways that minimize the internal inconsistency among his interpersonal relations, among his interpersonal cognitions, or among his beliefs, feelings and actions (p. 1).

Consistency theories stress the need of individuals to maintain balance or consistency, but different consistency theories have different emphases (Kiesler, Collins, & Miller, 1969). Some stress the need for individuals to be ''personally consistent.'' Others focus on the consistency between attitudes, between behaviors and among attitudes and behaviors. Yet others emphasize the need for consistency in perceptions about the world. Most balance theories assume that unbalance produces ''psychological tension'' that the individual can reduce by ''re-arranging'' his psychological world. Examples of the need for consistency are the Democrat who does not vote for Republicans, or an atheist who does not go to church.

Heider (1946, 1958) formulated the original consistency theory that has served as the prototype for the development of other models. See Feldman (1966) and Kiesler, Collins, and Miller (1969) for a discussion of other consistency theories.

Heider proposed that there are two types of relationships between people and events: (1) sentiment relations, which are how a person feels about or evaluates a person or object; and (2) unit relations, which refer to the perceptions a person has about the unity of persons, events, or objects. Heider described unit formation as:

> . . . separate entities [that] comprise a unit when they are perceived as belonging together. For example, members of a family are seen as a unit; a person and his deed belong together (p. 176).

Balance is achieved when ''. . . the perceived units and the expressed sentiments co-exist without stress; there is thus no pressure toward change, either in the cognitive organization or in the sentiment'' (p. 176). Heider used a set of symbols to describe the relationship between the perceiver (p), another person (o), and some object (x). According to Heider, balance is achieved when there is a homogeneity of the sentiment relation between the three relationships (p likes o, p likes x and o likes x). Imbalance results for example when p likes o, p dislikes x and o likes x. Imbalance leaves the person, ". . . with a feeling of disturbance that becomes relieved only when change within the situation takes place in such a way that a state of balance is achieved" (p. 180).

Keisler, Collins, and Miller (1969) pointed out several problems with Heider's theory. They concluded:

1. It is very unclear when a unit relationship exists and when it does not.
2. . . . the liking relationship is unclear as well.
3. No distinction was originally made between the complement and the opposite of a relationship.
4. It is unclear precisely what will occur when a state of imbalance exists.
5. There is no provision for degree of balance.
6. The basic model pays little attention to the complexity of the individual case. . .
7. There is no provision for variation in intensity or extremeness of the relationship.
8. There is conceptual 'looseness' about what unbalance is exactly.
9. There is no attention paid to the evaluation of the objects and people involved in the relationship other than liking or disliking (p. 166–168).

Kiesler, Collins and Miller discussed each of these problems and concluded that:

> the model lacks much of the precision we have come to expect of a formal theory. Also, the model has not stimulated much research conceived with directly testing it as a theory, and this research, although sparse, has not supported the theory unequivocally . . . . The positive point, and perhaps the most important point, is that the theory has stimulated a great deal of thinking about cognition and cognitive consistency. In this sense, the model has been important to psychology and to the study of attitude change (p. 168).

Cognitive Dissonance Theory

One of the most controversial theories in social psychology is Festinger's (1957) theory of cognitive dissonance, a type of consistency theory, in which cognitions are defined as, "any knowledge, opinion, or belief about one's self or about one's behavior" (p. 3). Festinger's theory states that dissonance occurs when an individual holds two cognitions that are inconsistent with one another. There are four sources of dissonance (examples of each are provided):

1. Logical Inconsistency—Two cognitions are dissonant because the opposite of one is logically inconsistent; both cannot be "true". For example, dissonance may occur in an individual who believes that men and women are created equal, but also believes in the natural superiority of females.

2. Cultural Mores—Knowing that one's actions are in conflict with what is acceptable to a particular cultural group. Thus, dissonance would occur when an individual knows that eating with his fingers at a formal dinner party is not acceptable etiquette in our culture. In another culture eating with one's fingers might be appropriate and therefore would not arouse dissonance.

3. Inconsistency between one specific opinion and a more general opinion (by definition the one specific opinion is in conflict with a more general opinion). The life-long Democrat who votes Republican would be an example of this source of dissonance.

4. Past Experience—Knowing that an occurrence does not agree with what one knows "should be" based on prior knowledge. A person who is bitten by a bee, yet feels no pain would experience dissonance because he knows from past experience that a bee sting causes pain.

The theory assumes that dissonance results in psychological discomfort, which, in turn, motivates the individual to: (1) seek to reduce the dissonance or achieve consonance by adding or changing cognitions; and (2) avoid information or situations that might increase the dissonance.

Festinger discussed the implications of dissonance theory: (1) in situations of forced compliance; (2) for involuntary or voluntary exposure to new information; and (3) for the social group. And the theory has generated a large amount of empirical support.

Forced Compliance. In "forced compliance" situations there is a discrepancy between the person's public behavior and private beliefs. For example, a person may be faced with a situation in which behaving in a certain way would require acting in a manner that is contrary to his beliefs or attitudes. An individual can either comply or not; in either case dissonance may occur. Theoretically, the magnitude of the resulting dissonance will depend on the importance of the behavior or attitude and the nature of the reward for complying or punishment for noncompliance: (1) the more important the opinion, the greater the dissonance; and (2) the smaller the reward, the greater the dissonance for compliance.

Dissonance which results from forced compliance may be reduced in two ways. First, the individual may change a cognition related to his behavior. He could change, deny, or distort the behavior. Thus the over-eater, who knows that his being greatly overweight is unhealthy, could go on a diet; deny his behavior; or eat as much, but less often. Second, by "magnification" the person convinces himself that the rewards or punishments were so great that he had no choice but to comply.

Involuntary or Voluntary New Information.   Festinger pointed out that via the mass media or interpersonal interactions individuals involuntarily might be exposed to new information which may produce dissonance because it is obverse to their cognitions. In this case, dissonance can be reduced by denying the validity of the information, purposeful misperception of the information or changing one's opinion. Voluntary exposure to new information may result from a need to use this information, or it may represent an attempt to reduce dissonance. For example a person who enrolled in a college course may seek dissonance reducing information about the advantages of the course selected over another college course offering.

Social Group Support.   Festinger stated that a person's social group is both a major source of dissonance for an individual and also the major vehicle for reducing dissonance. Agreement with group members decreases dissonance, but disagreement increases dissonance. The amount of dissonance which results from group disagreements depends on the: (1) "testable physical reality" of the disagreement (a belief that glass is fragile is testable, but a belief in reincarnation is not); (2) the number of individuals in the group who may agree with the dissenter; (3) the relevance of the disagreeing person or the issue to the group; (4) the attractiveness (defined here as meaning cohesiveness "denoting the total of attractions that pull the members to, and keep them in, the group" [p. 180]) of the disagreeing person in terms of his importance in the group; and (5) the extent of the disagreement (if one person says "black" and the other says "white" the disagreement is greater and more dissonance producing than if the issue is more like "black" versus "dark grey"). Dissonance resulting from group disagreements can be reduced by: (1) the group changing their opinion to agree with the disagreeing person; (2) the disagreeing person changing his opinion to agree with the group; or (3) making the disagreeing person "noncomparable" to the group (by rejecting or derogating him).

Research.   There is an abundant amount of research related to dissonance theory. Often the theory has been tested using a forced compliance situation in which subjects write counterattitudinal essays.[2] In these experiments writing the essays is expected to cause dissonance; the subjects experience an attitude change which occurs to reduce this dissonance. Numerous studies have sup-

---

[2]Other formulations cannot be presented in this brief summary.

ported the effects (See Insko, 1967). Laboratory experiments suggest that dissonance may be reduced by behaviors that alter dissonance without a cognitive change occurring (Steele, Southwick, & Critchlow, 1981), and that the effect may be diminished by making subjects aware of their attitudes before (Snyder & Ebbesen, 1972) or after (Wixon & Laird, 1976) the counterattitudinal behavior. Other evidence suggests that dissonance reducing attitudinal changes may be the result of a need for positive self-regard rather than a need for cognitive consistency (Steele & Liu, 1983).

Based on his review of the literature on dissonance theory, Insko (1967) stated that ". . . overall conclusions about the implications of this research would be premature" (p. 284). This lack of implications may be due to a number of factors. For example, Aronson (1969) pointed out that individual differences contribute to the amount of dissonance that can be tolerated by a person. Therefore, it is difficult to determine whether an individual will attempt to reduce dissonance; and, if he does, how he will attempt to do so. According to Aronson:

1. People differ in their ability to tolerate dissonance. It seems reasonable to assume that some people are simply better than others at shrugging off dissonance; i.e., it may take a greater amount of dissonance to bring about dissonance-reducing behavior in some people than in others.

2. People probably differ in their preferred mode of dissonance reduction; e.g., some people may find it easier to derogate the source of a communication than to change their own opinion. Others may find the reverse situation easier.

3. What is dissonant for one person may be consonant for someone else; i.e., people may be so different that certain events are regarded as dissonant for some but not others (p. 26).

Although it is not clear how dissonance theory may apply to attitudes toward the handicapped, there is some indication that it should be examined as a possible means of modifying negative attitudes. Culbertson (1957) found that the use of counterattitudinal role playing reduced the highly negative attitudes of subjects toward blacks who, like the handicapped, are a minority group in our society.

Functional Theory

Functional theories of attitude change focus on the functions attitudes may serve (see Insko, 1967; Kiesler, Collins, and Miller, 1969; Triandis, 1971). Attitude change depends on the relationship between the characteristics of the individual and the information they receive about an attitude object. The functional theory formulated by Katz and his associates (Katz, 1960; Katz & Stotland, 1959; Sarnoff & Katz, 1954) proposes that attitudes serve four functions:

1. The instrumental, adjustive, or utilitarian function refers to the notion that individuals develop positive attitudes toward attitude objects which satisfy their needs and negative attitudes toward those that are not need responsive.

2. The ego-defensive or externalization function refers to the person's self-protective attempt against acknowledged basic truths about himself or the realities of his world.
3. The knowledge function satisfies a person's need to organize and understand his environment.
4. A value-expression function wherein a person gains satisfaction from expressing attitudes that correspond to personal values and the self-concept of the person.

Data supporting Katz el al's. theory of attitude change is lacking. In reviewing functional theory, Insko (1967) pointed out that:

The basic assumption . . . is that in order to know how to change attitudes you have to know what type of attitude you are trying to change. This assumption sounds so plausible that it is surprising that more theorists have not been attracted by it. Perhaps one of the difficulties lies in deciding just how attitudes should be classified. It is conceivable that future theorists might find factor analysis of some use in this respect, although from the present vantage point there does not seem to be any compelling reason for supposing that a factor analytic classification would be the most fruitful one. This, however, is an approach that conceivably might be of value'' (p. 344).

Insko also noted that Cattell (1957) has made some effort in this direction.

Information Integration Theory

According to information integration theory (Anderson, 1971; Fishbein & Ajzen, 1975), a person's attitude toward an object is the result of all of the information or beliefs he/she has about the object. The intent of these theorists is mathematically to explain how information is combined so that predictions can be made about attitude changes that may occur as a result of an attitude modification procedure. As a mathematical theory which views individuals as information processors, the theory assumes individuals assign weight (a person's affective evaluation of the information) to the information they have about an attitude object. Attitudes change when individuals are provided with new information. It is not clear, however, how this information is combined or whether individuals add up all their information (Anderson, 1971) or average it (Fishbein & Ajzen, 1975).

SUMMARY

There are many definitions of attitude because these definitions have emerged out of different theoretical orientations. The issue of attitude formulation and change is complex; attitudes may consist of different components and serve different functions for different persons. Theory "is a set of interrelated constructs (concepts), definitions and propositions that present a systematic view of phenomena by specifying relations among variables, with the purpose of explaining and predicting phenomena" (Kerlinger, 1973, p. 9). Unfortunately, as Insko (1967) pointed out after reviewing different theories, "the field of attitude change is a long way from having any one theory that is a serious contender as a respectable general theory" (p. 348). And as a result of their critical review of various theoretical orientations, Kiesler, Collins and Miller concluded:

> . . . for the most part theorizing in this area is still at a relatively low level: assumptions made are not explicit; relations between theoretical constructs are not spelled out; and the details necessary for precise predictions are often missing (p. 343).

REFERENCES

Adorno, T. W., Frenkel-Brunswick, E., Levinson, D. J., & Sanford, R. N. (1950). *The authoritarian personality*. New York: Harper.

Ajzen, I., & Fishbein, M. (1970). The prediction of behavior from attitudinal and normative variables. *Journal of Experimental Social Psychology, 6*, 466–487.

Ajzen, I., & Fishbein, M. (1982). Attitude-behavior relations: A theoretical analysis and review of empirical research. *Psychological Bulletin, 84*, 888–918.

Allport, G. W. (1935). Attitudes. In C. Murchison (Ed.), *Handbook of Social Psychology*. Worcester, MA: Clark University Press.

Anderson, N. H. (1971). Integration theory and attitude change. *Psychological Review, 78*, 171–206.

Aronson, E. (1969). The theory of cognitive dissonance: A current perspective. *Advances in Experimental Social Psychology, 4*, 1–34.

Bem, D. J. (1965). An experimental analysis of self-persuasion. *Journal of Experimental Social Psychology, 1*, 199–218.

Bogardus, E. S. (1931). *Fundamentals of social psychology* (2nd ed.). New York: Century.

Calder, B. J., & Ross, M. (1973). *Attitudes and behavior*. New York: General Learning Press.

Cattell, R. (1957). *Personality and motivation structure and measurement*. New York: Harcourt, Brace & World.

Cooper, J., & Croyle, R. T. (1984). Attitudes and attitude change. In M. R. Rosenzweig & L. W. Porter (Eds.), *Annual Review of Psychology*. Palo Alto, CA: Annual Reviews Inc.

Culbertson, F. (1957). Modification of an emotionally held attitude through role playing. *Journal of Abnormal Social Psychology, 54*, 230–233.

Doob, L. W. (1947). The behavior of attitudes. *Psychological Review, 54*, 135–156.

Doob, L. W. (1967). The behavior of attitudes. In M. Fishbein (Ed.), *Readings in attitude theory and measurement*. New York: Wiley.

Fazio, R. H., Powell, M. C., & Herr, P. M. (1983). Toward a process model of the attitude behavior relationship: Accessing one's attitude upon mere observations of the attitude object. *Journal of Personality and Social Psychology, 44*, 724–735.

Feldman, S. (Ed.). (1966). *Cognitive consistency: Motivational antecedents and behavioral consequents*. New York: Academic Press.

Festinger, L. (1957). *A theory of cognitive dissonance*. California: Stanford University Press.

Fishbein, M., & Ajzen, I. (1975). *Belief, attitude, intention and behavior: An introduction to theory and research*. Reading, MA: Addison-Wesley.

Greenwald, A. G., Brock, T. C., & Ostrom, T. M. (Eds.) (1968). *Psychological foundations of attitudes.* New York: Academic Press.

Heider, F. (1946). Attitudes and cognitive organization. *Journal of Psychology, 21,* 107–112.

Heider, F. (1958). *The psychology of interpersonal relations.* New York: Wiley.

Hovland, C. I., Janis, I. L., & Kelley, H. H. (1953). *Communication and persuasion.* New Haven, CT: Yale University Press.

Hull, C. L. (1943). *Principles of behavior.* New York: Appleton-Century.

Insko, C. A. (1967). *Theories of attitude change.* Englewood Cliffs, NJ: Prentice-Hall.

Katz, D. (1960). The functional approach to the study of attitudes. *Public Opinion Quarterly, 24,* 163–204.

Katz, D., & Stotland, E. (1959). A preliminary statement to a theory of attitude structure and change. In S. Koch (Ed.), *Psychology: A study of a science* (Vol. 3). New York: McGraw-Hill.

Kerlinger, F. N. (1973). *Foundations of behavioral research.* New York: Holt, Rinehart & Winston.

Kiesler, C. A., Collins, B. E., & Miller, N. (1969). *Attitude change: A critical analysis of theoretical approaches.* New York: Wiley.

Lott, B. E., & Lott, A. J. (1960). The formation of positive attitudes toward group members. *Journal of Abnormal and Social Psychology, 61,* 297–300.

McGuire, W. J. (1966). The current status of cognitive consistency theories. In S. Feldman (Ed.), *Cognitive consistency: Motivational antecedents and behavioral consequents.* New York: Academic Press.

McGuire, W. J. (1969). The nature of attitude and attitude change. In G. Lindzey & E. Aronson (Eds.), *The handbook of social psychology* (2nd ed.). Reading, MA: Addison-Wesley.

Regan, D. T., & Fazio, R. (1977). On the consistency between attitudes and behavior: Look to the method of attitude formation. *Journal of Experimental Social Psychology, 13,* 28–45.

Sarnoff, D., & Katz, D. (1954). The motivational bases of attitude change. *Journal of Abnormal and Social Psychology, 49,* 115–124.

Sherif, C. W., Sherif, M., & Nebergall, R. E. (1965). *Attitude and attitude change: The social judgment-involvement approach.* Philadelphia, PA: W. B. Saunders.

Snyder, M. (1974). The self-monitoring of expressive behavior. *Journal of Personality and Social Psychology, 30,* 526–537.

Snyder, M. (1979). Self-monitoring process. *Advances in Experimental Social Psychology, 12,* 85–128.

Snyder, M., & Ebbesen, E. B. (1972). Dissonance awareness: A test of dissonance theory versus self-perception theory. *Journal of Experimental Social Psychology, 8,* 502–517.

Snyder, M., & Kendzierski, D. (1982). Acting on one's attitudes: Procedures for linking attitude and behavior. *Journal of Experimental Social Psychology, 18,* 165–183.

Staats, A. W., & Staats, C. K. (1958). Attitudes established by classical conditioning. *Journal of Abnormal and Social Psychology, 57,* 37–40.

Steele, C. M., & Liu, T. J. (1983). Dissonance processes as self-affirmation. *Journal of Personality and Social Psychology, 45,* 5–19.

Steele, C. M., Southwick, L. L., & Critchlow, B. (1981). Dissonance and alcohol: Drinking your troubles away. *Journal of Personality and Social Psychology, 41,* 831–846.

Triandis, H. C. (1971). *Attitude and attitude change.* New York: Wiley.

Weiss, R. F. (1962). Persuasion and the acquisition of attitudes: Models from conditioning and selective learning. *Psychological Reports, 11,* 709–732.

Wicker, A. W. (1969). Attitudes versus actions: The relationship of verbal and overt behavioral responses to attitude objects. *Journal of Social Issues, 25,* 41–78.

Wixon, D. R., & Laird, J. D. (1976). Awareness and attitude change in the forced compliance paradigm: The importance of when. *Journal of Personality and Social Psychology, 34,* 376–384.

Zanna, M. P., Olson, J. M., & Fazio, R. H. (1980). Attitude-behavior consistency: An individual perspective. *Journal of Personality and Social Psychology, 38,* 432–440.

2

The Importance of Professional and Peer Attitudes Toward Handicapped Students

The attitudes handicapped students hold toward themselves can affect their social, psychological, and academic growth and ultimately their functioning in society. Those attitudes are greatly influenced by the attitudes and opinions others hold. Whereas, at one time, the attitudes of handicapped students were mainly influenced by the family and the few school personnel and peers with whom they interacted, the possible influence of others in the environment has now greatly increased. Many handicapped students who formerly received educational services in segregated settings are now placed for at least part of the school day in regular classrooms.

The purpose of this chapter is to review the research that has explored the effects of teacher and peer attitudes on handicapped students. First a brief historical overview of events leading up to legislation mandating that handicapped students be placed in the most normal or least restrictive setting possible is presented. This is followed by discussions of teacher and peer attitudes in the classroom setting, and the likelihood that the handicapped student will be assigned to a low status position. In the remainder of the chapter a review of the effects of social status on a student is presented.

BRIEF HISTORICAL OVERVIEW

Prior to 1700, handicapped individuals were sometimes neglected, abandoned, ignored, abused, or accepted; but there were no educational or training programs. The time between the 1800s and the 1940s was characterized by fluctuating periods of optimism and skepticism about the potential for education, training, and social integration of handicapped individuals. Following World War II, there was a renewed interest in the status of handicapped persons, and during this time research efforts, as well as state legislative provisions for special education services in the public schools, were accelerated.

Public Law 85-926 was passed in 1958 and provided funds for training leadership personnel to prepare teachers of the mentally retarded. An amendment to this law in 1963, PL 88-164, extended funding to train personnel in other areas of special education.

Legislation passed in the 1960s provided funding for programs for the handicapped, and in 1966 the Bureau of Education for the Handicapped was established within the federal Office of Education by Congress. The 1960s were also characterized by the development of public school programs for learning disabled and emotionally disturbed students.

During the early 1970s there were several legal decisions guaranteeing the mentally retarded the right to an education, regardless of the extent of their handicap (Parc vs. Commonwealth of Pennsylvania, 1971; Wyatt vs. Stickney, 1971; and Mills vs. Board of Education of the District of Columbia, 1972). Another case, Diana vs. State Board of Education (1970), addressed the assessment procedures used to place students in special education classes. The court ruled that scores obtained on tests that were culturally biased or not administered in the student's primary language could not be used as a basis for such placements. Discrimination against handicapped persons was prohibited by the Vocational Rehabilitation Act of 1973 (Section 504 of PL 93-112).

Public Law 94-142, the Education for All Handicapped Children Act, was enacted in 1975. The purpose of this legislation was to ensure that handicapped children 3 through 21, regardless of the nature and degree of their handicap, would have access to free and appropriate public education. Ysseldyke and Algozzine (1984) delineated the four major provisions of the legislation which are summarized below:

1. Protection in Evaluation Procedures Provisions - tests and other procedures used to evaluate a handicapped student's special needs cannot be discriminatory either racially or culturally. Trained personnel must select and administer evaluation materials in the child's native language or mode of communication of the child. The regulations for the evaluation procedures used with handicapped children were published in the *Federal Register* on August 23, 1977 (U. S. Office of Education, 1977). Summarily, these regulations require that a child receive a complete evaluation by a trained multidisciplinary team consisting of at least one teacher or specialist knowledgeable about the suspected disability, before placement in a special program. The child must be evaluated in all areas related to the handicap; the evaluation must address areas of educational need, not just intelligence; and the instruments used in the evaluation must have been validated for the specific purposes for which they are used.

2. Due Process Provisions - parents must give written permission before a handicapped child can be evaluated or placed in a special program. Parents also

have the right: to examine all relevant records on their child, to obtain an independent evaluation, and to a due process hearing to challenge the evaluation or placement of their child. In most states both parents and school personnel have the right to an appeal. A "surrogate parent" must be appointed to safeguard these rights when the parent or guardian of the child is not available, or when the child is a ward of the state.

3. Individualized Education Program (IEP) Provision—a written individualized education plan must be developed for a handicapped student receiving special education services. The IEP must include a statement about a child's present level of educational functioning, short and long-term performance goals, the specific types of special education or related services the handicapped child will receive, projected dates for the initiation and duration of services and the procedures which will be used to measure the child's progress. The IEP must be reviewed annually.

4. Least Restrictive Environment Provision—handicapped children must be educated with nonhandicapped students to the extent possible. Handicapped students can only be educated out of the normal classroom situation if, even when supplementary aids and/or services are provided, an adequate program, responsive to the individual needs of the child, cannot be achieved within the regular setting.

The latter provision has had the greatest impact both on professionals and peers in public schools. From the standpoint of the handicapped students, their educational experience is likely to be very different from what might have occurred prior to the legislation. Consequently, this provision is discussed in the following section.

The Mainstreaming Procedure

The concept of the least restrictive environment mandated by Public Law 94-142 requires that handicapped children be educated within regular classrooms or educational environments that are as close to normal as possible depending upon their individual needs. The term "mainstreaming" emerged among professionals to refer to this procedure. According to the legislation a minimum number of placement alternatives must be made available for handicapped students. These include, in addition to regular classrooms, special classes and special schools, home instruction, and instruction in hospitals and institutions. Children who cannot educationally profit from a regular classroom placement must receive services in an educational setting which is closest to normal; i.e., the regular classroom is preferable to the resource room, and the special class is preferable to an institutional placement.

Operationally, the legislation may result in mildly handicapped students spending the major portion of the school day within the regular classroom. They may also be provided with some individualized assistance from a special education teacher in a resource room. The amount of time for special education services will vary, of course, depending upon the needs of the handicapped child, but an hour daily of this type of support is not uncommon. The student may also receive instruction outside of the regular classroom from other subject matter specialists such as the reading teacher. Sometimes, special education consultants collaborate with classroom teachers to design a program tailored to meet the needs of the handicapped student in which case, the handicapped student may not need to be provided with services outside of the regular classroom.

Moderately handicapped children may be assigned primarily to a special classroom but mainstreamed into regular classes for as much time as possible. At times the child's deficiencies may limit his/her participation in the regular classroom to nonacademic subjects (e.g., art, music), and some physically handicapped students may not be able to participate in the regular physical education program.

Not all handicapped children can profit from mainstream experiences. Consequently, for these, the law requires that placement alternatives in addition to the regular and special classroom be made available.

ATTITUDES IN CLASSROOMS

Attitudes are likes and dislikes. Teachers and students form attitudes toward each other; these attitudes are reflected in classroom interactions, which, in turn, reinforce the self-attitudes of the pupils and the attitudes of others toward them. Henry (1957) maintained that elementary classrooms are ". . . one of the most powerful instruments for developing attitudes." According to Henry, the elementary classroom situation:

> . . . does not merely sustain attitudes that have been created in the home, but reinforces some, de-emphasizes others, and makes its own contribution. In this way it prepares the conditions for and contributes toward the ultimate organization of peer- and parent-directed attitudes into a dynamically interrelated attitudinal structure supportive of the culture (p. 117).

Some students gain the approval of both their teachers and peers; others are relegated to a lower status position within the classroom group. Popular students, those assigned high status by teachers and/or peers, will engage in more positive interactions. Less-liked students or those with a lower social status will experience fewer positive interactions. Such students might be ignored, neglected, or even actively rejected, thus experiencing many negative interactions.

What happens when a student is rejected? Lippitt and Gold (1959) talked about the "classroom social structure as a mental health problem." Their examination of the classroom from a perspective of the socially rejected student, the classroom group, and the teacher led them to conclude that each person makes a contribution to the "unhealthy situation." Rejected students contribute their behaviors of "hostility," "aggressiveness," or "withdrawing noncontribution" toward peers. Classmates tend to rapidly label and maintain an "evaluative consensus" toward a student, are lacking in skills of providing helpful or supportive feedback to rejected students, and lack group standards for the acceptance and support of deviant behavior. Teachers contribute to the mentally unhealthy situation by not focusing on developing positive classroom relationships, ignoring the use of group strategies designed to facilitate interpersonal interactions, and failing to model positive behaviors toward low status students.

Prejudice toward handicapped individuals, as Gellman (1959) pointed out, is well established in our society. According to Gellman, the "roots of prejudice" toward handicapped persons may be found in child rearing practices that encourage an early development of negative attitudes toward those who are handicapped. It is likely that by the time a child comes to school, he/she prefers to interact with nonhandicapped peers. These attitudes will be very difficult to change given the reinforcing effect of the classroom environment on societal values. The handicapped student in the regular classroom situation is therefore subject to both teacher and peer rejection.

ATTITUDES AND MAINSTREAMING

One of the reasons for mainstreaming handicapped students into the regular classroom is to facilitate positive interactions among handicapped and nonhandicapped pupils (Warren, 1979). The achievement of this goal is highly dependent on the attitudes of professionals and peers toward handicapped students, and attitudes are often influenced by contact with such children. Yet many professionals, including administrators, school psychologists, as well as classroom teachers, have had very little contact with handicapped students, let alone training or coursework in the area of special education. Likewise, nonhandicapped classroom students may have had little, if any contact with handicapped pupils. There is abundant evidence (see Chapter 4) that both classroom teachers and peers may reject a handicapped student in their classroom.

It seems that the significance of the attitudinal issue is becoming recognized. Goodspeed and Celotta (1982) studied the perceptions of college of education faculty and classroom teachers about the competencies necessary for teachers to have if mainstreaming was to succeed. Findings indicated that out of 11 categories, attitudes were ranked fourth in importance by college professors and third by teachers. Both groups thought that teachers need to be familiar with: (1) the self-attitudes of handicapped students; (2) the attitudes of teachers, parents, and peers toward handicapped students; and (3) procedures to implement attitude modification. They also felt that teachers should be able to measure attitudinal changes. Another significant barrier to successful mainstreaming is parents of nonhandicapped children who are concerned about the potentially harmful effects of having their child educated with handicapped children. "They fear their child may be slowed educationally, that he will 'catch' retardation if not a spinal deformity" (Orelove, 1978, p. 700).

THE NATURE OF CLASSROOM SOCIAL STATUS

A pupil's social status influences his interactions with peers and school personnel, and vice versa. Social status is also related to academic achievement, personal adjustment, and interpersonal skills. Johnson (1981) referred to student-student interaction as "the neglected variable in education" and stressed the effects of peer relationships on educational aspirations and achievement, social competency, acquisition of values and future psychological adjustment. Johnson and Johnson (1980) further noted that, "In order for peer relationships to be constructive influences . . . they must promote feelings of belonging, acceptance, support, and caring, as opposed to feelings of rejection, abandonment, and alienation" (p. 91). And, Richey and Richey (1980) discussed the importance of having a best friend in adolescence:

> . . . it is apparent that the best friend is a more or less constant companion, a confidant with whom one can share very private information, a critic/advisor whose counsel is acceptable, a standard against which to measure one's self, an ego support whose affection and respect for one are known and reliable, an understanding ally, and a moral support in times of emotional crisis. Their quarrels give them practice in self-restraint and afterwards lessons in reconciliation. Obviously, these are important functions in anyone's emotional maturation (p. 537).

Unfortunately, handicapped students are likely to be rejected by their peers and their assignment to a lower social status position may influence their development.

Social Status and School Achievement.   A student's social status may influence school achievement (Glick, 1969; Yellott, Liem, & Cowen, 1969). Ide et al. (1981) analyzed 10 studies at the elementary and junior high school level and concluded that peers influence both the aspirations and achievement of students. A relationship between peer rejection and students' failure to actualize their learning potential has been shown in other studies (Epperson, 1963; Schmuck, 1963). And, rejected high school students are more likely to drop out of school (Barclay, 1966; Ullmann, 1957).

Social Status and Adjustment.   Social status may influence the psychological adjustment of students. Relationships have been demonstrated between social status and mental health in adulthood (Cowen et al., 1973; Kohn & Clausen, 1955; Rolf, 1976), suicide (Stengle, 1971), and delinquency (Roff, Sells & Golden, 1972). One study (Kuhlen & Bretsch, 1947) showed rejected adolescents reported having more personal problems (e.g., being unhappy, getting tired easily, having their feelings hurt too easily, never feeling well) than accepted students, and that there were differences in the problems related to social acceptance for males and females. Hansell (1981) demonstrated adolescent peer friendships are important for personality development. His finding also suggested that there may be gender differences with friendships being more important for personality development among females.

Social Status and Interpersonal Competence.   The amount of social interaction students have with peers will influence the extent to which they develop skills in social interaction (Newman & Doby, 1973). At the same time, students may develop inappropriate behaviors to cope with peer rejection (Kafer, 1982). And the coping behaviors may evoke responses from peers which will result in their maintaining these negative behaviors (Kohn, 1966).

Social Status and Teacher Attitudes.   Some research suggests there is a relationship between teacher and peer attitudes toward class members. Gronlund (1953) found that sixth graders and their teachers were largely in agreement about the most and least preferred students. Gronlund concluded that there are apparently aspects of a student's behavior that are important for acceptance by both teachers and peers. But it seems that teacher perceptions of students may dominate the attitudes classmates form toward one another. Hawkes (1971) reported that the sociometric choices of fifth and sixth graders were most closely related to the teacher's ratings of the social and academic adjustment of students; achievement, IQ, and student work habits did not emerge as important factors in the pattern of peer choices. Brown and Macdougall (1973) and Green et al. (1980) also found a significant relationship between peer and teacher acceptance of elementary students. According to Flanders and Havumaki (1960), positive interactions with the classroom teacher increase a student's status with peers; students praised by the teacher were chosen more often on a sociometric test by their classmates. And it has been shown that students are aware of the differential treatment high and low achievers may receive from classroom teachers (Silberman, 1969; Weinstein & Middlestadt, 1979; Weinstein et al., 1982).

Studies also have demonstrated the significant influence of teachers on peer attitudes toward handicapped students. Based on an experiment to test the effect teacher attitude statements may have on classmates, Gallagher (1969) concluded that peer attitudes toward children with speech defects will be: (1) most positive when the teacher does not express any attitude; (2) more positive if the teacher expresses a positive statement; (3) less positive when the teacher makes neutral statements; and (4) least positive when the teacher makes negative remarks. Gallagher's results support Rutherford's (1954) conclusion that speech-defective children are accepted by classmates to the degree that teachers accept them. In another experiment (Foley, 1979), peer acceptance ratings of children labeled "normal," "mentally retarded", or "emotionally disturbed" were significantly higher for all groups when teacher behaviors toward each group were depicted positively rather than negatively. Morrison, Forness and MacMillan (1983) explored the variables responsible for the assignment of social status to mildly handicapped students. They summarized the results for the path analysis:

> Observed behavior and measured achievement influence teacher ratings of cognition and behavior, which in turn influence student ratings of cognition and behavior. Given this pattern of influence, peer perceptions of behavior and teacher perceptions of cognitive competence then influence children's social status (pp. 70–71).

There seems to be ample evidence that teachers can influence the attitudes peers have toward handicapped peers; therefore, developing teacher awareness of their influence on student attitudes and interactions in the classroom is essential.

Social Status and Self-Attitudes.   Studies of nonhandicapped populations are in general agreement that children recognize their social status in the classroom (Epperson, 1963; Schmuck, 1963). Handicapped children may be similarly aware of their status, although there is some debate as to the ability of some handicapped children to make accurate assessments of their social status in the peer group. Peer social status may influence students' attitudes toward school, their confidence in their ability to learn, school related anxiety (Zeichner, 1978), and aggressive behavior in the classroom (Horne & Powers, 1983). There is also the probability that self-attitudes influence peer social status.

Stability of Social Status.   Studies of students' social status with peers across grade levels suggest that there is a marked degree of stability: students who are popular in the early grades tend to be among the popular students in later grades (Wertheimer, 1957). There is also evidence that mainstreamed handicapped students who are rejected by peers do not become more socially accepted even after two or three years (Bryan, 1976; Monroe & Howe, 1971).

Since social status is based on relatively stable student attributes, it may be hypothesized that teacher attitudes toward a student will be similar from year to year. Regardless of whether or not attitudes govern peer responses, handicapped students may continue to experience a low social status assignment throughout their school experience. Therefore it is not surprising that handicapped students have significantly more negative attitudes toward teachers, school in general, and toward academic subjects than do nonhandicapped students; and these attitudes may hinder learning (Guthery, 1971).

SUMMARY

Mainstreaming handicapped students into the regular classroom situation is a relatively new educational procedure. It is expected that teachers and students form positive and negative attitudes toward each other, but it is more likely that mainstreamed handicapped students will be assigned to a position of low social status. It appears that this assignment may effect their overall social, emotional, and intellectual development. Given the stability of social status assignments, it is realistic to suppose that many handicapped students will be subjected to a negative school experience unless the attitudes of peers and professionals are changed.

REFERENCES

Barclay, J. R. (1966). Interest patterns associated with social desirability. *Personnel and Guidance Journal, 45*, 56–61.

Brown, J. A., & Macdougall, M. A. (1973). Teacher consultation for improved feelings of self-adequacy in children. *Psychology in the Schools, 10*, 320–326.

Bryan, T. H. (1976). Peer popularity of learning disabled children: A replication. *Journal of Learning Disabilities, 9*, 307–311.

Cowen, E. L., Pederson, A., Babigian, H., Izzo, L. D., & Trost, M. A. (1973). Long-term follow-up of early detected vulnerable children. *Journal of Consulting and Clinical Psychology, 41*, 438–446.

Epperson, D. C. (1963). Some interpersonal and performance correlates of classroom alienation. *School Review, 71*, 360–376.

Flanders, N. A., & Havumaki, S. (1960). The effect of teacher-pupil contacts involving praise on the sociometric choices of students. *Journal of Educational Psychology, 51*, 65–68.

Foley, J. (1979). Effect of labeling and teacher behavior on children's attitudes. *American Journal of Mental Deficiency. 83*, 380–384.

Gallagher, B. (1969). Teachers' attitudes and the acceptability of children with speech defects. *The Elementary School Journal, 69*, 277–281.

Gellman, W. (1959). Roots of prejudice against the handicapped. *Journal of Rehabilitation, 25*, 4–6, 25.

Glick, O. (1969). Person-group relationships and the effect of group properties on academic achievement in the classroom. *Psychology in the Schools, 1*, 197–203.

Goodspeed, M. T., & Celotta, B. K. (1982). Professors' and teachers' views of competencies necessary for mainstreaming. *Psychology in the Schools, 19*, 402–407.

Green, K. D., Forehand, R., Beck, S. J., & Vosk, B. (1980). An assessment of the relationship among measures of children's social competence and children's academic achievement. *Child Development, 51*, 1149–1156.

Gronlund, N. E. (1953). Relationship between the sociometric status of pupils and teachers' preferences for or against having them in class. *Sociometry, 16,* 142–150.

Guthery, G. H. (1971). Differences in attitude of educationally handicapped, mentally retarded, and normal students. *Journal of Learning Disabilities, 4,* 330–332.

Hansell, S. (1981). Ego development and peer friendship networks. *Sociology of Education, 54,* 51–63.

Hawkes, T. H. (1971). Teacher expectations and friendship patterns in the elementary classroom. In M. L. Silberman (Ed.), *The experience of schooling.* New York: Holt, Rinehart & Winston.

Henry, J. (1957). Attitude organization in elementary classrooms. *American Journal of Orthopsychiatry, 27,* 117–133.

Horne, M. D., & Powers, J. E. (1983). Teachers' ratings of aggression and students' own perceived status. *Psychological Reports, 53,* 275–278.

Ide, J. K., Parkerson, J., Haertel, G. D., & Walberg, H. J. (1981). Peer group influence on educational outcomes: A quantitative synthesis. *Journal of Educational Psychology, 73,* 472–484.

Johnson, D. W. (1981). Student-student interaction: The neglected variable in education. *Educational Researcher, 10,* 5–10.

Johnson, D. W., & Johnson, R. T. (1980). Integrating handicapped students into the mainstream. *Exceptional Children, 47,* 90–98.

Kafer, N. F. (1982). Interpersonal strategies of unpopular children: Some implications for social skills training. *Psychology in the Schools, 19,* 255–259.

Kohn, M. (1966). The child as determinant of his peers' approach to him. *Journal of Genetic Psychology, 109,* 91–100.

Kohn, M., & Clausen, J. (1955). Social isolation and schizophrenia. *American Sociological Review, 20,* 265–273.

Kuhlen, R. G., & Bretsch, H. S. (1947). Sociometric status and personal problems of adolescents. *Sociometry, 10,* 122–132.

Lippitt, R., & Gold, M. (1959). Classroom social structure as a mental health problem. *Journal of Social Issues, 15,* 40–58.

Monroe, J. D., & Howe, C. E. (1971). The effects of integration and social class on the acceptance of retarded adolescents. *Education and Training of the Mentally Retarded, 6,* 20–24.

Morrison, G. M., Forness, S. R., & MacMillan, D. L. (1983). Influences on the sociometric ratings of mildly handicapped children: A path analysis. *Journal of Educational Psychology, 75,* 63–74.

Newman, H. G., & Doby, J. T. (1973). Correlates of social competence among trainable mentally retarded children. *American Journal of Mental Deficiency, 77,* 722–732.

Orelove, F. P. (1978). Administering education for the severely handicapped after P. L. 94–142. *Phi Delta Kappan, 59,* 699–702.

Richey, M. H., & Richey, H. W. (1980). The significance of best-friend relationships in adolescence. *Psychology in the Schools, 17,* 536–540.

Roff, M., Sells, B., & Golden, M. M. (1972). *Social adjustment and personality development in children.* Minneapolis, MN: University of Minnesota Press.

Rolf, J. E. (1976). Peer status and the directionality of symptomatic behavior: Prime social competence predictors of outcome for vulnerable children. *American Journal of Orthopsychiatry, 46,* 74–88.

Rutherford, D. R. (1954). *A sociometric study of children with speech deviations in third grade classrooms.* Unpublished masters thesis, University of Oklahoma.

Schmuck, R. (1963). Some relationships of peer liking patterns in the classroom to pupil attitudes and achievement. *School Review, 71,* 337–359.

Silberman, M. L. (1969). Behavioral expression of teachers' attitudes toward elementary school students. *Journal of Educational Psychology, 60,* 402–407.

Stengle, F. (1971). *Suicide and attempted suicide.* Middlesex, ENG: Penguin.

Ullmann, C. A. (1957). Teachers, peers, and tests as predictors of adjustment. *Journal of Educational Psychology, 48,* 257–267.

Warren, S. A. (1979). What is wrong with mainstreaming? A comment on a drastic change. *Mental Retardation, 17,* 301–303.

Weinstein, R. S., Marshall, H. H., Brattesani, K. A., & Middlestadt, S. E. (1982). Student perceptions of differential treatment in open and traditional classrooms. *Journal of Educational Psychology, 74,* 678–692.

Weinstein, R. S., & Middlestadt, S. E. (1979). Student perceptions of teacher interactions with male high and low achievers. *Journal of Educational Psychology, 71,* 421–431.

Wertheimer, R. R. (1957). Consistency of sociometric status position in male and female high school students. *Journal of Educational Psychology, 48,* 385–390.

Yellott, A. W., Liem, G. R., & Cowen, E. L. (1969). Relationships among measures of adjustment, sociometric status and achievement in third graders. *Psychology in the Schools, 6,* 315–321.

Ysseldyke, J. E., & Algozzine, B. (1984). *Introduction to special education.* Boston: Houghton Mifflin.

Zeichner, K. M. (1978). Group membership in the elementary school. *Journal of Educational Psychology, 70,* 554–564.

3 How Attitudes Toward Handicapped Students Are Measured*

There are many instruments that measure attitudes toward handicapped persons. Also, a variety of measurement techniques or procedures have been developed to measure attitudes toward a variety of attitude objects (e.g., religious concepts, political issues, occupational groups); these have also been used to develop instruments to measure attitudes toward handicapped persons. This chapter reviews a variety of attitude measurement techniques used in studies of professional, peer, and parental attitudes toward the handicapped.

Issues related to the technical qualities (e.g., reliability, validity, etc.) of the measurement procedures have not generally been raised since the intent was to present an overview of the available techniques. Furthermore, it was intended that by using examples and illustrations taken from attitudinal investigations, the reader would be helped to develop an awareness of the procedures which are typically used in investigations of the attitudes that professionals, peers, and parents may have toward the handicapped.

ATTITUDE SCALES

Three major types of attitude scales have been used to measure attitudes toward handicapped students: (1) summated rating scales; (2) equal-appearing interval scales; and (3) cumulative or Guttman scales. The most commonly used technique is the summated rating scale, followed by equal-appearing interval scales.

---

*Adapted from: Horne, M. D. *How attitudes are measured: A review of investigations of professional, peer, and parent attitudes toward handicapped children.* ERIC Clearinghouse on Tests, Measurement and Evaluation/Educational Testing Service, Princeton, New Jersey, 1981.

Although some studies have used Guttman methodology, this technique is probably used least frequently.

Before proceeding with a discussion of various attitude scales, some comment about the measurement characteristics of different types of scales is in order. Attitude scales may be nominal, ordinal, interval, or ratio in nature. Nominal scales allow only for classification of responses into two or more categories. For example, we may examine "yes" and "no" responses to questions about the categories "handicapped" and "nonhandicapped." Ordinal scales are measures that consider the ordering of responses. For instance, students may be asked to rank order the five pupils they like best in their classroom listing the person they like the very best first, the next best second, and so on. Such ordering, however, does not take into consideration the distance between the five responses which may be very unequal. That is, the distance (or degree of liking) between the first and second choice may be small, but there may be a much greater distance (or degree of liking) between the second and third choices. Interval scales are developed so that the actual distances (numerically) between the response choices or items are known, although it cannot be determined whether one point on the scale is twice as large as another because interval scales do not have a true zero. A ratio scale has a true zero and equal intervals. A more technical discussion of these measurement properties may be found in a basic measurement text. Attitude scales used in studies about attitudes toward handicapped population have used ordinal or interval type scales.

Likert-type Scales

One of the major types of attitude scales uses a method of summated ratings. Likert (1932) developed one type of summated rating scale which is ordinal in nature and used quite often in studies of attitudes toward the handicapped. When Likert's procedure is used, subjects are asked about the extent to which they agree or disagree with an attitude statement. For example, using a five-point scale, respondents would react to an attitude statement (e.g., Placing physically handicapped children in regular classrooms has a harmful effect on nonhandicapped classmates), by selecting from five choices as follows:

strongly agree	agree	uncertain	disagree	strongly disagree
(5)	(4)	(3)	(2)	(1)

Numerical values are assigned each choice (as indicated in the parentheses) and results for all of the hypothetical respondents are summed for the statement or summed and averaged to obtain an attitude score. The number of response alternatives may vary from two (e.g., agree, disagree) up to seven (e.g., strongly agree, agree, slightly agree, not sure, slightly disagree, disagree, strongly disagree). This is done at the discretion of the test developer, and usually reflects a consideration of the population for whom the scale is being developed. For instance, using more than two or three response choices with young children may confuse the children; but adult samples can discriminate among the seven response choices and the researcher will obtain results which more accurately reflect the respondents position toward the attitude statement. Researchers have also varied the response mode; rather than requiring a qualitative response mode, respondents provide a quantitative response (i.e., always, sometimes, seldom, never).

When Likert (1932) developed the method of summated ratings, a procedure whereby attitude statements were assigned a positive or negative value was also designed. In order to determine the positive or negative value of attitude statements, the investigator develops attitude statements and makes a judgment about whether the statements are positive or negative. Then the statements are administered to a sample of individuals and their responses recorded.

A group of high scorers (or those with positive attitudes) and a group of low scorers (or those with negative attitudes) are identified within this sample. These high and low groups serve as criterion groups for evaluating each of the attitude statements. A statistical procedure (the t test) is used to determine if a particular attitude statement differentiates between the high group (or those with positive attitudes) and the low group (or those with negative attitudes). Those statements which discriminate best are used in the final scale.

Unfortunately, most researchers purporting to use Likert scales have not adhered to these procedures in studies of attitudes toward handicapped individuals. Therefore their scales contain statements and response alternatives that only resemble those developed by Likert.

There are numerous examples of the use of Likert-type scales to measure educator attitudes toward exceptional groups (Berman & Fry, 1978; Carroll & Reppucci, 1978; Whiteman & Lukoff, 1964). For example, Efron and Efron (1967) designed a 70-item questionnaire to study teacher attitudes toward mentally retarded individuals. The teachers responded to each of the attitude statements using a six-point continuum (strongly agree, agree, not sure but probably agree, not sure but probably disagree, disagree, and strongly disagree) to respond to such items as "It would be kinder to establish separate communities for retardates where they would not feel so out of place" (p. 103).

Likert-type scales have also been used to measure adult community member attitudes (Gottlieb & Corman, 1975; Gottlieb & Siperstein, 1976), high school and elementary-aged student attitudes (Foley, 1979; Sheare, 1974) and parental attitudes (Gumz & Gubrium, 1972) toward handicapped groups.

Equal-Appearing Interval Scales

The original social distance scale which enabled an ordinal level of measurement of attitudes was developed by Bogardus (1925). According to Bogardus, the concept of "social distance" referred, ". . . to the degrees and grades of understanding and feelings that persons experience regarding each other" (p. 216). Bogardus developed seven statements to measure social distance toward various nationality groups. The statements, from most to least positive, asked respondents to indicate whether or not they would accept an individual from a nationality group: "to close kinship by marriage," "to my club as personal chums," "to my street as neighbors," "to employment in my occupation in my country," "to citizenship in my country," "as visitors only to my country," or "would exclude from my country."

Shortly thereafter, a method was developed for assigning specific scale values to items or statements representing different degrees of favorable attitudes along a psychological continuum ranging from positive to negative (Thurstone & Chave, 1929). When Thurstone and Chave's method is used, statements are created and then sorted by judges who indicate how positive or negative the item is. The procedure is quite time consuming, and a formula procedure for scaling suggested by Edwards (1957) is considerably easier to use.

Bogardus (1932) modified Thurstone and Chave's method to develop *A Social Distance Scale* which measured attitudes toward race, occupations, and religion. Sixty statements were developed and then rated by judges. The final scale consisted of seven equal-interval scale value items: (1) Would marry; (2) Would have as regular friends; (3) Would work beside in an office; (4) Would have several families in my neighborhood; (5) Would have merely as speaking acquaintances; (6) Would live outside my neighborhood; and (7) Would have live outside my country. Respondents selected one statement which best described their feelings toward each race, occupation, and religion.

More recently, Tringo (1970) developed the *Disability Social Distance Scale* based on the Bogardus (1925) scale. He selected some of the original items, added more negative statements and used Thurstone and Chave's sorting and scaling procedures to arrive at scale values for the group of attitude statements. The nine items and their scale values are shown in Table 3.1. The instrument was administered to subjects from various backgrounds (e.g., high school students, undergraduates in varied disciplines, undergraduate education majors, undergraduate physical therapy majors, graduate students and rehabilitation workers) to determine attitudes toward 21 disability groups.

The *Perception of Social Closeness Scale* (Horne, 1981) was developed, using Thurstone & Chave's procedure, to measure classroom social distance. It has the advantage of providing interval level measurement of pupil and teacher attitudes toward every other class member. The instrument has been used to measure peer and self status (Horne, Seidner & Harasymiw, 1978; Horne & Powers, 1983) and student attitudes toward disability and occupation groups (Harasymiw, Horne & Lewis, 1976a; Harasymiw, Horne & Lewis, 1976b; Harasymiw, Horne & Lewis, 1977). Table 3.2 contains the five-item scale and the interval values for the statements. There is also a seven item form.

TABLE 3.1
The Disability Social Distance Scale

Scale Value	Items
.33	Would marry
.57	Would accept as a close kin by marriage
.85	Would have as a next door neighbor
1.06	Would accept as a casual friend
1.21	Would accept as a fellow employee
2.95	Would keep away from
3.14	Would keep in an institution
3.65	Would send out of my country
4.69	Would put to death

From Tringo (1970). The hierarchy of preferance toward disability groups. *Journal of Special Education*, *4*, 295-306.

Social distance scales that are ordinal in nature and modeled after Bogardus' 1925 scale also have been devised and administered to children (Horne, 1978; Siperstein & Gottlieb, 1977; Westervelt & McKinney, 1980) and adults (Hollinger & Jones, 1970; Shears & Jensema, 1969).

The *Comfortable Interpersonal Distance Scale* (Duke & Nowicki, 1972) represents a visual approach to social distance measurement. This instrument requires that the respondent indicate on a diagram how close he would like to be to other people. It was used by Schaefer and Brown (1976) to measure the attitudes of young emotionally disturbed boys toward other students with different ethnic origins, who were all residing in a residential treatment center. The boys pointed to where they wanted a classmate to sit on a diagram of the classroom. Their attitude score toward another student was indicated by how far away from them they preferred a classmate sit (the possible range was 0 to 74 millimeters).

TABLE 3.2
Perception of Social Closeness Scale

Scale Value	Items
2.04	Would like to invite to my home
3.01	Would like to spend time with on the playground
4.74	Would like to spend time with once in a while
5.39	Would like to be more like other students
6.80	Would like to leave me alone

From Horne (1981). Assessment of classroom status: Using the perception of social closeness scale. (ERIC Document Reproduction Service No. ED 200 616).

Guttman Scales

Cumulative or Guttman scales (see Guttman, 1944, 1947, and 1950) consist of a series of statements which are thought to be unidimensional. In the case of attitude statements, this means that statements span a continuum of favorability from most positive to most negative. If the statements form a continuum, or are cumulative, it is possible to predict responses to individual items from a total or final score. A coefficient of reproducibility is computed to determine the degree to which individual patterns of scores may be reproduced from the total score; that is, the extent to which the ordering of the statements form an accurate continuum (coefficients greater than .9 are considered acceptable). It is important to understand that cumulative scales provide ordinal level measurement. The items may resemble those found, for example, in Tringo's (1970) previously discussed social distance scale, but the interval or psychological distance between the items is unknown.

An example of a Guttman scale is the social tolerance scale constructed by Yamamoto and Dizney (1967); it has the following continuum of tolerance levels: classmate, fellow organizational member, co-worker, roommate, date, marriage partner. Student teachers read descriptive paragraphs about unlabeled disturbed and normal individuals (i.e., paranoid schizophrenic, depressed neurotic, simple schizophrenic, phobic compulsive, normal healthy), and for each description indicated whether or not they would tolerate the person at each level. In this scale, a respondent who answered "yes" to "marriage partner" would be expected to answer "yes" to all preceding statements. Another who answered affirmatively to "roommate" but negatively to "date," would be expected to answer "yes" to classmate, fellow organizational member and co-worker (the levels below "roommate") and "no" to marriage partner (the level above "date"). The subject described in the first example would be assigned a higher tolerance score than would the second example. Not surprising were the results for this study indicating all types of individuals were significantly less tolerated than "normal healthy" persons.

This social tolerance scale was also used in an investigation (Yamamoto & Wiersma, 1967) exploring the relationship between self esteem (also measured using a Guttman scale), tolerance and attitudes toward the disabled. Contrary to expectations, higher self esteem was related to intolerance.

RANK ORDER SCALES

Frequently, investigators measure attitudes by asking respondents to rank-order items. For example, Barsch (1964) designed the *Handicapped Ranking Scale* to study parental attitudes about the severity of different disabilities. In this scale, ten handicapping conditions of childhood were listed and the parents were asked to rank the disabilities from one to ten in order of the degree of severity (i.e., from most severe to least severe). Similarly, in another study, undergraduate students' attitudes toward different disability groups were measured by requiring students to rank fifteen conditions "in the order of acceptability to you" (Abroms & Kodera, 1979).

Ranking procedures also have been used to study such things as perceptions about the need to provide services to handicapped students, preferences toward working with different handicapped groups (Orlansky, 1979), teacher knowledge about handicaps (Kvaraceus, 1956) and the perceptions of regular and special classroom teachers about the relative importance of different classroom goals (Fine, 1967).

Picture Ranking Procedures

Children's attitudes toward those with a handicap have sometimes been studied using pictures which are ranked. For example, Richardson, Goodman, Hastorf, and Dornbusch (1961) developed a series of drawings to investigate the attitudes of black, white, and Puerto Rican handicapped and non-handicapped children. Male and female drawings which were identical except for the gender depicted were prepared of a child who: (1) had no physical handicap; (2) used crutches and wore a brace on the left leg; (3) was sitting in a wheelchair with a blanket covering both legs; (4) had a hand missing; (5) had a facial disfigurement; and (6) was obese. Children responded to drawings of their own sex by ranking the depicted children from most to least preferred.

The drawings which Richardson et al. (1961) developed have subsequently been administered to adults and children in research about the cultural uniformity of attitudes (Chigier & Chigier, 1968; Goodman, Dornbusch, Richardson & Hastorf, 1963), in a study of the relative effect of race versus physical handicaps on student attitudes (Richardson & Royce, 1968), and an investigation of age relatedness of handicap preferences (Richardson, 1970).

The picture ranking procedure represents a good alternative for measuring young children's attitudes since children as young as two years can respond to pictures (Jones & Sisk, 1967). According to Chigier and Chigier (1968), the picture ranking test has several advantages: (1) the test is easy to administer to large groups in a short period of time; (2) the procedure overcomes language barrier problems and cultural factors related to dress and skin coloring; and (3) children enjoy the task. However, in one study (Matthews & Westie, 1966) a set of pictures similar to those first used by Richardson et al. (1961) and a seven-item social distance scale were administered. Findings suggested the social distance approach may be more valid when testing adults.

THE Q-SORT TECHNIQUE

The Q-sort technique is a more precise ranking procedure which requires that the subject sort a pile of cards containing words or statements according to some criterion. For example, respondents are asked to sort the statements (generally between 60 and 140 in number) into a specified number of piles (the number of statements per pile also may be specified) indicating the extent to which they agree or disagree with the statement. Since intra- and inter-individual comparisons of the way the cards are sorted may be undertaken by the researcher, Q-sorting represents an effective procedure to use in studies of attitude change where the effects may be quite minimal and vary from individual to individual.

Q methodology also has been discussed as a utilitarian approach to theory testing because factors or underlying ideas behind the ideas may be revealed. See Stephenson (1953, 1964) for a complete discussion of structured versus unstructured Q-sorts.

Q-sorting has been used very infrequently in research on attitudes toward handicapped persons. In one of the few studies (Schaver & Scheibe, 1967), Block's (1961) 70-item Q-sort procedure was used to study college students' attitudes toward mental illness, before and after volunteer work in a summer camp for the mentally ill. Results showed there were no significant differences. In another study, Stevens and Gardner (1982) developed a 50-statement Q-sort to study teacher attitudes toward hyperkinesis. As shown in Table 3.3 the statements considered symptoms/traits, etiology/constitution, and assessment/treatment. The teachers sorted the 50 cards into seven piles from "most-relevant-to-hyperkinesis" to "least-relevant-to-hyperkinesis." Results showed the teachers had different beliefs about the causes for hyperkinesis.

TABLE 3.3
Q Sort Statements

Common stem: Children who are thought to be Hyperkinetic...

Symptoms/Traits

tend to be restless.
tend to have a short attention span.
tend to be disruptive in the classroom.
tend to be impulsive.
tend to have exceptionally high energy level.
tend to be rowdy.
tend to have a low IQ.
tend to not be interested in education.
tend to lack persistence.
tend to be obnoxious.
tend to be naturally rambunctious.
tend to be excitable.

Etiology/Constitution

tend to be male.
tend to be from broken homes.
tend to be from large families (5 or more children).
tend to be from small families (1 or 2 children).

continued...

tend to be from lower socioeconomic status families.
tend to have mothers who are also thought to be hyperkinetic.
tend to be from middle socioeconomic status families.
tend to have diagnosed visual problems.
tend to have diagnosed auditory problems.
tend to be the youngest in the family.
tend to be the middle child in a family.
tend to be undernourished.
tend to have two working parents.
tend not to have a lot of clothes.
tend to live in poorer neighborhoods.
tend to have gone to a nursery school.
tend to suffer from too much parental discipline.
tend to come from a warm, loving, accepting home environment.
tend to watch too much television.
tend to eat junk food.
tend to have several siblings.
tend to have a neurological dysfunction.
tend to have a blood disorder.
could learn not to be hyperkinetic.
tend to need a good spanking.
tend to come from unstructured environments.
tend to have allergies.
tend to suffer from a developmental lag.
tend not to have experienced good medical care in their
    early years.

Common stem: Children who are thought to be Hyperkinetic...

Assessment/Treatment

are more difficult to help if treatment has not started before
    the child is nine years old.
tend to be recognized by their mothers as being a behavioral
    problem.
tend to be referred for evaluation by their teachers.
tend to be referred for evaluation by their mothers.
tend to be referred for evaluation once they have started
    kindergarten.
tend to be easily identified by age three.
tend to respond best to drug therapy.
tend to respond best to family counseling.

From Stevens and Gardner (1982). A study of attitudes toward hyperkinesis using Q methodology. *Behavioral Disorders, 8,* 9-18.

PAIRED COMPARISONS

In the paired comparisons method, all the persons or objects to be rated are paired with each other in all possible combinations. Respondents are asked to select the one from each pair they prefer on the basis of some criterion. The procedure results in a preference ranking, but scale values indicating the degree of acceptance or the actual psychological distances between the stimuli may also be computed. For a complete discussion of the computational procedures see Edwards (1957).

Perhaps the major problem with the paired comparisons method is that it is time consuming for the investigator and tiring for the respondent. If for example, 15 exceptionalities are compared, respondents must be presented with 105 comparisons or n(n-1) ÷ 2. Indeed, it may be the time factor which explains why the paired comparisons method has not been used in many studies of attitudes toward handicapped individuals.

A study by Jones, Gottfried, and Owens (1966) illustrates the use of the paired comparisons method to measure high school students' attitudes toward thirteen disability groups. One of the ten interpersonal situations shown in Table 3.4 preceded each pairing and subjects were required to circle which of the two disability groups they would accept in the given situation. Results showed the gifted and nonexceptional were preferred most.

TABLE 3.4
Social Distance-Type Interpersonal Situations

1. I would accept this person as close kin by marriage
2. I would accept this person as a neighbor
3. I would exclude this person from my country
4. I would accept this person in my fraternity, sorority or club
5. I would accept this person as a coworker in my occupation
6. I would accept a child of this type as a playmate for my children
7. This person is most in need of help
8. I would marry this person
9. I would accept this person as a visitor only to my country
10. I would invite this person to visit my home

From Jones, Gottfried, and Owens (1966). The social distance of the exceptional: A study at the high school level. *Exceptional Children, 32,* 551-556.

THE SEMANTIC DIFFERENTIAL TECHNIQUE

Osgood, Suci, and Tannenbaum (1957) designed the semantic differential procedure to measure affect associated with any attitude object. According to Osgood et al., there are many dimensions or factors of meaning associated with attitude, but the major ones are evaluation, potency, and activity. These factors may be represented using bipolar adjectives or scales. Evaluative object pairs, such as good-bad, clean-dirty, and nice-ugly, focus on goodness or value. Other adjectives represent potency, or the idea or meaning of the concept (e.g., large-small, strong-weak, or heavy-light), and finally some adjectives express activity (e.g., active-passive, fast-slow, and sharp-dull). Osgood et al. identified 50 adjective pairs, tested them, and provided their factor loadings on each of these dimensions.

Coefficients of test-retest reliability coefficients of .87, .83, .91 were reported in investigations of attitudes toward blacks, the church, and capital punishment. Validity studies of evaluative scales showed correlation coefficients of .74 to .82 with Thurstone scales and .78 with Guttman scales respectively (Osgood & Suci, 1955).

Perhaps because the semantic differential technique is so easy to use, it is one of the most commonly used procedures in attitude investigations. Once the concept to be measured is identified, adjective pairs may be selected by the researcher. The criteria for selecting the bipolar adjectives have to do with factor representativeness and relevance to the concept being investigated. Generally evaluation, potency, and activity pairs are chosen; however, in attitudinal research it is common to use only the evaluation factor. Usually the adjective pairs presented by Osgood and his colleagues provide an adequate resource, but investigators also have substituted their own. Although factorial identity and content should be determined, this rarely occurs.

Osgood et al. (1957) recommended a seven-point scale when using the semantic differential technique; but, three-, five-, and nine-point scales have been used by some investigators. When the semantic differential technique is used, the concept is placed at the top of the page and the subject is asked to indicate his attitude position. An example of the format is presented in Table 3.5.

The semantic differential technique has been used with professionals, peers and parents to measure their attitudes toward various exceptionalities (Casey, 1978; Halpin, Halpin & Tillman, 1973; Noe, 1970; Novak, 1974, 1975), identify hierarchies of attitudes toward disabilities (Buttery, 1978), and to explore the efficacy of attitude modification procedures (Brooks & Bransford, 1971). It also has been used to study the similarities of attitudes in diverse groups (Greenbaum & Wang, 1965) and the effect of contact with disabled persons (Panda & Bartel, 1972; Strauch, 1970) and psychological adjustment (Gottlieb, 1969; Gottlieb, Cohen & Goldstein, 1974) have on attitudes. The semantic differential technique also has been an effective rating device for case studies (Jaffe, 1972) and vignettes (Jaffe, 1966; 1967).

In one study where the procedure was used with young children, 20 pairs of bipolar adjectives were presented in the form of a phrase (e.g., "don't need help," "need help," "need lots of help"); children circled one of the three

TABLE 3.5

The Semantic Differential Technique Sample Item [A] and Scoring Sample [B]

A. Directions: Place a check mark ($\checkmark$) in the place which best shows how you feel about learning disabilities.*

Learning Disabilities

bad**	___	___	___	___	___	$\checkmark$	___ good
dirty	___	___	___	___	___	___	$\checkmark$ clean
nice	___	$\checkmark$	___	___	___	___	___ ugly

B. As illustrated below the score for each adjective pair may range from -3 to +3. When three evaluative scales are used, for example, they may range from -9 to +9. Thus for the above illustration, the bad/good and nice/ugly checks would be scored +2 and the dirty/clean as +3. The overall score for the three adjectives then would be +7.

bad	-3	-2	-1	0	+1	+2	+3	good
dirty	-3	-2	-1	0	+1	+2	+3	clean
nice	+3	+2	+1	0	-1	-2	-3	ugly

* The directions are in abbreviated form. Variations are developed according to the characteristics of the population being studied.
** Random polarity is used to eliminate response bias.

options presented (Rapier, Adelson, Carey, & Croke, 1972). According to Di-Vesta (1966), children down to the second grade level can be tested using bipolar adjectives.

THE ADJECTIVE CHECKLIST TECHNIQUE

When the adjective checklist technique is used, positive and negative adjectives (not bipolar or factor loaded as in the case of the semantic differential procedure previously discussed) are selected to describe some particular person, group or product (Gough, 1960). The procedure has been used to measure attitudes since at least the 1930 s.

Parish, Bryant, and Shirazi (1976) chose adjectives from the *Adjective Checklist* developed by Gough (1952) to develop the *Personal Attribute Inventory* to measure affective reactions. College students were asked to rate the adjectives as positive or negative labels of persons. The Inventory consists of 50 positive and

TABLE 3.6
The Personal Attribute Inventory*

Read through this list and select exactly 30 words which seem
to you typical of _____.** Indicate your selection by placing an X in the appropriate space next to each word.

___active	___healthy	___rude
___affectionate	___helpful	___self-centered
___alert	___hostile	___self-confident
___appreciative	___humorous	___self-controlled
___awkward	___imaginative	___self-pitying
___bitter	___impatient	___selfish
___calm	___industrious	___shallow
___careless	___initiative	___shiftless

*   Only 24 of the 100 choices are indicated.
** Any individual or group of individuals may be noted here.
Reprinted with permission of authors and publisher from: Parish, Bryant, and
Shirazi (1976). The personal attribute inventory. *Perceptual and Motor Skills*,
43, 715-720.

50 negative adjectives which were randomly selected from those for which
students showed 95 percent agreement. Administration of the test requires that
respondents select 30 words from the 100-word list which are most descriptive of
a group or person; the attitude score is the total number of negative adjectives
selected. The reliability and validity of the Inventory, obtained using the scale to
measure attitudes toward blacks, was adequate. The format of the *Personal
Attribute Inventory* in abbreviated form is shown in Table 3.6.

The Personal Attribute Inventory has been used to study the effect of coursework on the attitudes of college students toward exceptional children (Parish,
Eads, Reece, & Piscitello, 1977) and teacher attitudes (Parish, Dyck, & Kappes,
1979).

Variations of the Adjective Checklist Procedure

Worchel and Worchel's (1961) modification of the *Index of Adjustment and
Values* (Rogers & Dymond, 1954) demonstrated a combined use of adjectives
and Likert-type rating methods. The Index, a measure of self-concept, was
adapted to measure the attitudes of parents toward mentally retarded children,
children in general, and their concept of a desirable child. The instrument con-

sisted of three statements: (1) My child . . .; (2) Most children are . . .; and (3) I wish my child were . . . . Forty adjectives were listed following the three statements (e.g., anxious, busy, cruel, docile, jealous, and nervous) along with a seven-point Likert-type scale to identify the degree to which parents thought each trait was applicable to their child. A measure of parental attitudes was obtained by examining the discrepancies between ratings for the three statements.

Another variation of the adjective checklist procedure was used in an investigation supporting the negative effect of labels on teacher attitudes (Combs & Harper, 1967). A checklist which contained twenty positive and five negative adjectives was developed to rate behavioral descriptions. The negative adjectives were selected from a group of negative terms which a sample of teachers had previously rated, and the positive adjectives were selected from those used by Worchel and Worchel (1961). Teachers rated each adjective in terms of its applicability to behavioral descriptions using a five-point Likert-type scale; their score was the sum of the ratings for the negative terms.

Adjective Checklists for Student Populations

Adjective checklists also have been used with students. Davidson and Lang (1960) used the technique to investigate students' perceptions of their teachers' feelings toward them. Other studies have measured students' attitudes toward particular exceptional student groups (Gottlieb & Gottlieb, 1977, and the effect of physical appearance (Siperstein & Gottlieb, 1977) and labels (Gottlieb, 1974) on their attitudes.

SOCIOMETRIC PROCEDURES

Sociometric questionnaires have been used extensively in investigations of classroom relationships (Gronlund, 1959). Peer nomination (Moreno, 1934), an often used procedure, requires group members to indicate choices for companions (usually 3 choices are requested) on the basis of some criterion (e.g., McGinley & McGinley, 1970, asked students which classmates they prefer to work with). According to Moreno (1934), valid responses are most likely to be obtained when realistic criteria are specified; asking students to name classmates they like best or to name their best friends would not be considered a sociometric question but rather a less valid "near-sociometric" question.

The peer nomination method has been very useful in determining the attitudes of classroom members toward each other. Stars (students who receive more choices than could be expected by chance), isolates (students who receive fewer choices than could be expected by chance), neglectees (students who are not chosen) and rejectees (students who receive negative choices) are identified within the group. See Gronlund (1959) for a comprehensive discussion of sociometric testing and Marcus (1980) for a presentation of a computerized scoring method.

Noll and Scannell (1972), however, have pointed out the limitations of the peer nomination technique. A major shortcoming is that when children are required to make a specified number of choices they may make nominations which do not really reflect true feelings of liking or disliking for their classmates; instead they are complying with the directions they were given. A second limitation, according to Noll and Scannell, involves using questions in which students may be asked to name 'rejects' or students with whom they prefer not to associate. Noll and Scannell believed that negative questions should be eliminated because they tend to "... emphasize negative feelings which would appear to have some undesirable aspects" (p. 458). On the other hand, if negative choices are eliminated it becomes impossible to distinguish between isolates and students who are actively rejected. This distinction is particularly important in research on handicapped student status in the regular classroom.

The roster-rating approach (Roistacher, 1974) calls for presenting students with a list of all the class members for rating. This method controls for students being eliminated as choices due to forgetfulness on the part of classmates, something which may occur when using the nominating technique. Also, since responses for each student are obtained from every other class member, the relative status of the student in the classroom (usually an average of the ratings assigned to students by classmates is computed) is measured more accurately. The approach is correlated with peer nomination techniques (Justman & Wrightstone, 1951; Young, 1947) and is not really any more time consuming. Morrison's (1981) findings suggested that peer ratings may give a more exact assessment of the social status of handicapped students mainstreamed for only part of the school day because peer nomination procedures can be greatly influenced by the extent to which students know each other. One consideration when using a sociometric device is evidence indicating that ratings of children only by members of their gender may provide a more accurate measure of peer preferences (Bruininks, Rynders & Gross, 1974; Gronlund, 1959; Singleton & Asher, 1977).

Sociometric Procedures Used in Studies of Handicapped Student Status

The classroom status of handicapped students has been investigated using both the peer nomination method and the roster-rating approach. First, two types of peer nomination procedures are reviewed. Then the roster-rating approach and related measures are discussed.

Choosing Best- and Least-Liked Students.   Many investigators have asked students to identify classmates they would or would not like to work with, invite or not invite to their birthday party, or play or not play with (Bryan, 1974; 1978; Bryan et al., 1976; Johnson & Kirk, 1950; Morgan, 1978; Stilwell, Brown, & Barclay, 1973). For example, in an investigation of the status of learning disabled students (Hutton & Polo, 1976), classmates answered the following questions: (1) Which students in the class would you most like to work with on a work project—one that requires that you prepare a report to be given in class? (2) Which students in the class would you most like to be with in a play group—one in which you play games and have fun? (3) Which students would you least like to work with on a work project—one that requires you to prepare a report to be given in class? (4) Which students would you least like to be with in a play group—one in which you play games and have fun?

In some cases, children are assigned acceptance and rejection scores. Johnson (1950), for instance, individually interviewed students and computed acceptance and rejection scores based on their answers to questions about who they did and did not like, want or not want to sit next to or play with. Johnson also calculated a chance expectancy index (as reported by Bronfenbrenner, 1943) for each classroom studied to make comparisons. This formula is used to calculate the number of stars, isolates, and rejectees that could be expected to occur by chance in a class, thus providing a "frame of reference against which data from diverse sociometric situations may be projected without distortion" (Bronfenbrenner 1943, pp. 371–372). A very similar procedure was used in determining that learning disabled students were rejected by their classmates (Scranton & Rykman, 1979).

Choosing Best Liked Students.   Sometimes isolates, neglectees, and stars are identified using only positive questions. Perrin (1954), for example, found speech-impaired children were isolates in their classes. This finding was obtained by asking students in grades one through six to respond to the following: (1) What three children would you like best to play with? (2) What three children would you like best to sit next to you? In another similar investigation (Siperstein, Bopp & Bak, 1978) children were asked to name the students they like best, and to identify the "best athlete," "smartest," and best looking."

Roster-Rating Procedures.   When the roster-rating approach is used, students rate each class member. Sheare (1978) found learning disabled students were assigned lower status by peers on the *Peer Acceptance Rating Scale* (Sheare, 1975). Students were given a list of the names of class members and chose a rating: (1) I like this person a lot; (2) I like this person; (3) Don't know very well; (4) Don't care for this person; and (5) Don't like this person at all. Sometimes students are asked to choose between fewer ratings; for example they might rate each classmate as a "friend," "alright," or "don't like" (Gottlieb & Budoff, 1973; Leyser & Gottlieb, 1980).

Visual stimuli have been incorporated into some roster-rating scales; when this approach is used students are required to circle a picture of a face with a smile, frown, neutral expression or a question mark to indicate whether they liked, disliked, were neutral about, or didn't know a student in their class (Ballard, Corman, Gottlieb, Kaufman, 1977; Gottlieb, Semmel, & Veldman, 1978).

The *Ohio Social Acceptance Scale* (Fordyce, Yauck, & Raths, 1946; Lorber, 1973) requires students to rate each of their classmates using six descriptive paragraphs ranging in degrees from high acceptance to active rejection. After each paragraph is read, students select individuals in their class who fit the particular description. The scale, in its original or modified form, has been used in several attitudinal investigations (Baldwin, 1958; Rucker, Howe & Snider, 1969; Rucker & Vincenzo, 1970).

Perceived Status.   How students think their peers feel about them, or perceived status, also has been measured using the roster-rating approach. The *Peer Acceptance Scale* (Bruininks, Rynders & Gross, 1974) contains stick figures of: (a) two children playing well together; (b) two children writing; and (c) two children who have their backs toward each other. This instrument, shown in Table 3.7, was used to compare the actual and perceived status of mainstreamed learning disabled students (Bruininks, 1978). Class members indicated their responses by circling the appropriate number above the line drawings which appeared next to the name of each student in the class. The measure was administered twice, first to obtain students' rating of their peers, and again to find out how they thought each classmate rated them.

Miller (1956) devised four scales to identify the social status of superior, typical and retarded students as well as to determine the group's ability to predict

TABLE 3.7
The Peer Acceptance Scale

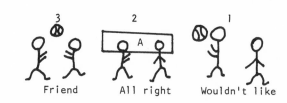

| A STUDENT'S NAME | Friend | All right | Wouldn't like |

From Bruininks (1978). Actual and perceived peer status of learning disabled students in mainstream programs. *Journal of Special Education,* *12,* 51–58.

their own status, the status of their peers, and their ability to predict other students' learning rates. Subjects were provided with the names of all the students in the class and circled statements from the four scales (e.g., the least positive items from each scale were: Scale 1—"if you don't want that person as a friend at all"; Scale 2—"if that person doesn't want you as a friend at all"; Scale 3—"if the person is very unpopular, chosen as a friend by no one"; and Scale 4—"if the person learns new things with great difficulty."

Chennault (1968) modified Miller's scales and used two instruments to study the effects of an attitude modification program. One instrument was used to measure feelings classmates had toward peers and another to identify how they thought their peers felt about them.

Variations in Sociometric Approaches

Considerably lengthier sociometric questionaires have queried students about classmates evidencing a variety of attributes. For example, Centers and Centers (1963) developed seventeen questions about appearance, social relationships, and popularity to inquire about the social status of amputee children in twenty-eight regular classrooms.

Sociometric procedures also have been used to query teachers and parents about their feelings toward students. Soldwedel and Terrill (1957) administered sociometric instruments to physically handicapped and non-physically handicapped students as well as to their parents and compared the responses of the groups. Students were asked whom they would like to sit by, play with, and take home to a party. Parents were asked to identify which students in the class their child had picked for each question and which student they would like their child to pick.

In another investigation (Marge, 1966), parallel questions were developed for students and teachers. For example, one question asked teachers to "Name three children in your class who would be good work or study leaders"; the complement for children was "Name three children in your class with whom you like to work or study at school."

McCandless and Marshall (1957) modified the peer nomination technique for testing preschool children. Young children were shown photographs of their classmates and asked to point to their friendship choices. Another approach for pre-schoolers (Asher, Singleton, Tinsley & Hymel, 1979) also required children to point to pictures of classmates they liked and did not like to play with. The children also rated each of their classmates as to how much they liked playing with a particular classmate. Faces (i.e., happy, neutral, or sad) were selected by the children to indicate the degree of liking for play with a particular child. Thus when this latter procedure is used, three sociometric scores can be obtained for each class member: (1) the number of positive choices from class members; (2)

the number of negative choices; and (3) an average rating score from all the classmates.

INTERVIEWS

There are two types of interview procedures. In the unstructured interview the interviewer is free to structure the questions surrounding the purpose of the investigation. Structured interviews involve the use of interview schedules that generally contain yes–no, agree–disagree, on open-end type items. Although unstructured interviews have been used to study such things as the efficacy of mainstreaming (Barngrover, 1971), and special class programming (Keogh, Becker, Kukic, & Kukic, 1974), educational researchers have used the structured approach more frequently. Some studies illustrate how interviews have been used. Hollinger and Jones (1970), for example, developed a structured interview to assess differences in the perceptions community members had about the labels "slow learner" and "mentally retarded." Agree-disagree and yes-no type items were included in the interview schedule and respondents were asked to define the terms "slow learner," and "mentally retarded." They were also administered a social distance scale.

Meyers, Sitkei and Watts (1966) also were interested in attitudes toward mental retardation and developed five questions about what parents should do about educating their retarded children. The questions were used in interviews with a random sample of community members and parents of a child enrolled in a special classroom.

In another study which involved interviewing community members, thirty-one yes–no and open-end items were used to explore relationships between formal education and attitudes toward mental illness (Freeman & Kassebaum, 1960).

Parent feelings about institutionalizing a retarded child have also been explored in the interview situation (Mercer, 1966). To understand the stress this event created in the family, open-ended questions were directed toward the feelings parents had prior to and after institutionalizing their child. Fairfield (1983) explored feelings of parents of handicapped children using a 50-item interview questionnaire and found that information about parents' early memories about handicaps may be helpful in understanding the current attitudes and concerns parents have about their handicapped child.

Although interview procedures have not generally been used to explore student attitudes toward handicapped children, information gathered about children's friendships using the interview procedure (Hayes, 1978; Hayes, Gershman, & Bolin, 1980) suggests that an understanding of students' attitudes toward handicaps and handicapped children could be increased using the interview approach.

BEHAVIORAL OBSERVATIONS

Numerous observational systems have been developed to study classroom interactions (see Simon & Boyer [1974] for a presentation of 99 observation systems). These systems identify categories of teacher and/or student behaviors and specific observable behaviors or subcategories of behavior which may be subsumed under each category. A sampling plan is developed and used in the classroom by observers who record the actual occurrence of the specified behaviors. Generally speaking there are three types of sampling plans. When event sampling is used, the occurrence of specific events or behaviors are recorded; in time sampling, observations are undertaken at specified or random times; and in point-time sampling the two are combined.

For example in one investigation (Khleif, 1976) occurrences of "role distance" behaviors (e.g., observations of the teacher's tone of voice, type of verbal interactions, movement patterns and gestures) toward slow learners and normal students were recorded. In another investigation (Lyon, 1977), teacher nonverbal behaviors (eye-contact, facial expressions, head movements, and physical contact) toward handicapped students were observed and rated as positive, neutral, or negative at 10-second intervals. The physical distances between the students and teachers during interaction were also measured.

A system was recently developed to observe interactions among preschool handicapped and nonhandicapped students (Dunlop, Stoneman, & Cantrell, 1980). Observers recorded behaviors related to five behavior categories over the course of the school year for two random 6–minute periods each week. The behavior categories included observations of solitary activity, direct interactions of a dominant nature, direct interactions cooperative in nature, adult-child interactions and an "other" category that included any behavior not fitting into the previous four categories. The subcategories of behavior recorded under the category entitled "Direct Interaction/Cooperative" are presented in Table 3.8 to illustrate how observation systems are constructed. Although initial observations indicated there were significant differences in handicapped and nonhandicapped student interactions, observations over time revealed that the initial impressions were not representative of their interactions. Thus, the findings supported a need for observational studies to consider the longitudinal development of classroom relationships. This is underscored by the findings of a sociometric instrument administered at the beginning of the year wherein nonhandicapped students were chosen twice as often. A logical inference that nonhandicapped children interacted less with peers would be incorrect.

Observational procedures also have been used to monitor student conversations with peers. Studies of learning disabled students' conversations with peers (Bryan, 1978; Bryan, Wheeler, Felcan, & Henek, 1976) suggest learning disabled students experience fewer positive interactions.

TABLE 3.8
Observation Instrument for Preschool Student Interactions--
Category of "Direct Interaction/Cooperative"

---

1. Parallel sharing of play materials. Child uses same materials as one or more other children, but plays independently without interacting or conversing with them.

2. Initiates cooperative activity. Child suggests activity involving a companion, asks companion to join him or her in an ongoing activity, or otherwise begins a cooperative interaction.

3. Companion engages child in cooperative activity. Child complies with request or suggestion of a cooperative activity by a companion, is joined by a companion in his or her ongoing play, or otherwise responds positively to attempts to cooperate or share on the part of a companion.

4. Cooperative appropriate object play. Child is engaged in cooperative play with a companion that involves the appropriate use of materials (defined in another subcategory), in which the initiator is not known or the activity is a continuation of an interaction previously coded in subcategories 2 or 3.

5. Cooperative inappropriate object play. Child is engaged in cooperative play with a companion that involves the inappropriate use of materials (defined in another subcategory), regardless of which child initiated the interaction.

6. Cooperative play not involving objects. Child is engaged in cooperative play with a companion not involving toys or other materials, in which the initiator is not known, or the activity is a continuation of an interaction previously coded in subcategories 2 or 3.

7. Cooperative fantasy play. Child is engaged in cooperative play with a companion that involves make believe, in which the initiator is not known, or the activity is a continuation of an interaction previously coded in subcategories 2 or 3.

8. Parenting/teaching. Child verbally or physically instructs a companion in an activity or gives a companion information or suggestion which would alter the performance of a task.

9. Conversation. Child is engaged in conversation with a companion without being simultaneously involved in any other form of cooperative interaction.

10. Positive physical contact. Hugging, kissing, touching while dancing, and one child having his or her arm around a companion's shoulder are the only behaviors constituting this category.

From Dunlop, Stoneman, and Cantrell (1980). Social interaction of exceptional and other children in a mainstreamed preschool classroom. *Exceptional Children, 47,* 132-141.

When behavioral observations of mother-child interactions have been undertaken, findings generally indicated differential patterns of interaction for mothers of handicapped and nonhandicapped students (Doleys, Cartelli, & Doster, 1976; Forehand, King, Peed, & Yoder, 1974; Marshall, Hegrenes, & Goldstein, 1973).

PROJECTIVE METHODS

Projective methods are relatively unstructured procedures of obtaining responses thought to tap the inner world of the individual and to reveal feelings, emotions, desires, and attitudes of which the individual is not aware. This information is secured by interpreting the subject's drawing or their responses to pictures, or sentence completion tasks. Lindzey (1959) classified projective methods according to the type of response required; that is, whether or not the technique required association (word association techniques are the most common approach), construction (e.g., the creation of a story or picture), completion (sentence completion), choice or ordering (subject chooses an answer), or expressive techniques (where the emphasis is on the manner or style of expression the subject evidences in constructing something such as a painting, and the product is not important).

Although projective techniques have not been extensively used in studies of attitudes toward persons with a handicap, there are some examples. Billings (1963) used projective techniques with children in grades 1, 3, and 6. The instruments developed for the study included the *Tell Me a Story* technique (in the first administration students were asked to write stories about a girl in a picture, and in the second administration were told the picture was of "a little crippled girl") and the *Complete This Sentence* procedure (students completed ten sentences, three of which were about a crippled child). Judges, who evaluated the stories and sentences, found children had negative attitudes toward the crippled child.

The *Thurston Sentence Completion Form* (Thurston, 1959) was developed to measure the attitudes of parents of handicapped children about familial and community reactions, treatment and expectations. This test consists of forty-five sentences for completion. Some sample items are: (1) "My biggest fear is . . ."; (2) "The thing that most parents find hardest to accept about the handicap of their child is . . ."; and (3) "If I could be granted one wish for my child it would be . . . ." The responses may be accepted at "face value" as telling how the parent feels or subjectively interpreted by trained psychological examiners.

MAINSTREAMING QUESTIONNAIRES

There have been a variety of procedures used to measure professional, peer, and parent attitudes; mainstreaming questionnaires represent a current trend in the literature. Indeed, legislation (P. L. 93–380 and P. L. 94–142 and the subsequent implementation of state mandates for the appropriate education of all handicapped children) has resulted in the development and administration of a variety of questionnaires designed to query teachers about all aspects of these laws. These questionnaires employ all types of measurement formats to gather data about various aspects of mainstreaming. Reliability and validity data have been reported for only a few of these questionnaires.

Table 3.9 contains the thirty attitude statements contained in a mainstreaming questionnaire focusing on handicapped student behavior in the classroom and its effect on teachers and peers (Larrivee & Cook, 1979). The instrument required

TABLE 3.9
A Survey of Teacher's Opinions Relative to Mainstreaming Special Needs Children

1. Many of the things teachers do with regular students in a classroom are appropriate for special-needs students.

2. The needs of handicapped students can best be served through special, separate classes.

3. A special-needs child's classroom behavior generally requires more patience from the teacher than does the behavior of a normal child.

4. The challenge of being in a regular classroom will promote the academic growth of the special-needs child.

5. The extra attention special-needs students require will be to the detriment of the other students.

6. Mainstreaming offers mixed group interaction which will foster understanding and acceptance of differences.

7. It is difficult to maintain order in a regular classroom that contains a special-needs child.

8. Regular teachers possess a great deal of the expertise necessary to work with special-needs students.

9. The behavior of special-needs students will set a bad example for the other students.

10. Isolation in a special class has a negative effect on the social and emotional development of a special-needs student.

11. The special-needs child will probably develop academic skills more rapidly in a special classroom than in a regular classroom.

12. Most special-needs children do not make an adequate attempt to complete their assignments.

13. Integration on special-needs children will require significant changes in regular classroom procedures.

14. Most special-needs children are well behaved in the classroom.

15. The contact regular-class students have with mainstreamed students may be harmful.

16. Regular-classroom teachers have sufficient training to teach children with special needs.

17. Special-needs students will monopolize the teacher's time.

18. Mainstreaming the special-needs child will promote his/her social independence.

19. It is likely that a special-needs child will exhibit behavior problems in a regular classroom setting.

20. Diagnostic-prescriptive teaching is better done by resource-room or special teachers than by regular-classroom teachers.

21. The integration of special-needs students can be beneficial for regular students.

22. Special-needs children need to be told exactly what to do and how to do it.

23. Mainstreaming is likely to have a negative effect on the emotional development of the special-needs child.

continued...

24. Increased freedom in the classroom creates too much confusion.

25. The special-needs child will be socially isolated by regular-classroom students.

26. Parents of a special-needs child present no greater problem for a classroom teacher than those of a normal child.

27. Integration of special-needs children will necessitate extensive retraining of regular teachers.

28. Special-needs students should be given every opportunity to function in the regular-classroom setting, where possible.

29. Special-needs children are likely to create confusion in the regular classroom.

30. The presence of special-needs students will promote acceptance of differences on the part of regular students.

From Larrivee and Cook (1979). Mainstreaming: A study of variables of affecting teacher attitude. *Journal of Special Education, 13*, 315-324.

teachers to respond using a 5-point Likert scale (strongly agree to strongly disagree). Adequate evidence for reliability and validity for this instrument is presented by the authors, and the technical merits of the instrument have also been supported in another investigation about qualities of the questionaire (Green, Rock, & Weisenstein, 1983).

There are numerous other examples of mainstreaming questionnaires in the literature (Graham, Hudson, Burdg & Carpenter, 1980; Gickling & Theobald, 1975; Harasymiw & Horne, 1976; Hudson, Graham, & Warner, 1979; May & Furst, 1977; Ringlaben & Price, 1981). Questionnaires also have been developed to measure attitudes toward mainstreaming particular handicapped student groups (Berryman & Neal, 1980; Olley, Devellis, Devellis, Wall, & Long, 1981; Vacc & Kirst, 1977), the frequency and importance of support services for mainstreaming (Speece & Mandell, 1980), and attitudes toward all aspects of Individual Educational Programs (IEPs) and related diagnostic and prescriptive considerations (Semmel, 1979).

PHYSIOLOGICAL REACTIONS AND THE "BOGUS PIPELINE"

Although most of the available attitude measurement procedures are represented in the literature on attitudes toward handicapped individuals, physiological reactions such as galvanic skin responses and pupillary dilation that have been used in studies of racial prejudice have not generally been employed in collecting data about attitudes toward handicapped persons.

In a unique study, Gargiulo and Yonker (1983) examined the attitudes of special education teachers, regular class teachers and college seniors majoring in regular or special education toward handicapped students using self-report and physiological measures. There were no differences in the responses of the four groups on a Likert-type scale to questions about the degree of stress they would experience when working with different kinds of handicapped students depicted in a slide presentation. However, the continuous pulse, but not temperature, data collected during the slide presentation indicated preservice teachers perceived teaching handicapped students as more stressful than did experienced teachers. These findings suggest that further use be made of physiological data collection procedures in studies of attitudes toward people with a handicap.

Another procedure, the "bogus pipeline," which has been used in research on racial stereotyping (Schlenker, Bonoma, Hutchinson, & Burns, 1976; Sigall & Page, 1971), also may be a good approach to incorporate into research on handicapped persons. This procedure was developed by Jones and Sigall (1971) to overcome the response bias problems inherent in self-report measures. The pipeline into a subject's covert feelings is really a deception technique whereby subjects are convinced that new developments in electromyography make it possible to measure accurately the direction and intensity of their attitudes.

SOME COMMONLY USED MEASURES

Some of the many instruments designed to measure attitudes have been more frequently used in investigations of professional, peer, and parent attitudes. The following are general descriptions of these instruments, as well as other measures which may be helpful in studying attitudes.

Olley et al. (1981) developed the *Autism Attitude Scale for Teachers* (AAST) to measure the attitudes of classroom teachers toward autistic children and the possible effect of inservice training on their feelings toward these students. There are two forms available and the authors reported the instrument to be reliable and valid.

The *Attitudes to Blindness Scale* (ATBS) was developed by Cowen, Underberg, & Verrillo (1958) to measure parental attitudes toward blindness, and uses items from scales developed by Steingisser (1954) and Fitting (1954). Item-test correlations of +.44 to +.75 and split-half reliabilities of .83 and .91 are reported. The ATBS consists of thirty statements (e.g., a blind person might as well accept the fact that blindness makes people pretty helpless) with a 4-point Likert-type response format. The scale has been used to measure the attitudes of teachers (Kuhn, 1971) and high school students (Marsh & Friedman, 1972) toward blindness .

Yuker, Block and Campbell (1960) published the original *Attitude Toward Disabled Persons Scale* (ATDP), a Likert-type scale for measuring attitudes of disabled and non-disabled persons. Two monographs have made available information about new developments in the scales and their uses (Yuker, Block, &

Young, 1970; Block, 1974). The ATDP is probably one of the best known and most widely used instruments for attitude measurement.

The ATDP groups all forms of disability into a single category called physically disabled. The intent is to provide a measure focusing on the concept of disability in a general way. The scales consist of statements designed to measure the extent to which respondents regard the physically disabled as different or inferior to the nondisabled. There are three forms of the scale; Forms A and B consist of thirty statements and Form O contains twenty statements. Respondents indicate the extent to which they agree (+3, I agree very much; +2, I agree pretty much; +1, I agree a little; −1, I disagree a little; −2, I disagree pretty much; −3, I disagree very much) with statements such as "Disabled persons are usually easier to get along with than other people" and "Most disabled persons feel sorry for themselves." Scoring procedures result in a single total attitude score. Numerous investigations of the reliability and validity of the scales reported in the monographs demonstrate the measure is relatively reliable and valid (the monographs should be consulted for a comprehensive report on investigations using the ATDP).

Wilson and Alcorn (1969) used the scale to measure the effects of simulation projects on the attitudes of college students. They found no significant treatment effects and speculated about whether or not the findings were attributable to the nature of the project or to the insensitivity of the ATDP to "quick attitude change." Other studies (Donaldson, 1976; Donaldson & Martinson, 1977; Evans, 1976; Higgs, 1975), however, seem to support the instrument's sensitivity to attitudinal shifts.

Attitude changes in very young students also have been measured using the ATDP. When Simpson, Parrish, and Cook (1976) administered the scale to second- and third-grade students, they substituted the word "handicapped" for "disabled" to facilitate the children's understanding, and asked them to indicate their responses by choosing from six smiling or frowning faces.

Attitudes Toward Handicapped Individuals Scale (ATHI)

The Attitudes Toward Handicapped Individuals Scale (ATHI) is a modification of the ATDP by Lazar, Gensley and Orpet (1971). The 20-item instrument contains statements similar to those found on the ATDP scale and uses the same Likert-type format and scoring procedure. In the ATHI, the term "disabled" was changed to "handicapped" in order to give broader meaning to the statements. Lazar, Stodden, and Sullivan (1976) reported a product-moment correlation between the ATHI and ATDP (Form O) of .802 and a coefficient of stability (test-retest) over a period of two weeks of .732; both significant at the .01 level. These authors used the ATHI in an investigation of the attitudes of administrators toward handicapped students.

The ATHI was also used in an investigation supporting gender differences in attitudes toward handicapped pupils (Skrtic, Sigler, & Lazar, 1975) and to explore the relationship among attitudes, personality, and educational background variables (Parker & Stodden, 1977). When used to study the attitudes of parents who had a child in a class for the educable mentally retarded (Lazar et al., 1976), both mothers and fathers evidenced high acceptance scores toward their child.

The *Barclay Classroom Climate Inventory* (BCCI) was designed by Barclay (1977) to measure the social and affective climate of a classroom. The BCCI incorporates measures of student self-reports, peer judgments, and teacher expectations. A computerized scoring procedure is necessary to analyze and interpret the collected data. Data from the measure indicates the amount of support a student receives and perceives as receiving from others in the classroom as well as problems a student may have in the areas of self-competency, group interaction, self-control, verbal skills, physical skills, vocational awareness, cognitive motivation, and school attitude. The instrument provides a methodology for exploring the impact of the classroom on the mainstreamed handicapped child and the impact the handicapped child has on the classroom. See Barclay & Kehle (1979) for a review of three studies on the effects of mainstreaming handicapped students using the BCCI.

Harth (1971) developed the *Mental Retardation Attitude Inventory* (MRAI) to measure attitudes toward retarded individuals. Starting with a scale that measured ten dimensions or components of attitudes toward black persons (Woodmansee & Cook, 1967), Harth sought to determine the relevancy of these dimensions for mentally retarded persons. Five subtests each with 10 items were selected from the Woodmansee-Cook Scale (Integration-Segregation Policy, Overfavorableness, Social Distance, Private Rights and Subtle Derogatory Beliefs). The items were rewritten, primarily by changing the term ''blacks'' to ''retarded,'' and then subjected to expert review. The reliability of the MRAI was derived from administering the measure to undergraduate students enrolled in general and special education. Pearson product-moment coefficients supported the relationship between subtest items, independence of the subtests, and a relationship with the total-test attitude score. Validity of the scale was demonstrated by comparing the MRAI scores of general and special education students.

When Kennon and Sandoval (1978) administered the MRAI to white and black regular and special class teachers, there were no significant differences between the groups' attitudes toward mental retardation; however, white teachers demonstrated lower social distance scores toward retarded person on some subscales, and teachers who had contact were more positive than teachers who had little or no contact with retarded students in their classes.

The original *Minnesota Teacher Attitude Inventory* (Cook, Leeds, & Callis, 1951) was developed as a measure of teacher attitudes thought to be predictive of interpersonal relationships with students. Phillips (1976) revised the Inventory in order to investigate factors associated with classroom teachers' attitudes toward speech-handicapped school children, and their understanding of speech disorders and remediation procedures. The revision involved rephrasing items, substituting key words and using some items in their original form. It contains 50 items, with three distractors (10 items measuring understanding of speech handicaps and 20 items on remedial procedures that might be used). Responses indicated attitudes were significantly related to having had a course in speech remediation, as well as to age, teaching experiences, and access to a speech pathologist.

The *Parental Attitude Research Instrument* (PARI) was developed by Schaefer and Bell (1958) to determine attitudes toward child rearing. It consists of 23 five-item scales: encouraging verbalization; fostering dependency; seclusion of the mother; breaking the will; martyrdom, fear of harming baby; marital conflict; strictness; irritability; excluding outside influences; deification; suppression of aggression; rejection of homemaking role; equalitarianism; approval of activity; avoidance of communication; inconsiderateness of husband; suppression of sex; ascendance of the mother; intrusiveness; comradeship and sharing; acceleration of development; dependency of mother. These are related to attitudinal factors of authoritarian control (suppressive, punitive attitudes), hostility-rejection (attitudes of strictness, hostility toward family members), and democratic sharing or equalitarianism.

The instrument has been used in numerous investigations of the attitudes of mothers of normal and handicapped children (see Chapter 7). Because Shaefer and Bell's normative sample consisted of only 100 military personnel wives, some investigators have focused on gathering additional data about the scale (Zuckerman, 1959; Zuckerman, Ribback, Monashsin, & Norton, 1958). Becker and Krug (1965) provided a comprehensive review of the PARI and concluded that there are some difficulties in the design and structure of the test, although the instrument does correlate with other measures of parent attitudes. They suggested that new approaches be developed to measure parent attitudes.

Rucker and Gable (1974) developed the *Rucker-Gable Educational Programming Scale* (RGEPS) to measure teacher attitudes toward mentally retarded, emotionally disturbed, and learning disabled children. Respondents are presented with thirty brief descriptions of children who exhibit behaviors typical of these three groups of students. They are asked to read about each child and to select the most appropriate educational placement for the child from a continuum of services (regular classroom placement, regular classroom placement with consultation, regular classroom placement with consultation and short-term direct services, regular classroom placement with resource room placement for up to 2 hours per day, part-time enrollment in a special class, and full-time special class placement).

The teacher's attitude score is indicated by the placement selection made since this is considered a measure of the degree of social distance the teacher prefers to maintain between himself and the student. Consequently higher or more positive attitude scores are indicated by placements in the regular classroom. In addition to the total attitude score, subscores are obtained for attitudes toward mental retardation, emotional disturbance, learning disability, mild, moderate and severe handicaps. A knowledge score is obtainable by computing the discrepancy between the placement made by the respondent and an expert opinion score on the placement provided by the test referent groups. Split-half internal consistency reliabilities for teachers range from .53 to .91 on the subscales, and is .86 for the total score.

The RGEPS has been used to investigate classroom teacher attitudes (Gillung & Rucker, 1977; Johnson & Cartwright, 1979; Shaw & Gillung, 1975) and administrator attitudes (Morris & McCauley, 1977). The scale has also been revised to measure attitudes toward children with other handicapping conditions (Hirshoren & Burton, 1979).

Haring, Stern, and Cruickshank (1958) designed five instruments to measure the efficacy of a workshop designed to change teacher attitudes: (1) *The General Information Inventory* measured information teachers had about exceptional students; (2) *The Classroom Integration Inventory* was administered to identify levels of acceptance for exceptional students; (3) *The Activities Index* was used to determine the personality structure of the teachers; (4) *The Picture Judgment Test* was used to measure attitudes toward handicapped and nonhandicapped students; and (5) *The Critical Incident Technique* was used to identify the degree to which teachers said they applied techniques learned in the workshop. Since a comprehensive review of the procedure is provided by the authors these are not discussed in detail. Findings of this study were that both knowledge about exceptional students and classroom experiences working with these students were important for attitude change to occur.

When Jordan and Proctor (1969) administered modifications of the *Classroom Integration Inventory* and the *General Information Inventory*, they found that special education teachers were more knowledgeable than regular classroom teachers, but did not have more positive attitudes.

SUMMARY

This chapter has focused on a presentation of the various procedures which have been used to measure attitudes toward individuals with a handicap. Numerous options are available. There can be no endorsement of any one procedure because making a selection depends upon the context of the situation and the sample being tested as well as the intent of the user.

REFERENCES

Abroms, K. I., & Kodera, T. L. (1979). Acceptance hierarchy of handicaps: Validation of Kirk's statement, "Special education often begins where medicine stops." *Journal of Learning Disabilities, 12,* 24–29.

Asher, S. R., Singleton, L. C., Tinsley, B. R., & Hymel, S. (1979). A reliable sociometric measure for preschool children. *Developmental Psychology, 15,* 443–444.

Baldwin, W. K. (1958). The social position of the educable mentally retarded child in the regular grades. *Exceptional Children, 25,* 106–108, 112.

Ballard, M., Corman, L., Gottlieb, J., & Kaufman, M. J. (1977). Improving the social status of mainstreamed retarded children. *Journal of Educational Psychology, 69,* 605–611.

Barclay, J. R. (1977). *Appraising individual differences in the classroom: A manual of the Barclay Classroom Climate Inventory* (4th ed.). Lexington, KY: Educational Skills Development.

Barclay, J. R., & Kehle, T. J. (1979). The impact of handicapped students on other students in the classroom. *Journal of Research and Development in Education, 12,* 80–92.

Barngrover, E. (1971). A study of educators' preferences in special education programs. *Exceptional Children, 37,* 754–755.

Barsch, R. H. (1964). The handicapped ranking scale among parents of handicapped children. *American Journal of Public Health, 54,* 1560–1567.

Becker, W. C., & Krug, R. S. (1965). The parent attitude research instrument - A research review. *Child Development, 36,* 329–365.

Berman, D. S., & Fry, P. B. (1978). Pariah or paragon? Student teachers' evaluations of enrolling mentally ill students. *Psychology in the Schools, 15,* 529–532.

Berryman, J. D., & Neal, W. R. (1980). The cross validation of the attitudes toward mainstreaming scale (atms). *Educational and Psychological Measurement, 40,* 469–474.

Billings, H. K. (1963). An exploratory study of the attitudes of non-crippled children toward crippled children in three selected elementary schools. *Journal of Experimental Education, 31,* 381–387.

Block, J. (1961). *The q-sort method in personality assessment and psychiatric research.* Springfield, IL: C C Thomas.

Block, J. R. (1974). *Recent research with the attitudes toward disabled persons scale: Some research abstracts.* Albertson, NY: Human Resources Center.

Bogardus, E. S. (1925). Measuring social distances. *Journal of Applied Sociology, 9,* 216–226.

Bogardus, E. S. (1932). A social distance scale. *Sociology and Social Research, 17,* 265–271.

Bronfenbrenner, V. (1943). A constant frame of reference for sociometric research. Part 1. *Sociometry, 6,* 363–397.

Brooks, B. L., & Bransford, L. A. (1971). Modification of teachers' attitudes toward exceptional children. *Exceptional Children, 38,* 259–260.

Bruininks, R. H., Rynders, J. E., & Gross, J. C. (1974). Social acceptance of mildly retarded pupils in resource rooms and regular classes. *American Journal of Mental Deficiency, 78,* 377–383.

Bruininks, V. L. (1978). Actual and perceived peer status of learning disabled students in mainstream programs. *Journal of Special Education, 12,* 51–58.

Bryan, T. H. (1974). Peer popularity of learning disabled children. *Journal of Learning Disabilities, 7,* 621–625.

Bryan, T. H. (1978). Social relationships and verbal interactions of learning disabled children. *Journal of Learning Disabilities, 11,* 107–115.

Bryan, T. H., Wheeler, R., Felcan, J., & Henek, T. (1976). "Come on dummy": An observational study of children's communications. *Journal of Learning Disabilities, 9,* 661–669.

Buttery, T. J. (1978). Affective response to exceptional children by students preparing to be teachers. *Perceptual and Motor Skills, 46,* 288–290.

Carroll, C. F., & Reppucci, N. D. (1978). Meanings that professionals attach to labels for children. *Journal of Consulting and Clinical Psychology, 46,* 372–374.

Casey, K. (1978). The semantic differential technique in the examination of teacher attitudes to handicapped children. *Exceptional Child, 25,* 41–52.

Centers, L., & Centers, R. (1963). Peer group attitudes toward the amputee child. *The Journal of Social Psychology, 61,* 127–132.

Chennault, M. (1968). Improving the social acceptance of unpopular educable mentally retarded pupils in special classes. *American Journal of Mental Deficiency, 72,* 455–458.

Chigier, E., & Chigier, M. (1968). Attitudes to disability of children in the multi-cultural society of Israel. *Journal of Health and Social Behavior, 9,* 310–317.

Combs, R. H., & Harper, J. L. (1967). Effects on attitudes of educators toward handicapped children. *Exceptional Children, 33,* 399–403.

Cook, W., Leeds, C., & Callis, R. (1951). *Minnesota Teacher Attitude Inventory.* New York: Psychological Corp.

Cowen, E. L., Underberg, R. P., & Verrillo, R. T. (1958). The development and testing of an attitude to blindness scale. *The Journal of Social Psychology, 48,* 297–304.

Davidson, H. H., & Lang, G. (1960). Children's perceptions of their teacher's feelings toward them related to self-perception, school achievement and behavior. *Journal of Experimental Education, 29,* 106–118.

DiVesta, F. J. (1966). A developmental study of the semantic structures of children. *Journal of Verbal Learning and Verbal Behavior, 5,* 249–259.

Doleys, D. M., Cartelli, L. M., & Doster, J. (1976). Comparison of patterns of mother-child interaction. *Journal of Learning Disabilities, 9,* 371–375.

Donaldson, J. (1976). Channel variations and effects on attitudes toward physically disabled individuals. *Audio-Visual Communication Review, 2,* 135–143.

Donaldson, J., & Martinson, M. C. (1977). Modifying attitudes toward physically disabled persons. *Exceptional Children, 44,* 337–341.

Duke, M. P., & Nowicki, S. (1972). A new measure and social learning model for interpersonal distance. *Journal of Experimental Research in Personality, 6,* 119–132.

Dunlop, K. H., Stoneman, Z., & Cantrell, M. H. (1980). Social interaction of exceptional and other children in a mainstreamed preschool classroom. *Exceptional Children, 47,* 132–141.

Edwards, A. (1957). *Techniques of attitude scale construction.* New York: Appleton-Century-Croft.

Efron, R. E., & Efron, H. Y. (1967). Measurement of attitudes towards the retarded and an application with educators. *American Journal of Mental Deficiency, 72,* 100–107.

Evans, J. H. (1976). Changing attitudes toward disabled persons: An experimental study. *Rehabilitation Counseling Bulletin, 19,* 572–579.

Fairfield, B. (1983). Parents coping with genetically handicapped children: Use of early recollections. *Exceptional Children, 49,* 411–415.

Fine, M. J. (1967). Attitudes of regular and special class teachers toward the educable mentally retarded child. *Exceptional Children, 33,* 429–430.

Fitting, E. A. (1954). *Evaluation of adjustment to blindness.* New York: American Foundation for the Blind, Res. Ser. 2.

Foley, J. M. (1979). Effect of labeling and teacher behavior on children's attitudes. *American Journal of Mental Deficiency, 83,* 380–384.

Fordyce, W. G., Yauck, W. A., & Raths, L. (1946). A manual for the Ohio guidance tests for the elementary grades. Columbus, OH: Ohio State Department of Education.

Forehand, R. L., King, H. E., Peed, S., & Yoder, P. (1974). Mother-child interactions: Comparisons of a non-compliant clinic group and a non-clinic group, *Behavior Research Therapy, 13,* 79–84.

Freeman, H. E., & Kassebaum, G. G. (1960). Relationship of education and knowledge to opinions about mental illness. *Mental Hygiene, 44,* 43–47.

Gargiulo, R. M., & Yonker, R. J. (1983). Assessing teachers' attitude toward the handicapped: A methodological investigation. *Psychology in the Schools, 20,* 229–240.

Gickling, E. E., & Theobald, J. T. (1975). Mainstreaming: Affect of effect. *Journal of Special Education, 9*(3), 317–328.

Gillung, T. B., & Rucker, C. N. (1977). Labels and teacher expectations. *Exceptional Children, 43,* 464–465.

Goodman, N., Dornbusch, S. M., Richardson, S. A., & Hastorf, A. H. (1963). Variant reactions to physical disabilities. *American Sociological Review, 28,* 429–435.

Gottlieb, J. (1969). Attitudes toward retarded children: Effects of evaluators psychological adjustment and age. *Scandinavian Journal of Educational Research, 13,* 170–182.

Gottlieb, J. (1974). Attitudes toward retarded children: Effect of labeling and performance. *American Journal of Mental Deficiency, 79,* 268–273.

Gottlieb, J., & Budoff, M. (1973). Social acceptability of retarded children in non-graded schools differing in architecture. *American Journal of Mental Deficiency, 78,* 15–19.

Gottlieb, J., Cohen, L., & Goldstein, L. (1974). Social contact and personal adjustment as variables relating toward emr children. *Training School Bulletin, 71,* 9–16.

Gottlieb, J., & Corman, L. (1975). Public attitudes toward mentally retarded children. *American Journal of Mental Deficiency, 80,* 72–80.

Gottlieb, J., & Gottlieb, B. W. (1977). Stereotypic attitudes and behavioral intentions toward handicapped children. *American Journal of Mental Deficiency, 82,* 65–71.

Gottlieb, J., Semmel, M. I., & Veldman, D. J. (1978). Correlates of social status among mainstreamed mentally retarded. *Journal of Educational Psychology, 70,* 396–405.

Gottlieb, J., & Siperstein, G. N. (1976). Attitudes toward mentally retarded persons: Effects of attitude referent specificity. *American Journal of Mental Deficiency, 80,* 376–381.

Gough, H. G. (1952). *The Adjective Checklist.* Palo Alto, CA: Consulting Psychologists Press.

Gough, H. G. (1960). The adjective checklist as a personality assessment research technique. *Psychological Reports, 6,* 107–122.

Graham, S., Hudson, F., Burdg, N. B., & Carpenter, D. (1980). Educational personnel's perceptions of mainstreaming and resource room effectiveness. *Psychology in the Schools, 17,* 128–134.

Green, K., Rock, D. L., & Weisenstein, G. R. (1983). Validity and reliability of a scale assessing attitudes toward mainstreaming. *Exceptional Children, 50,* 182–183.

Greenbaum, J. J., & Wang, D. D. (1965). A semantic-differential study of the concepts of mental retardation. *Journal of General Psychology, 73,* 257–272.

Gronlund, N. E. (1959). *Sociometry in the classroom.* New York: Harper.

Gumz, G. J., & Gubrium, J. F. (1972). Comparative parental perceptions of a mentally retarded child. *American Journal of Mental Deficiency, 77,* 175–180.

Guttman, L. (1944). A basis for scaling qualitative data. *American Sociological Review, 9,* 139–150.

Guttman, L. (1947). On Festinger's evaluation of scale analysis. *Psychological Bulletin, 44,* 451–465.

Guttman, L. (1950). The basis for scalogram analysis. In S. A. Stouffer et al. (Eds.), *Measurement and prediction.* Princeton, NJ: Princeton University Press.

Halpin, G. H., Halpin, G., & Tillman, M. H. (1973). Relationships between creative thinking, intelligence, and teacher rated characteristics of blind children. *Education of the Visually Handicapped, 5,* 33–38.

Harasymiw, S. J., & Horne, M. D. (1976). Teacher attitudes toward handicapped children and regular class integration. *Journal of Special Education, 10,* 393–400.

Harasymiw, S. J., Horne, M. D., & Lewis, S. C. (1976a). Disability social distance hierarchy for population subgroups. *Scandinavian Journal of Rehabilitation Medicine, 8,* 33–36.

Harasymiw, S. J., Horne, M. D., & Lewis, S. C. (1976b). A longitudinal study of disability group acceptance. *Rehabilitation Literature, 37,* 98–102.

Harasymiw, S. J., Horne, M. D., & Lewis, S. C. (1977). Occupational attitudes in population subgroups. *The Vocational Guidance Quarterly, 26,* 147–156.

Haring, N. G., Stern, G. G., & Cruickshank, W. M. (1958). *Attitudes of educators toward exceptional children.* Syracuse, NY: Syracuse University Press.

Harth, R. (1971). Attitudes toward minority groups as a construct in assessing attitudes towards the mentally retarded. *Education and Training of the Mentally Retarded, 6,* 142–147.

Hayes, D. S. (1978). Cognitive bases for liking and disliking among preschool children. *Child Development, 49,* 906–909.

Hayes, D. S., Gershman, E., & Bolin, L. J. (1980). Friends and enemies: Cognitive bases for preschool children's unilateral and reciprocal relationships. *Child Development, 51,* 1276–1279.

Higgs, R. W. (1975). Attitude formation - contact or information? *Exceptional Children, 41,* 496–497.

Hirshoren, A., & Burton, T. (1979). Willingness of regular teachers to participate in mainstreaming handicapped children. *Journal of Research and Development in Education, 12,* 93–100.

Hollinger, C. S., Jones, R. L. (1970). Community attitudes toward slow learners and mental retardates: What's in a name? *Mental Retardation, 8,* 19–23.

Horne, M. D. (1978). Cultural effect on attitudes toward labels. *Psychological Reports, 43,* 1051–1058.

Horne, M. D. (1981). *Assessment of classroom status: Using the perception of social closeness scale.* (ERIC Document Reproducation Service No. ED. 200 616).

Horne, M. D., & Powers, J. E. (1983). Teacher's ratings of aggression and students' own perceived status. *Psychological Reports, 53,* 275–278.

Horne, M. D., Seidner, C. J., & Harasymiw, S. J. (1978). Peer status in research on locus of control. *Perceptual and Motor Skills, 47,* 487–490.

Hudson, F., Graham, S., & Warner, M. (1979). Mainstreaming: An examination of the attitudes and needs of regular classroom teachers. *Learning Disability Quarterly, 2,* 58–62.

Hutton, J. B., & Polo, L. (1976). A sociometric study of learning disability children and type of teaching strategy. *Group Psychotherapy and Psychodrama, 29,* 113–120.

Jaffe, J. (1966). Attitudes of adolescents toward the mentally retarded. *American Journal of Mental Deficiency, 70,* 907–912.

Jaffe, J. (1967). 'What's in a name' - Attitudes toward disabled persons. *Personnel and Guidance Journal, 45,* 557–560.

Jaffe, J. (1972). The effects of work conferences on attitudes towards the mentally retarded. *Rehabilitation Counseling Bulletin, 15,* 220–227.

Johnson, A. B., & Cartwright, C. A. (1979). The roles of information and experience in improving teachers' knowledge and attitudes about mainstreaming. *Journal of Special Education, 13,* 453–462.

Johnson, G. O. (1950). Study of the social position of mentally-handicapped children in regular grades. *American Journal of Mental Deficiency, 55,* 60–89.

Johnson, G. O., & Kirk, S. A. (1950). Are mentally handicapped children segregated in the regular grades? *Exceptional Children, 17,* 65–68, 87–88.

Jones, E. E., & Sigall, H. (1971). The bogus pipeline: A new paradigm for measuring affect and attitude. *Psychological Bulletin, 76,* 349–364.

Jones, R. L., Gottfried, N. W., & Owens, A. (1966). The social distance of the exceptional: A study at the high school level. *Exceptional Children, 32,* 551–556.

Jones, R. L., & Sisk, D. A. (1967). Early perceptions of orthopedic disability. *Exceptional Children, 34,* 42–43.

Jordan, J. E., & Proctor, D. I. (1969). Relationships between knowledge of exceptional children, kind and amount of experience with them, and teacher attitudes toward their classroom integration. *Journal of Special Education, 3,* 433–439.

Justman, J., & Wrightstone, J. W. (1951). A comparison of three methods of measuring pupil status in the classroom. *Educational and Psychological Measurement, 11,* 362–367.

Kennon, A. F., & Sandoval, J. (1978). Teacher attitudes toward the educable mentally retarded. *Education and Training of the Mentally Retarded, 13,* 139–145.

Keogh, B. K., Becker, L. D., Kukic, M., & Kukic S. (1974). Programs for eh and emr pupils: Review and recommendations. *Academic Therapy, 9,* 325–333.

Khleif, B. B. (1976). Role distance of classroom teachers of slow learners. *Journal of Research and Development in Education, 9,* 69–73.

Kuhn, J. (1971). A comparison of teacher's attitudes toward blindness and exposure to blind children. *The New Outlook, 65,* 337–340.

Kvaraceus, W. C. (1956). Acceptance-rejection and exceptionality. *Exceptional Children, 22,* 328–331.

Larrivee, B., & Cook, L. (1979). Mainstreaming study of the variables affecting teacher attitude. *Journal of Special Education, 13,* 315–324.

Lazar, A. L., Gaines, L., Haughton, D. D., D'Alonzo, B. J., & Pemos, G. (1976). *A study of parental attitudes toward their handicapped child.* Long Beach, CA: California State University, ERIC Document Reproduction Service No. ED 123 853.

Lazar, A., Gensley, J., & Orpet, R. (1971). Changing attitudes of young mentally gifted children toward handicapped persons. *Exceptional Children, 37,* 600–602.

Lazar, A. L., Stodden, R. L., & Sullivan, N. V. (1976). A comparison of attitudes held by male and female future school administrators toward instructional goals, personal adjustment, and the handicapped. *Rehabilitation Literature, 37,* 198–201.

Leyser, Y., & Gottlieb, J. (1980). Improving the social status of rejected pupils. *Exceptional Children, 46,* 459–461.

Likert, R. A. (1932). A technique for the measurement of attitudes. *Archives of Psychology, 140,* 44–53.

Lindzey, G. (1959). On the classification of projective techniques. *Psychological Bulletin, 56*(2), 158–168.

Lorber, N. M. (1973). Measuring the character of children's peer relations using the Ohio social acceptance scale. *California Journal of Educational Research, 24,* 71–77.

Lyon, S. (1977). Teacher nonverbal behavior related to perceived attributes. *Journal of Learning Disabilities, 10,* 173–177.

Marcus, E. J. (1980). Mapping the social structure of a class: A practical instrument for assessing some effects of mainstreaming. *Journal of Special Education, 14,* 311–324.

Marge, D. K. (1966). The social status of speech-handicapped children. *Journal of Speech and Hearing Research, 9,* 165–177.

Marsh, V., & Friedman, R. (1972). Changing public attitudes toward blindness. *Exceptional Children, 38,* 426–428.

Marshall, N. R., Hegrenes, N. R., & Goldstein, S. (1973). Verbal interactions: Mothers and their retarded children vs. mothers and their nonretarded children. *American Journal of Mental Deficiency, 77,* 415–419.

Matthews, V., & Westie, C. (1966). A preferred method for obtaining rankings: Reactions to physical handicaps. *American Sociological Review, 31,* 851–854.

May, B. J., & Furst, E. J. (1977). *Evaluation and revision of an inventory for measuring attitudes toward mainstreaming.* Fayetteville, AR: University of Arkansas. (ERIC Document Reproduction Service No. ED 160 642).

McCandless, B. R., & Marshall, H. R. (1957). A picture sociometric technique for preschool children and its relation to teacher judgements of friendship. *Child Development, 28,* 139–147.

McGinley, P., & McGinley, H. (1970). Reading groups as psychological groups. *Journal of Experimental Education, 39,* 35–42.

Mercer, J. R. (1966). Patterns of family crisis related to reacceptance of the retardate. *American Journal of Mental Deficiency, 71,* 19–32.

Meyers, C. E., Sitkei, E. G., & Watts, C. A. (1966). Attitudes toward special education and the handicapped in two community groups. *American Journal of Mental Deficiency, 71,* 78–84.

Miller, R. V. (1956). Social status and socioempathic differences among mentally superior, mentally typical and mentally retarded children. *Exceptional Children, 23,* 114–119.

Moreno, J. L. (1934). *Who shall survive? A new approach to the problem of human interrelations.* Washington, DC: Nervous and Mental Disease Publishing Co.

Morgan, S. R. (1978). A descriptive analysis of maladjusted behavior in socially rejected children. *Behavior Disorders, 4,* 23–30.

Morris, P. S., & McCauley, R. W. (1977). *Placement of handicapped children by Canadian mainstream administrators and teachers: A Rucker-Gable survey.* Paper presented at the Annual International Convention of the Council for Exceptional Children, Atlanta, Georgia. (ERIC Document Reproduction Service No. ED 139 139).

Morrison, G. M. (1981). Sociometric measurement: Methodological consideration of its use with mildly learning handicapped and nonhandicapped children. *Journal of Educational Psychology, 73,* 193–201.

Noe, F. P. (1970). A denotative dimension of meaning for the mentally ill–healthy role in society. *Psychological Reports, 26,* 519–531.

Noll, V. H., & Scannell, D. P. (1972). *Introduction to educational measurement* (3rd ed.). New York: Houghton Mifflin.

Novak, D. W. (1974). Children's reactions to emotional disturbance in imaginary peers. *Journal of Consulting and Clinical Psychology, 42,* 462.

Novak, D. W. (1975). Children's responses to imaginary peers labeled as emotionally disturbed. *Psychology in the Schools, 12,* 103–106.

Olley, J. G., Devellis, R. F., Devellis, B. M., Wall, A. J., & Long, C. E. (1981). The autism attitude scale for teachers. *Exceptional Children, 47,* 371–372.

Orlansky, M. D. (1979). Active learning and student attitudes toward exceptional children. *Exceptional Children, 46,* 49–52.

Osgood, C. E., & Suci, G. (1955). Factor analyses of meaning. *Journal of Experimental Psychology, 50,* 325–338.

Osgood, C. E., Suci, G. J., & Tannebaum, P. H. (1957). *The measurement of meaning.* Urbana, IL: University of Illinois.

Panda, K. C., & Bartel, N. R. (1972). Teacher perception of exceptional children. *The Journal of Special Education, 6,* 261–266.

Parker, L. G., & Stodden, R. J. (1977). Attitudes towards the handicapped. *Journal for Special Education of the Mentally Retarded, 14,* 24–28.

Parish, T. S., Bryant, W. T., & Shirazi, A. (1976). The personal attribute inventory. *Perceptual and Motor Skills, 42,* 715–720.

Parish, T. S., Dyck, N., & Kappes, B. M. (1979). Stereotypes concerning normal and handicapped children. *Journal of Psychology, 102,* 63–70.

Parish, T. S., Eads, G. M., Reece, N. H., & Piscitello, M. A. (1977). Assessment and attempted modification of future teachers' attitudes toward handicapped children. *Perceptual and Motor Skills, 44,* 540–542.

Perrin, E. H. (1954). The social position of the speech defective child. *Journal of Speech and Hearing Disorders, 19,* 250–252.

Phillips, P. P. (1976). Variables affecting classroom teachers' understanding of speech disorders. *Classroom Teachers, 7,* 142–149.

Rapier, J., Adelson, R., Carey, R., & Croke, K. (1972). Changes in children's attitudes toward the physically handicapped. *Exceptional Children, 39,* 219–223.

Richardson, S. A. (1970). Age and sex differences in values toward physical handicaps. *Journal of Health and Social Behavior, 11,* 207–214.

Richardson, S. A., Goodman, N., Hastorf, A. H., & Dornbusch, S. M. (1961). Cultural uniformity in reaction to physical disabilities. *American Sociological Review, 26,* 241–247.

Richardson, S. A., & Royce, J. (1968). Race and physical handicap in children's preference for other children. *Child Development, 39,* 467–480.

Ringlaben, R. P., & Price, J. R. (1981). Regular classroom teachers' perceptions of mainstreaming effects. *Exceptional Children, 47,* 302–304.

Rogers, C. R., & Dymond, R. F. (1954). *Psychotherapy and Personality Change.* Chicago,IL: University of Chicago Press.

Roistacher, R. C. (1974). A microeconomic model of sociometric choice. *Sociometry, 39,* 219–238.

Rucker, C. N., & Gable, R. K. (1974). *Rucker-Gable educational programming scale manual.* Storrs, CT: Rucker-Gable Associates.

Rucker, C. N., Howe, C. E., & Snider, B. (1969). The participation of retarded children in junior high academic and nonacademic regular classes. *Exceptional Children, 35,* 617–623.

Rucker, C. N., & Vincenzo, F. M. (1970). Maintaining social acceptance gains made by mentally retarded children. *Exceptional Children, 36,* 679–680.

Schaefer, C., & Brown, S. (1976) Investigating ethnic prejudice among boys in residential treatment. *Journal of Social Psychology, 100,* 317–318.

Schaefer, F. E., & Bell, R. Q. (1958). Development of a parental attitude research instrument. *Child Development, 29,* 339–361.

Schaver, P. R., & Scheibe, K. E. (1967). Transformation of social identity: A study of chronic mental patients and college volunteers in a summer camp setting. *Journal of Psychology, 66,* 19–37.

Schlenker, B. R., Bonoma, T. V., Hutchinson, D., & Burns, L. (1976). The bogus pipeline and stereotypes toward blacks. *Journal of Psychology, 93,* 319–329.

Scranton, T. R., & Ryckman, D. B. (1979). Sociometric status of learning disabled children in integrative programs. *Journal of Learning Disabilities, 12,* 49–54.

Semmel, D. S. (1979). *Variables influencing educators' attitudes toward individualized educational programs for handicapped children.* Paper presented at the American Educational Research Association Annual Meeting, San Francisco.

Shaw, S. F., & Gillung, T. B. (1975). Efficacy of a college course for regular class teachers of the mildly handicapped. *Mental Retardation, 13,* 3–6.

Sheare, J. B. (1974). Social acceptance of emr adolescents in integrated programs. *American Journal of Mental Deficiency, 78,* 678–682.

Sheare, J. B. (1975). *The relationship between peer acceptance and self-concept in children in grades 3 through 6.* Unpublished doctoral dissertation, The Pennsylvania State University.

Sheare, J. B. (1978). The impact of resource room programs upon the self-concept and peer acceptance of learning disabled students. *Psychology in the Schools, 15,* 406–412.

Shears, L. M., & Jensema, C. J. (1969). Social acceptability of anomalous persons. *Exceptional Children, 36,* 91–96.

Sigall, H., & Page, R. (1971). Current stereotypes: A little fading, a little faking. *Journal of Personality and Social Psychology, 18,* 247–255.

Simon, A., & Boyer, E. G. (Eds.). (1974). *Mirrors for behavior III: An anthology of observation instruments.* Wyncote, PA: Communication Materials Center.

Simpson, R. L., Parrish, N. E., & Cook, J. J. (1976). Modification of attitudes of regular class children towards the handicapped for the purpose of achieving integration. *Contemporary Educational Psychology, 1,* 46–51.

Singleton, L. C., & Asher, S. R. (1977). Peer preferences and social interaction among the third-grade children in an integrated school district. *Journal of Educational Psychology, 69,* 330–336.

Siperstein, G. N., Bopp, N. J., & Bak, J. J. (1978). The social status of learning disabled children. *Journal of Learning Disabilities, 11,* 49–53.

Siperstein, G. N., & Gottlieb, J. (1977). Physical stigma and academic performance as factors affecting children's first expressions of handicapped peers. *American Journal of Mental Deficiency, 81,* 455–462.

Skrtic, T. M., Sigler, G. R., & Lazar, A. L. (1975). Attitudes of male and female tmr teachers toward the handicapped. *Journal for Special Educators of the Mentally Retarded, 11,* 171–174.

Soldwedel, B., & Terrill, I. (1957). Physically handicapped and non-handicapped children in the same elementary school. *Exceptional Children, 23,* 371–383.

Speece, D. L., & Mandell, C. J. (1980). Resource room support services for regular teachers. *Learning Disability Quarterly, 3,* 49–53.

Steingisser, E. R. (1954). *The influence of set upon attitudes toward the blind as related to self-concept.* Unpublished M. A. thesis, University of New Hampshire.

Stephenson, W. (1953). *The study of behavior: Q-techniques and its methodology.* Chicago: University of Chicago Press.

Stephenson, W. (1964). Application of Q method to the measurement of public opinion. *Psychological Record, 14,* 265–273.

Stevens, G., & Gardner, S. (1982). A study of attitudes toward hyperkinesis using Q methodology. *Behavioral Disorders, 8,* 9–18.

Stilwell, W. E., Brown, P. W., & Barclay, J. R. (1973). Effects of three classroom management methods on classroom interaction of fifth graders. *Psychology in the Schools, 10,* 365–372.

Strauch, J. P. (1970). Social contact as a variable in the expressed attitudes of normal adolescents toward emr pupils. *Exceptional Children, 36,* 495–500.

Thurston, J. R. (1959). A procedure for evaluating parental attitudes toward the handicapped. *American Journal of Mental Deficiency, 64,* 148–155.

Thurstone, L. L., & Chave, E. J. (1929). *The Measurement of Attitude.* Chicago: University of Chicago Press.

Tringo, J. L. (1970). The hierarchy of preference toward disability groups. *Journal of Special Education, 4,* 295–306.

Vacc, N. A., & Kirst, N. (1977). Emotionally disturbed children and regular classroom teachers. *The Elementary School Journal, 78,* 309–317.

Westervelt, V. D., & McKinney, J. D. (1980). Effects of a film on nonhandicapped children's attitudes toward handicapped children. *Exceptional Children, 46,* 294–297.

Whiteman, M., & Lukoff, I. F. (1964). Attitudes toward blindness in two college groups. *The Journal of Social Psychology, 63,* 179–191.

Wilson, E. D., & Alcorn, D. (1969). Disability simulation and development of attitudes toward the exceptional. *Journal of Special Education, 3,* 303–307.

Woodmansee, J. J., & Cook, S. W. (1967). Dimensions of verbal racial attitudes: their identification and measurement. *Journal of Personality and Social Psychology, 7,* 240–250.

Worchel, T. L., & Worchel, P. (1961). The parental concept of the mentally retarded child. *American Journal of Mental Deficiency, 65,* 782–788.

Yamamoto, K., & Dizney, H. F. (1967). Rejection of the mentally ill: A study of attitudes of student teachers. *Journal of Counseling Psychology, 14,* 264–268.

Yamamoto, K., & Wiersma, J. (1967). Rejection of self and of deviant others among student teachers. *Journal of Special Education, 1,* 401–408.

Young, L. L. (1947). Sociometric and related techniques for appraising social status in an elementary school. *Sociometry, 10,* 168–177.

Yuker, H. E., Block, J. R., & Campbell, W. J. (1960). *A scale to measure attitudes toward disabled persons.* Albertson, NY: Human Resources Center.

Yuker, H. E., Block, J. R., & Young, J. H. (1970). *The measurement of attitudes toward disabled persons.* Albertson, NY: Human Resources Center.

Zuckerman, M. (1959). Reversed scales to control acquiescence response set in the parental attitude research instrument. *Child Development, 30,* 523–532.

Zuckerman, M., Ribback, B. B., Monashkin, I., & Norton, J. A. (1958). Normative data and factor analysis on the parental attitude research instrument. *Journal of Consulting Psychology, 22,* 165–171.

4 Attitudes of Professionals and Peers Toward Handicapped Students

Federal legislation (P. L. 94–142) passed in 1975 and the subsequent implementation of state mandates for the appropriate education of all handicapped children in accordance with the "least restrictive alternative" concept provided for handicapped student participation within the regular classroom to the extent possible. What must be of concern, however, is the quantity and qualities of social interaction among handicapped students, their nonhandicapped peers, and school personnel. Indeed, the regular classroom may be more restrictive if handicapped students are assigned to a status of a "second class citizen." The purpose of this chapter is to review the research that has explored the attitudes of professionals and peers toward handicapped class members and the self-attitudes of handicapped students. The issues of mainstreaming, community member attitudes, and the representation of handicapped individuals in the media are also discussed.

PROFESSIONAL ATTITUDES

This section opens with the findings of hierarchy studies which have involved comparisons of the attitudes nonhandicapped populations have toward a variety of different disability groups. Teacher and peer attitudes toward selected handicapped student groups are then considered.

Is There a Hierarchy of Preference?

Several studies provide evidence that a fairly consistent hierarchy of preference toward disability groups may exist. After normal and gifted individuals, those with physical disabilities such as asthma, arthritis, and heart trouble are among the more preferred or accepted. Mental retardation and mental illness seem to be among the least accepted handicaps, ranking just above those disabilities viewed as self-imposed, namely, ex-convict, alcoholism, drug addiction, and homosexuality, which are the most rejected by societal members (Harasymiw, Horne, & Lewis, 1976; Grand, Bernier, & Strohmer, 1982; Schneider & Anderson, 1980).

The rankings in terms of acceptability, severity, manageability, etc. obtained from diverse groups are reported in Table 4.1. These data were reported in studies dating from 1956 to 1983. When comparisons were made among several sub-population groups (Barsh, 1964; Harasymiw, Horne, & Lewis, 1976; Tringo, 1970), high positive correlations among the rankings obtained from heterogeneous groups were reported. For studies in which somewhat heterogeneous samples have been included but separate rankings not computed (Abroms & Kodera, 1979; Shears & Jensema, 1969; Warren & Turner, 1966), as well as for those investigations in which, generally speaking, the groups were homogeneous (Antonak, 1980; Kvaraceus, 1956; Harasymiw & Horne, 1976; Horne, 1983; Warren, Turner, & Brody, 1964), results are also similar.

There also are numerous other studies which support a congruency of attitudes in diverse groups, including professionals who have been specifically trained to work with handicapped populations. For example, Greenbaum & Wang (1965) found that parents with a mentally retarded child, professionals involved in treating retarded persons (psychologists, physicians, vocational counselors), paraprofessionals working in institutional settings, and business executives all had negative attitudes toward the mentally retarded and mentally ill, and were especially rejecting of the latter. In a study by Parker & Stodden (1977) no differences were demonstrated in the attitudes toward disabilities held by pre- and in-service groups in elementary education, counselor education, vocational rehabilitation and special education. Other investigations have demonstrated that: (1) teacher attitudes may be similar to those of the general public (Conine, 1969); (2) rehabilitation workers were not more positive toward the physically disabled than hospital workers (Bell, 1962); and, (3) education and seminary students similarly evidenced negativity toward blindness (Kang & Masoodi, 1977).

A Closer Look at Which Exceptionalities Teachers Prefer

Investigations of teacher attitudes have usually involved comparisons of their attitudes toward two or three selected handicapped student group populations. However, it is difficult to say exactly which exceptionality groups are regarded most positively by classroom teachers. Shotel, Iano & McGettigan (1972) found that after contact with each group, teachers preferred learning disabled students over those who were emotionally disturbed and over the educable mentally retarded, who were the least preferred. Teachers demonstrated a similar ranking based on questionnaire (Vandivier & Vandivier, 1981). Hirshoren and Burton (1979) also found teachers were more accepting of disturbed than retarded students. In another study (Parish, Eads, Reece, & Piscitello, 1977), those labeled physically handicapped were rated more positively than learning disabled and mentally handicapped by future teachers. In contrast, physical education teachers understandably indicated they felt more able to work with educable mentally retarded students than with students with a physical handicap (Aloia, Knutson, Minner, & Von Seggern, 1980). Parish, Dyck, and Kappes (1979) completed two surveys: one of Kansas teachers and another of attendees at the 1978 International Conference of the Association for Children with Learning Disabilities. The results were the same for both groups; the labels gifted, normal, and physically handicapped were perceived significantly more positively than the labels of mentally retarded, learning disabled, and emotionally disturbed students (ranked in this order of decreasing positivity). These results are somewhat surprising in that the mentally retarded were more positively rated than the learning disabled by teachers with a demonstrated interest in learning disabilities.

Another investigation of attitudes (Williams & Algozzine, 1977) provided teachers with a definition and description for learning disabled, socially/emotionally disturbed, physically handicapped and educable mentally retarded children. After reading each description, teachers used a Likert-type scale to: (1) indicate what portion of the exceptional student's education should be in the regular classroom; and (2) rate "their ability to provide a meaningful educational program for the handicapped child." Results indicated teachers were more willing, and felt they were better equipped, to teach physically handicapped and learning disabled students than socially-emotionally disturbed or educable mentally retarded children.

When these findings are examined along with results reported for the hierarchy studies discussed in the previous section, it appears that although students who are gifted, stutter, have epilepsy, or a learning disability seem to be among the more favored (and emotionally disturbed students among the least favored), there is some variability. Consequently, it is necessary to look for specific factors that possibly influenced teacher attitudes. Among these are the knowledge and experience teachers have had with handicapped individuals (see Chaper 6) as well as the fact that studies use somewhat different labels as well as different measurement techniques. For example, blindness may connote a higher degree of severity than visual impairment. There is also evidence that responses to labels may be less positive than when sketches or vignettes are used to measure attitudes (Jaffe, 1967).

PEER ATTITUDES

As shown in Table 4.2, representative research on classmates' attitudes toward their handicapped peers has indicated the vast majority of studies completed in

TABLE 4.1
Rankings for Disability Groups Reported in Studies of Diverse Groups Percentage

	Kvaracous (1956) most prefer to teach[g]	Barach (1964) least to most severe[b]	Warren, Turner & Brody (1964) most to least prefer to work with[c]	Warren & Turner (1966) most to least prefer to work with[d]	Shears & Jensema (1969) most to least acceptable[e]	Tringo (1970) rankings obtained using social distance questionnaire[f]	Harasymiw, Horne & Lewis (1976) rankings obtained using social distance questionnaire[g]	Harasymiw & Horne (1976) most to least manageable in class[h]	Abroms & Kodera (1979) in order of acceptability[i]	Antonak (1980) most to least easy to integrate into regular classroom/into community[j]	Horne (1983) most to least manageable in the regular classroom[k]
Alcoholism		1	4(D)	2		20	20		10		
Antisocial											
Amputee						6	6		4		
Arthritis					1	2	3		2		
Asthma						3	2		11		
Blindness	6	4(SH)	5.5	3(SH)	3	7	7	9	12	4/8(VI)	7
Brain Injury	7	5		6					14	8/9(NI)	
Cancer	10				7	10	12				
Cerebral Palsy	4					15	15				
Cronically Ill	1										
Deafness		3(HH)	8	5(HH)	4	8	8	7	7	9/5	6
Diabetes						4	1		3	5/3(HI)	
Dwarf						14					
Epilepsy	5					13	13	3			3
Ex-convict						18	19				
Gifted		2(T)	1	1(T)				2	8	2/6	2
Hair Lip					6						
Heart Trouble	2					5	5				
Homosexual							14				
Hunchback					10	16					
Learning Disabled								4	5	6/4	4
Mental Illness	8	6(M)	2(ED)	4(M)	8	21	17	8(ED) 5(EMR)	13	11/11(ED)	8(ED) 5(EMR)
Mental Ret'dat'n	8	7(S)	7	7(S)	9	19	18	6(TMR) 10	15	10/10	10(TMR) 9
Multiple Handicapped										12/12(SPI)	
Old Age						11	9				
Paraplegic			3(PH)		2(WP)	12	10			7/2(PD)	
Polio	3		5.5								
Speech Defect					5(SST)	9	11	1(ST)	6	3/7(CD)	1(ST)
Stroke						17					
Tuberculosis							16		9		
Ulcer						1	4		1		

TABLE 4.1 (continued)

% Rankings are for the total sample studies

+ "normal" label ranked first

[a] graduate students enrolled in a course "The Education of the Exceptional Child" (N=84)

[b] parents, nurses, teachers, professional therapists, optometrists, undergraduate psychology students (N=2,500)

[c] sophomores in College of Education (N=80)

[d] psychologists, teachers of mentally retarded, social workers, students in nursing, medicine, psychology and education (N=403)

[e] psychology students and psychiatric technicians (N=94)

[f] high school students, undergraduates, graduate students, rehabilitation workers (N=955)

[g] adults from general population (N=1,030)

[h] elementary teachers in schools with mainstreamed children (N=191) and in school where mainstreaming was not instituted (N=161)

[i] students enrolled in introductory courses in special education, child development, and exceptional child development at two universities (N=138)

[j] graduate students enrolled in education department courses (N=122)

[k] teachers enrolled in an introductory special education course (N=139)

( ) BD = behaviorally disordered, CD = communication disordered, D = delinquent, ED = emotionally disturbed, EMR = educable mentally retarded, HH = hearing handicapped, HI = hearing impaired, M = mild, NI = neurologically impaired, PD = physically disabled, PH = physically handicapped, S = severe, SH = sight handicapped, SPI = severely and profoundly impaired, SST = severe stutterer, ST = stutterer, T = talented, TMR = trainable mentally retarded, VH = visually handicapped, VI = visually impaired, WP = wheelchair patient.

---

the last 30 years have utilized sociometric procedures to document the rejected status of the handicapped student in the regular classroom. Prior to 1950, there were very few studies on the classroom acceptance of handicapped students. Rather, early research focused on the relationship of intelligence and social acceptance, and made comparisons of performance in segregated and integrated settings.

The investigations of peer attitudes may be categorized according to the setting or circumstances in which the status of handicapped students was measured. Many investigations involved administering a sociometric questionnaire to classmates of handicapped students placed in the regular classroom; however, the status of handicapped students enrolled in open space schools and the possi-

TABLE 4.2

Representative Research on Classmates Attitudes Toward Their Exceptional Peers

Author	Sample	Instrumentation	Findings
Johnson, 1950	39 mr students and 698 1st through 5th graders in 25 classrooms	Sociometric Questionnaire	"Borderline," "upper," and "lower" mentally handicapped were isolated and rejected
Johnson & Kirk, 1950	12 mr students integrated in 6 classrooms in a progressive school which stressed social adjustment and 163 classmates	Sociometric Questionnaire	Mentally retarded are isolated and rejected
Perrin, 1954	37 students with speech defects and 408 classmates in grades 1 to 6	Sociometric Questionnaire	Students with speech defects are isolated and rejected
Force, 1956	63 physically handicapped and 361 nonhandicapped in 14 elementary classes	Near-Sociometric Questionnaire	Physically handicapped students were chosen significantly less often as friends, playmates, and workmates
Freeman & Sonnega, 1956	26 students attending a speech correction class and 107 classmates in 3rd and 4th grade	Sociometric Questionnaire	Children attending speech correction classes were chosen less by classmates as speakers to represent the class but were not chosen less when the basis of choice was friendship
Miller, 1956	40 superior, 40 typical and 40 mr students in 4th and 6th grades	Roster Ratings	Retarded in regular classes least chosen as friends but not rejected
Lapp, 1957	16 retarded children integrated into 3rd to 5th grade regular classes part time and 290 classmates	Sociometric Questionnaire	mr students had significantly lower acceptance scores

Study	Sample	Instrument	Findings
Soldwedel & Terrill, 1957	10 physically handicapped and 22 nonhandicapped 7th and 8th graders enrolled in the same class	Sociometric Questionnaire	No significant differences were found in choices among nonhandicapped and nonhandicapped for seating partners; there was a trend for physically handicapped to receive fewer choices as playmates
Baldwin, 1958	31 integrated mr students and 574 4th, 5th and 6th graders	Ohio Social Acceptance Scale	Integrated emrs have segregated status
Elser, 1959	45 hearing handicapped students and 1,258 nonhandicapped classmates in grades 3 to 7	Sociometric Questionnaire	Hearing handicapped not accepted by classmates
Billings, 1963	6 crippled children in regular classroom in grades 1, 2, 6 and 54 classmates	Projective Tests	Students have unfavorable attitudes toward crippled classmates
Centers & Centers, 1963	14 students with amputations enrolled in regular classrooms with 413 nonhandicapped students	Sociometric Questionnaire	Students with amputations were least liked and considered the saddest children in the classroom
Marge, 1966	36 speech handicapped students and 131 normal speakers in 3rd grade	Sociometric Questionnaire	Speech handicapped students receive significantly fewer choices as work partners, study partners, and guests for dinner; they were not chosen significantly less for playground games or as speakers. There were some speech handicapped "stars."
Renz & Simensen, 1969	14 emr special class students, 14 randomly drawn control students,	Interview	Emr students were not evaluated differently from normal peers

continued...

Author	Sample	Instrumentation	Findings
	and 57 randomly drawn interviewees		
Rucker, Howe, & Snider, 1969	23 retarded students and 1,010 7th and 8th graders	Ohio Social Acceptance Scale	Mentally retarded students integrated into junior high academic and non-academic classes are equally rejected
Goodman, Gottlieb, & Harrison, 1972	10 integrated and 8 segregated emr students and 83 1st to 3rd graders in a nongraded school	Peer Acceptance Scale	Emr students who were segregated and integrated were rejected by regular class students; those who were integrated were rejected more often
Jones, Lavine, & Shell, 1972	27 blind children integrated into 10 regular classrooms containing 247 students in grades 1 to 7	Sociomatric Questionnaire	Blind children were rejected; when they were assigned higher ratings, it was because isolates and rejectees chose them
Gottlieb & Budoff, 1973	40 boys and 40 girls in an open school and 28 boys and 28 girls in a traditional school who were not handicapped, 8 partially integrated and 4 segregated emr students in an open school, and 4 partially integrated and 8 segregated emr students in a traditional school	Sociometric Questionnaire	Partially segregated and integrated emr students in the open school were more often known by peers; all children in the open school were more often rejected and partially integrated students were rejected most often
Gottlieb & Davis, 1973	42 students in 4th, 5th, and 6th grades and a segregated and integrated	Observation of student choices for partners in a game	Integrated and segregated emr students were chosen less as partners for a

	emr student		game than nondisabled students
Bryan, 1974	84 white and black LD students, 84 matched controls and 1,430 non-disabled students in 3rd, 4th, and 5th grades	Sociometric Questionnaire	LD students received significantly more rejection votes and fewer social attraction votes than the control group
Iano et al., 1974	40 former educable class students, 80 regular class students, attending a resource room, and 606 'ordinary' regular class elementary students	Sociometric Questionnaire	Former special class students now mainstreamed and students not formerly diagnosed but receiving resource room services were rejected
Kennedy & Bruininks, 1974	15 hearing impaired students in 13--2nd and 3rd grade classrooms and 277 nondisabled classmates	Sociometric Questionnaire	Students with severe hearing losses were chosen significantly more often as friends than nondisabled students; children with mild to moderate losses were less accepted; there was no significant difference found between the total hearing impaired population and nondisabled classmates
Bryan, 1976	25 learning disabled students (from Bryan, 1974 sample) in 20 classrooms 1 year later and 185 non disabled classmates	Sociometric Questionnaire	Learning disabled student social status remained the same; one year later they received more rejection votes
Hutton & Polo, 1976	450 4th graders in 18 classes; each class had 13 nondisabled and 12 hearing disabled students	Sociometric Questionnaire	Learning disabled students were rejected by classmates

continued...

Author	Sample	Instrumentation	Findings
Bruininks, 1978	16 learning disabled students in grades 1 and 2, 7 learning disabled in grades 4 and 5, and 139 classmates	Peer Acceptance Scale	Learning disabled students had significantly lower social status
Reese-Dukes & Stokes, 1978	32 mainstreamed emr students and 32 randomly selected control students in 5th and 6th grade	Sociometric Questionnaire	Emr students were assigned significantly lower sociometric ratings
Sheare, 1978	41 learning disabled students integrated in 3rd, 4th and 5th grade classrooms and receiving resource room help and 41 nondisabled classmates	Peer Acceptance Rating Scale	Learning disabled students had significantly lower peer acceptance scores
Siperstein, Bopp, & Bak, 1978	22 learning disabled students and 155 nondisabled in 5th and 6th grade classes	Sociometric Questionnaire	Learning disabled students were significantly less popular; but not significantly more often isolated
Scranton & Rykman, 1979	42 learning disabled students and 42 classmates in	Sociometric Questionnaire	Learning disabled students were rejected by classmates

	grades 1 to 3 in open schools		
Prillaman, 1981	362 nonhandicapped students in grades 1 to 6 and 28 mainstreamed learning disabled students	Sociometric Questionnaire	There was no significant difference for LD students' status; although disproportionately more LD students were identified as isolates, some were "stars"
Randolph & Harrington, 1981	25 fifth grade students	Open-ended questions for projected response: "How would you feel if a new child who was blind or who was in a wheelchair was to join our class tomorrow?"	Isolated response factors showed students felt pity, desire to help, and sorrow; rejection was not evidenced
Schumaker, Wildgen, & Sherman, 1982	35 pairs of learning disabled and nondisabled junior high school students	In-class observations of target behaviors	LD students are not social isolates
Perlmutter, Crocker, Cordray, & Garstecki, 1983	55 learning disabled students, 12 behavior disordered and 107 nonhandicapped 10th grade classmates in 8 special education classes and 7 low-ability mainstreamed classrooms	Sociometric Questionnaire	Students rated nondisabled peers significantly higher; 6 LD students achieved sociometric ratings equal to the most popular non-LD students

ble positive effects of resource rooms and mainstreaming have also been studied. Two studies compared the status of learning disabled students in classrooms containing almost equal numbers of learning disabled and nonhandicapped students.

Handicapped Student Status in the Regular Classroom

In the majority of investigations, significant differences are observed for the status of handicapped versus nonhandicapped students in the regular classroom. Studies of the mentally retarded (Baldwin, 1958; Gottlieb & Davis, 1973; Lapp, 1957; Miller, 1956; Reese-Dukes & Stokes, 1978), learning disabled (Bruininks, 1978, Bryan, 1974, 1976; Siperstein, Bopp, & Bak, 1978; Sheare, 1978), speech handicapped (Perrin, 1954), hearing handicapped (Elser, 1959), blind (Jones, Lavine & Shell, 1972), and physically handicapped (Billings, 1963; Centers & Centers, 1963; Force, 1956) have shown that these handicapped students experience peer rejection at least to some degree.

Open Space, Nongraded Schools, and the Handicapped

In contrast to traditional schools, open-space and nongraded schools provide flexible groupings of children according to their performance level. Thus, they are thought to facilitate greater understanding and acceptance of individual differences. It has been suggested that the stigma of receiving special education services is minimized because students move freely from class to class and their peers do not necessarily know to which group students belong (Scranton & Ryckman, 1979).

Unfortunately, the promise of such plans has not been realized. When handicapped student status has been investigated within an open-space or nongraded environment, the results have not supported greater peer acceptance. Scranton and Ryckman (1979) found learning disabled students had significantly lower acceptance scores than their nonhandicapped peers. In another investigation (Goodman, Gottlieb, & Harrison, 1972), mentally retarded students in a nongraded elementary school were rejected; those who were integrated into the classroom were rejected more often than those in segregated classes. Another study (Gottlieb & Budoff, 1973), which compared peer acceptance of educable mentally retarded (EMR) children in an open and a traditional school, indicated that partially segregated and integrated EMR students in the open school were more often known and rejected by their peers. Partially integrated EMR students were rejected more often than the segregated group. Mentally retarded students attending a progressive school stressing social adjustment rather than achievement were also rejected by their peers (Johnson & Kirk, 1950).

Mainstreaming, Resource Rooms, and Handicapped Student Status

It was expected that mainstreaming handicapped students into the regular classroom would facilitate positive attitudes and interactions among handicapped and nonhandicapped students. Similarly, it was hoped that receiving resource room services would have a less stigmatizing effect than placement in a special education classroom. Indeed, an early study demonstrated that EMR junior high school students who had been integrated into nonacademic areas and extracurricular activities were not rejected by peers (Renz & Simenson, 1969). There is, however, more evidence to the contrary. Iano, Ayers, Hellern, McGettigan, & Walker (1974) found no differences in peer acceptance of EMR mainstreamed students who were formerly enrolled in a special class and ''undiagnosed'' students receiving resource room services; both groups were rejected by classmates. In another study, Gottlieb and Davis (1973) found that both integrated and segregated EMR fourth- through sixth-grade students were rejected by classmates. Similarly, Rucker, Howe, & Snider (1969) reported that 7th- and 8th-grade special class students were equally rejected in academic and non-academic classes. And a study by Sheare (1978) showed that learning disabled students who attended a resource room had lower peer acceptance scores than their non-disabled classmates.

Effect of Minority versus Majority Group Status on Peer Attitudes

The term ''minority group'' refers to a group that is smaller than some other group with which it is compared. Handicapped students constitute a minority group in the regular classroom and it is expected that when a student is a member of a minority group the likelihood of rejection increases. In one study (Richardson, Ronald, & Kleck, 1974) of peer relationships in a summer camp where there was almost an equal number of boys with and without handicaps, the nonhandicapped were preferred by peers but the handicapped campers were also accepted to a considerable degree depending on the visibility of their handicap. But Hutton & Polo (1976) found that learning disabled (LD) students in 4th grade classes where there was an almost equal number of LD and nonlearning disabled students were rejected by peers. On the other hand Perlmutter, Crocker, Cordray, & Garstecki's (1983) results indicated that LD 10th-graders were more accepted by their nonhandicapped peers in classes where there was a high ratio (more than 25%) of learning disabled classroom members than in classes with a low ratio of LD students.

Positive Findings for Handicapped Student Status

There are few studies in which the rejected status of handicapped students was not clearly evidenced. In one study (Jones, Lavine, & Shell, 1972), although blind children were generally rejected, a few were assigned higher ratings than their nonhandicapped peers. When the choices indicated on the sociometric questionaire were examined, however, it became apparent that these higher ratings for a few of the blind students were the result of choice preferences by children who were themselves rejectees or isolates. It was not clear why some, but not other, blind students were chosen.

Soldwedel and Terrill (1957) did not find differences in the choices of seating partners made by physically handicapped and nonhandicapped students enrolled in a single classroom, although there was a trend for the physically handicapped to receive fewer choices as playmates. The ratio of 10 physically handicapped to 22 nonhandicapped students could have contributed to the findings.

Sometimes the positivity of classmates toward a handicapped peer has depended upon the criterion activity. Freeman and Sonnega (1956) used a sociometric test to measure the classroom status of students who were attending a speech correction class. Results showed that the speech students were chosen less by classmates when the criterion was speaking ability; however, this was not the case when the basis of choice was friendship. In contrast, Marge (1966) found speech handicapped students were not chosen less by classmates who were asked to choose students to speak for them in class or be on their team for games. However, they were selected significantly less often as work partners, study partners, and guests for dinner. No explanation was offered for these results. Marge (1966) also found some speech handicapped were stars (students who receive many more choices from peers than could be expected by chance) in the group; but the number of these students was less than would be expected to occur given the ratio of speech handicapped to nonhandicapped in the classes.

Indeed it is very unusual to find children with exceptionalities evidencing popularity scores which exceed those of "normal" or nonhandicapped peers, or to find handicapped students among the stars of the class. However, Kennedy and Bruininks (1974) found severely hearing handicapped students were actually picked more often as friends by their first- and second-grade nonhandicapped classmates. Several reasons for this unexpected finding were suggested: the hearing handicapped students demonstrated socially desirable traits and skills required for school success; the characteristics of the classrooms facilitated acceptance; young students may be more accepting; or the pre-school experiences of the hearing handicapped enhanced their social acceptability. Inexplicably, students with mild to moderate losses were less accepted than those with severe to profound hearing losses.

Stars among mentally retarded students were reported by Johnson (1950). However, an analysis of the data indicated several plausible explanations: they were in classes having a larger number (4 or 5 versus 1 or 2) of mentally retarded students; popularity had been purchased to some extent since these "stars" gave things to other students; and most of the votes they received were from students with lower intelligence quotients.

In a few cases, stars have also been noted among learning disabled populations. For example, Prillaman (1981) did not find learning disabled students had lower sociometric status than non-disabled students. Furthermore, although disproportionately more learning disabled students were found to be isolates, there were a few (11% or 3 out of 28 learning disabled) who were stars. Perlmutter et al., (1983) found that some learning disabled subjects had sociometric rankings as high as those achieved by popular non-learning disabled students, although non-learning disabled subjects had overall received higher rankings than their handicapped classmates. In one study (Siperstein, Bopp, & Bak, 1978), no learning disabled student achieved star status, but neither were they overrepresented in the isolate category. An observational study (Schumaker, Wildgen, & Sherman, 1982) showed that LD junior high students interacted with peers as often as the nondisabled did.

When asked (Randolph & Harrington, 1981) how they would feel if a child who was blind or in a wheelchair were integrated into their class, students' responses did not evidence feelings of rejection. Of course, the findings might be different if and when a handicapped child joined the class.

Handicapped Student Status in the Regular Versus Special Classroom

The results of the few studies comparing the social position of the handicapped student in the regular classroom versus their social position in the special class have been inconclusive. Perrin (1954) found some speech-impaired children had higher status in their speech therapy classes than in the regular classroom, but others had lower status. Similarly, Lapp (1957) found mentally retarded students evidenced both greater acceptance and greater rejection in their special classroom than in the regular classes they participated in for a portion of the day. It was speculated that the results reflected the opportunity for students to get to know each other better in the small group situation. In another study (Rucker, Howe, & Snider, 1969) a comparison of social status scores for mentally retarded junior high school students in their special versus regular classroom where they were integrated for part of the school day showed they were assigned higher social status scores by their special class peers. Those with higher social status scores in the special class were also assigned higher status by students in the regular classes.

Indeed, it appears that many of the same variables that account for peer social status in regular classrooms (see Chapter 5) are important in determining the status of students in special or segregated settings. Intelligence and academic achievement (Dentler & Mackler, 1964; Hays, 1951; Marden & Farber, 1961) as well as attractiveness, cooperativeness, happiness and physical strength (Pandy, 1971) are important variables in determining the status of a student in a special setting. The students who are most liked in special classes are the ones who are friendly, kind, helpful, fair, and so forth (Barksdale, 1961). Among emotionally disturbed populations, the social status assigned by disturbed peers has been shown to be significantly higher for the more emotionally adjusted (Davids & Parenti, 1958; Smith & Olson, 1970) and among delinquents, higher for conforming individuals (McCorkle, Elias, & Bixby, 1958).

Which Exceptionalities Do Students Prefer?

Very few investigators have queried elementary-aged students about their feelings toward a variety of handicapping conditions. In one investigation (Harasymiw, Horne, & Lewis, 1976), where samples of third to fifth graders were included, the intercorrelations among adult and young student samples were significant. The rankings for the mean scores assigned disability groups by elementary-aged students using social distance type questionnaires appear in Table 4.3. It seems that the order of disability preference from most to least

TABLE 4.3
Rankings of Mean Attitude Scores Assigned Disability Groups by
Elementary Classroom Students

Group	Rankings of Suburban 3rd Grade Students (N=22)	Rankings of Inner City 3rd and 5th Grade Students (N=48)	Rankings of Inner City 3rd to 5th Grade Students (N=79)
Alcoholic	18	7	20
Amputee	5	5	10
Arthritis	6		6
Asthma	2		4
Blindness	3	3	7
Cancer	12	2	15
Cerebral Palsy	9	–	12
Deaf	4	4	9
Diabetes	14	–	5
Drug Addict	19	10	19
Epilepsy	15	–	16
Ex-convict	20	6	18
Gifted	–	–	1
Heart Disease	7	–	13
Hunchback	10	–	–
Mental Illness	17	9	14
Mental Retardation	11	8	17
Old Age	1	1	2
Stroke	13		11
Stutterer	–		3
Tuberculosis	16		–
Ulcer	8		8

From Harasymiw, Horne, and Lewis (1976). Disability social distance hierarchy for population subgroups. *Scandinavian Journal of Rehabilitation Medicine, 8*, 33-36.

accepted may be summarized as being: physical, sensory, psychological and social handicaps.

In another study (Miller, Richey, & Lammers, 1983) gifted 4th to 7th graders were tested with a social distance type scale to identify their attitudes toward six handicapped student groups. The order of preference from most to least accepted was: learning disabled, nonhandicapped, hearing impaired, physically handicapped, mildly retarded, and partially sighted. The authors speculated that the highest rating, surprisingly for the learning disabled, might have been the result of the pictorial characterization used for this handicap on the measurement instrument.

Parish, Ohlsen, and Parish (1978) used an adjective checklist to determine the preferences of fifth, sixth, and seventh graders. In this study the hierarchy from most to least preferred was: normal, physically handicapped, learning disabled, and emotionally disturbed.

Richardson, Goodman, Hastorf, & Dornbusch (1961) developed and administered a series of drawings to investigate student attitudes toward physically disabled children in culturally diverse student groups. Richardson's test was subsequently used in other investigations concerned with the cultural uniformity of attitudes. These studies included students confined to residential psychiatric institutions, institutions for retarded persons, and noninstitutionalized mentally retarded (Goodman, Dornbusch, Richardson, & Hastorf, 1963) high school students, (Matthews & Westie, 1966), Israeli students (Chigier & Chigier, 1968) and elementary-aged students (Richardson & Royce, 1968). The students were asked to identify which child they liked ''best,'' ''next best,'' and so forth. As indicated in Table 4.4, almost all the student groups indicated a preference for the child without a handicap. One exception was Richardson's mentally retarded group who were not institutionalized. It was speculated that because this group was not institutionalized but in environments where they had less opportunity to interact with others, they therefore had less opportunity to acquire societal attitudes or preferences for being handicapped. (All of Richardson's groups were significantly different in their rankings, supporting the hypothesis that negative attitudes toward handicapped persons reflect exposure to cultural values and the ability to learn from this exposure.) In the Matthews and Westie study, an effort was made to compare the results for Richardson's drawings and findings for a social distance scale which they conclude is a more valid device. As shown, when a social distance scale was administered, the nonhandicapped child was most preferred.

The relationship between student and adult rankings of disabilities (Harasymiw, Horne, & Lewis, 1976; Goodman et al., 1963) suggests that, with increasing age, children begin to acquire the normative values of society. The preferences, however, of younger students are not clear. (See Chapter 5 for a further discussion of the effect of the age variable.)

TABLE 4.4

Rank-Order of Preference by Student Groups Using the Richardson et al. (1961) Pictures

PICTURE	Richardson et al. (1961) 7 diverse student groups aged 10 and 11 years	Goodman et al. (1963) 50 male and female students confined to a residential psychiatric institution	Goodman et al. (1963) 70 males and females in institution for the mentally retarded	Goodman et al. (1963) 26 mentally retarded males and females not institutionalized	Mathews & Westie (1966) 144 high school students pictorial ranking/social distance scale results	Chigier & Chigier (1968) 11 culturally diverse student groups aged 10 or 11 years in Israel	Richardson & Royce (1968) Females and males aged 10 and 12
Child with no physical handicap	1*	1	1	3	2/1	1*	1*
Child with crutches and a brace on the left leg	2	3	4	1	4/3	5	3
Child sitting in a wheelchair with a blanket covering both legs	3	5	6	4-5	1/2	6	4
Child with the left hand missing	4	5	3	6	5/4	3	5
Child with a facial disfigurement	5	2	2	4-5	6/5	2	2
An obese child	6	4	5	2	3/6	4	6

* Rankings are for the total sample studied

WHY DO PEERS REJECT HANDICAPPED STUDENTS?

How Handicapped Students Behave

The nature of the behaviors exhibited by handicapped students seems particularly important in determining their status among or acceptance by classmates. In a few early studies, students were interviewed after they had been administered a sociogram and queried about why they had rejected students. For example, Johnson (1950) asked elementary school students to tell why they did not want to sit next to, play with, or did not like mentally retarded students. Their responses indicated that rejection was primarily due to the misbehaviors exhibited by their mentally retarded classmates. Of the 288 reasons given, only 34 dealt with academic or physical factors. The remainder of the responses had to do with misbehaviors such as "rough," "mean," "poor sport," "cheats," "shows off," "steals," and "swears." Johnson and Kirk (1950) also found students in both traditional and progressive schools cited misbehaviors ("he teases me," "he cheats in games," "he pulls my hair," "he hits me over the head with his lunch bucket," "he says bad things," "he takes my jump rope," "he steals my bicycle") as responses for rejecting retarded students. Similarly, Baldwin (1958) found that most of the reasons given by students for rejecting mentally retarded peers were behavioral in nature.

Student interviews, which followed the presentation of vignettes describing emotionally disturbed subjects also have provided evidence about the negative effect of handicapped students' deviant behaviors on peer attitudes (Coie & Pennington, 1976; Hoffman, Marsden, & Kalter, 1977; Marsden & Kalter, 1976). Students recognize emotional disturbance, may even perceive the degrees of severity (Hoffman, Marsden, & Kalter, 1977), and the implication of their subsequent rejection can be made. This is substantiated further by studies which have shown a relationship between sociometric ratings of students by peers and behavioral rating instruments designed to provide a measure of behaviors symptomatic of emotional disturbance (Hutton & Roberts, 1982; Morgan, 1978).

The relative effect of different misbehaviors on peer attitudes toward handicapped classmates is not clear. In one study (Vidoni, Fleming, & Mintz, 1983), 5th to 8th graders ranked the "seriousness" of 46 behaviors; the results appear in Table 4.5. According to descriptive reports, many of these behaviors characterize handicapped students, particularly mentally retarded and emotionally disturbed children. It seems that future studies might consider the perceptions students have of the severity or seriousness of specific deviant behaviors exhibited by various handicapped student groups; then the relationship these perceptions have to the assignment of classroom social status could be examined.

Academic competence has also been shown to be an important correlate of peer status, and many handicapped groups are characterized as performing poorly on academic tasks. Gottlieb, Semmel, and Veldman (1978) have at-

TABLE 4.5
Rankings for Seriousness of Behavior Problems by 5th to 8th Graders

Ranking	Behavior	Ranking	Behavior
1	Stealing	24	Slovenly in Appearance
2	Destroying School Materials	25	Tattling
3	Cruelty, Bullying	26	Laziness
4	Cheating	27	Resentfulness
5	Smoking	28	Stubornness
6	Truency	29	Thoughtlessness
7	Untruthfulness	30	Easily Discouraged
8	Impudence, Rudeness	31	Dreaminess
9	Temper Tantrums	32	Suggestible
10	Impertinence/Defiance	33	Sullenness
11	Disobedience	34	Unhappy, Depressed
12	Selfishness	35	Suspiciousness
13	Profanity	36	Imaginative Lying
14	Quarrelsomeness	37	Physical Cowardice
15	Inquisitiveness	38	Sensitiveness
16	Unreliableness	39	Interrupting
17	Lack of Interest in Work	40	Nervousness
18	Disorderliness in Class	41	Unsocial, Withdrawing
19	Carelessness in Work	42	Fearfulness
20	Overcritical of Others	43	Tardiness
21	Attracting Attention	44	Restlessness
22	Inattention	45	Whispering
23	Domineering	46	Shyness

From Vidoni, Fleming, and Mintz (1983). Behavior problems as perceived by teachers, mental health professionals, and children. *Psychology in the Schools, 20*, 93-98.

tempted to explain the relative contribution of academic competence and misbehavior to peer acceptance and rejection of educable mentally retarded students. According to these authors peer acceptance and rejection are not on the same continuum. This means, for example, that misbehaviors may be related to rejection but not to acceptance. Results suggested that for the sample of integrated EMR 3rd, 4th, and 5th graders, misbehavior was more closely related to rejection; academic competence was associated with acceptance. These authors suggested it might be easier to modify student behaviors to increase peer acceptance via training in academics. MacMillan and Morrison (1980), however, found: (1) misbehavior and academic competence were both linked to rejection in a special class population; and (2) academic competence was most closely associated with acceptance and rejection in a population of low achievers with IQ's in the normal range and enrolled in regular classes. Consequently, MacMillan and Morrison recommended that future research intended to clarify the correlates of social status must consider different groups of handicapped students who are also enrolled in different settings (i.e., regular class, special class, and resource room).

Other Salient Characteristics

In addition to the general classroom behavior or misbehavior cited by peers, some researchers have attempted to isolate more specifically those skills and characteristics which could also contribute to the rejection of handicapped students by classmates. But the variables thought to contribute to peer status have not been uniformly studied across handicapped student groups. This is understandable since handicapped student status in the regular classroom has only recently become a major educational issue (with the advent of Public Law 94-142); at the same time the data that have been gathered reflect the prerogatives of researchers. Consequently, these biases are reflected in the presentation of investigations related to problems in: (1) nonverbal communication; (2) verbal communication; (3) role-taking; and (4) social skills in general.

Nonverbal Communication. Several investigations have demonstrated that learning disabled students exhibit deficiencies in nonverbal communication; that is, the ability to recognize the meaning of nonverbal aspects of communication that may indicate the attitudes, feelings, and intentions of others. Thus, they cannot make appropriate responses. These nonverbal communications include interpreting the meaning of facial expression, hand and arm gestures, body posture and positioning (Axelrod, 1982; Bachara, 1976; Bryan, 1977; Gerber & Zinkgraf, 1982; Pearl & Cosden, 1982; Wiig & Harris, 1974).

Maheady and Maitland's (1982) review of the literature on the ability of learning disabled students to understand nonverbal communications, however, led them to conclude that the use of laboratory situations and test materials assumes the findings validly represent behavior in actual social situations. To overcome this shortcoming, they suggested that future data collection include actual classroom observations. They also speculated that social perception deficiencies may result from factors related to problems in listening, looking, integrating, grasping the meaning of stimuli, and attending, which should be considered in future research.

A few laboratory studies have focused on the nonverbal signals emitted by learning disabled students, but the results are inconclusive. Although Cernak, Co ster, and Drake (1980) found learning disabled boys were inferior in gestural abilities, Raskind, Drew, and Regan (1983) reported differences in only 1 of 31 nonverbal behaviors observed in videotapes of learning disabled students with and without behavior disorders and nondisabled 3rd, 4th, and 5th graders.

A logical assumption is that peer rejection of learning disabled students may be, to some degree, a result of the nonverbal deficiencies which some researchers have evidenced to exist in this population of students. However, since the relationship between nonverbal communication skills and peer acceptance and/or rejection in the classroom has not been empirically demonstrated, it remains for further research to clarify this issue.

Verbal Communication. Many handicapped student groups (e.g., mentally retarded, emotionally disturbed, hearing impaired, and speech impaired) are characterized by impaired verbal communication skills, at least to some degree. These language deficiencies may affect the verbal interactions of handicapped children with nonhandicapped peers, and these may be a contributing factor in the handicapped student being assigned a lower status position in the classroom. There is some indication that even learning disabled students, who can be regarded as exhibiting behaviors relatively less discrepant from those of nonhandicapped peers, may be rejected by peers because of their lack of verbal communication skills. For example in one study (Bryan, Wheeler, Felcan, & Henek, 1976), categories of questions or statements were developed and observed in a sample of learning disabled students and a control group of nonhandicapped peers. The results showed that learning disabled students' interactions with peers were characterized by the learning disabled using more competitive (e.g., "I'm going to beat you") and more rejecting statements (e.g., "You're a dummy"); they also made fewer helpful or considerate statements. In another laboratory experiment (Bryan, Donahue, & Pearl, 1981) the interactions of learning disabled and nondisabled classmates were observed in a contrived decision making situation. Compared to the nondisabled, the learning disabled students were less persuasive, more likely to agree than disagree with or argue against others' choices, and less likely to direct the group toward resolution of the problem or to keep the group on task. An experiment of conversation strategies (Bryan, Donahue, Pearl, & Sturm, 1981) showed that learning disabled students (as compared to nondisabled) evidenced differences in the strategies they used for initiating and sustaining conversation. For example, they asked fewer and less open-ended questions. It is not clear how such differences in communication strategies might affect the perceptions and the consequent sociometric status peers assign to learning disabled students; however, the evidence supports the potential influence of communication variables. If conversational differences can be shown to relate to peer rejection, efforts can be made to teach handicapped students to engage in more socially appropriate communication strategies.

Role-Taking.   It has been hypothesized that children who are better at understanding what others are thinking (cognitive role-taking) and feeling (affective role-taking) will interact more effectively with peers. For a review of the literature of the construct of role-taking see Enright & Lapsley (1980).

A few studies have attempted to explore the relationship between handicapped student's role-taking skills and the degree to which they are accepted by peers, but the relationship is not clear. One study (Bruck & Hebert, 1982) found that learning disabled students aged 7 to 10 years, evidenced poorer role-taking skills than normal peers, but the relationship between role-taking skills and teacher impressions of peer interactions was weak. In another study, Horowitz (1981) failed to demonstrate a relationship between the role-taking skills of 3rd and 4th grade learning disabled students and their sociometric ranking. When Affleck (1975) looked at relationships among retarded students, a connection between role-taking and interpersonal competence was clear.

Because so few studies have attempted to study the relationship between role-taking skills and peer acceptance in a variety of handicapped student groups, it is impossible to make any definitive statements. Indeed, it remains to be clarified whether or not handicapped student groups are deficient in these skills. Possible differences in the nature of the deficit among different handicapped student groups may also exist. For example, Dickstein and Warren (1980) reported learning disabled students have deficits when compared to normal students; but Ackerman, Elardo, and Dykman (1979) found there weren't any differences in normal students and a nonhyperactive learning disabled group but there were differences in a hyperactive group with no learning problems. In another study Paulauskas and Campbell (1979) failed to discover any differences in the role-taking abilities of hyperactive and control subjects aged 5 to 14 years, although teachers reported that the hyperactive subjects had problems in their interactions with peers.

Social Skills. Clinical as well as anecdotal observations suggest that handicapped students may manifest a variety of social and task related skill deficits. Therefore handicapped students may be rejected because of deficiencies in social skills.

The notion of specific social skill deficits in particular handicapped student groups has been given considerable attention in the literature. At the same time, there is no consensus about what skills or behaviors may be classified as being social skills. They may comprise the behaviors described above (including, therefore, nonverbal communication, verbal communication, and role-taking), but this depends on the researcher's conceptualization.

In one study (Schumaker, Hazel, Sherman, & Sheldon, 1982) social skills were defined as accepting and giving negative feedback, conversation, following instructions, giving positive feedback, negotiation, problem solving, and resisting peer pressure. When tested in a role-play situation, learning disabled students showed significantly poorer performance than the nonlearning disabled students; but their performance differed only on resisting peer pressure from that of a group of juvenile delinquents. Fincham's (1978) results indicate some differences in the sharing behavior of learning disabled and normal achievers.

The nature of social skill deficits in handicapped student groups has not been adequately documented; furthermore, the relationship to peer acceptance is not clear. See Chapter 6 for a further discussion of social skills and social skills training.

SELF-ATTITUDES OF HANDICAPPED STUDENTS

This section considers self-attitudes: how the handicapped student may think peers feel about him/her; the self-attitudes or self-concept of the handicapped student; and the possible effects of special class and resource room attendance on self-attitudes.

Perceived Peer Status

Perceived status, or how students think their peers feel about them, has been assessed in a few studies. But it is not clear whether or not handicapped students make accurate assessments of their status. In an early study, Miller (1956) explored the ability of intellectually superior, average, and mentally retarded 4th and 6th graders to predict their popularity and the popularity of their peers. The retarded students were less able to predict how popular their peers were than the superior or average students, and tended to overestimate their own status. Similarly, Rucker, Howe, and Snider (1969) found that EMR students who were integrated into academic and nonacademic junior high school classes significantly overestimated their acceptance by classmates in both settings. It was suggested that the students were either unaware of their low status or chose to deny it. Although Bruininks (1978) found elementary school LD students assigned themselves acceptance scores higher than their actual status, Horowitz (1981) found learning disabled 3rd and 4th graders could make realistic assessments of their social standing. Findings for a study done by Kennedy and Bruininks (1974) showed that hearing impaired students were accurate in the appraisals they made of their status, but in another study (Hus, 1979) they were not.

The foregoing evidence supports the need for further study to clarify the abilities of different handicapped student groups to make accurate predictions about how their peers feel toward them. If handicapped students are not aware of the low status they are assigned by classmates, they will probably not be motivated to make any changes in the nature of the interactions they have with peers. Consequently, they may not make any gains in peer acceptance.

Self-Concept or Self-Attitude

Numerous studies have attempted to measure the relationship between self-concept and academic achievement in nonhandicapped students. Although there are considerable difficulties related to the measurement of the "self-concept" construct (Wylie, 1974), it is generally acknowledged that there is a "persistent and significant relationship between the self-concept and academic achievement" (Purkey, 1970, p. 27).

It is often pointed out that handicapped children quite logically develop a poor self-assessment because of their characteristics such as lower intellectual ability, poor academic achievement and physical differences. There is however, little empirical evidence of the self-concept of handicapped students. Some studies have shown that handicapped student groups, for example the emotionally disturbed (Bloom, Shea, & Eun, 1979; Holdaway & Jensen, 1983) and physically handicapped (Siller, 1960), have lower self-attitudes. But there are also studies that have found that visually handicapped (Coker, 1979) and students with spina bifida (VanPutte, 1979) have positive self-concepts. Serafica and Harway (1979) concluded as a result of a comprehensive review of the literature on the self-concept of learning disabled students that: (1) these children are characterized by lower self-concepts; (2) the relationship between academic performance and self-concept in this group is not clear; and (3) further research is necessary. In another literature review, Garrison and Tesch (1978) concluded that the self-concept of deaf students: (1) may be lower than for hearing children; (2) could depend on the educational environment the child is in; (3) have not been studied from a developmental or longitudinal approach, yet may reflect a developmental lag; (4) have often been measured with devices not appropriate for deaf populations; and (5) must be further studied.

The need for more comprehensive study of the self-concept construct among handicapped populations is apparent. Other attributes besides the handicap, such as physical appearance (Coker, 1979) may also be factors in the self-concept developed by a handicapped student. To this point in time, the focus of research has primarily been on the effect of special class placement might have.

Effect of Special Class Placement and Resource Rooms

Several studies have been undertaken to identify the effect of special class placement on the self-concept of the student. Although an early study (Meyerowitz, 1962) reported EMR first graders placed in a special classroom demonstrated significantly more self-derogations than those placed in regular grades, other studies indicate that the mentally retarded students placed in special settings actually have more positive attitudes toward themselves. For example, Kern and Pfaeffle (1963) found that educable mentally retarded students placed in special schools had higher self-adjustment scores than special class students. The findings were attributed to a more accepting atmosphere in the special schools.

More recently Schurr, Towne, and Joiner (1972) reported that whereas EMR students placed in a special class had an increased academic self-concept at the end of their first and second year of attendance, students who were reassigned to regular classes showed a decrease in their self-concept.

In another study, Battle and Blowers (1982) tested the self-concepts of LD and EMR students before special class placement, and one and two years later; both groups evidenced significant gains in their self-perceptions. According to Battle and Blowers (1982) the findings may be attributed to two possible factors. First, they speculated, it may be that the smaller special class setting, because of the individualzed instruction leads to better academic performance which in turn positively effected self-perceptions; also the increased student-teacher interaction which characterizes a special class setting might have contributed to the students' perceptions about themselves. Secondly, the results may be viewed from the standpoint of Festinger's (1954) social comparison theory. Accordingly, assessment of one's self-worth is arrived at (in the absence of other more objective standards for comparison) as a result of observations of others in the environment. Similar individuals, more so than those perceived as different, are chosen for comparison; thus, special class children choose special class members to compare themselves with. Because of the similarities evidenced among the students in the special classroom, students have a comparison group of students within which their own skills might be perceived more favorably. Consequently special class placement can actually enhance the self-concept of a student.

Strang, Smith, and Rogers (1978) secured evidence supporting Festinger's theory. They tested a group of "academically handicapped" children (mean WISC-R full scale IQ was 86.96) placed in a special class all day and another group who were mainstreamed for one-half of the school day. The mainstreamed group exhibited significantly increased self-concept scores at the end of the school year, but this finding was not evidenced for those in the special class. This finding was attributed to the fact that those in the resource room had an opportunity to make multiple comparisons themselves. In order to determine whether or not the mainstreamed students' self-concepts were enhanced by their perception of mainstreaming as a success experience, or because they could selectively compare themselves to two groups (the regular and special class), another experiment was undertaken one year later. In this experiment, social comparisons for mainstreamed students were restricted by manipulating the salience of regular class membership. One group of mainstreamed students were permitted comparisons with both groups; the referent for the other group was only regular class members. Students with two reference groups (special and regular class students) increased in self-concept, but those who were restricted to regular class members as referents demonstrated lower self-concept scores. From the standpoint of Festinger's theory, the mainstreamed student group that could make comparisons between themselves and similar other special students were provided an opportunity for maintaining as well as enhancing their self-concept.

In another study (Coleman, 1983), the self-concepts of elementary students labeled "mildly handicapped" receiving one of three types of services including one hour of resource room assistance, two hours of resource room assistance, or enrolled in a self-contained class (no other information on the subjects is provided) were examined in comparison to a group of classroom underachievers not receiving any support services. It was hypothesized that, from the standpoint of Festinger's theory, students in the special class with a homogeneous reference group and those receiving support services enabling them to choose from two comparison groups would have higher self-concepts than the underachieving group. Findings indicated that the self-concept scores of the handicapped students were significantly higher than the underachievers' scores. Students receiving one hour of resource room assistance had the most positive self concepts, followed by students in the self-contained class and next those students receiving two hours of resource room assistance.

But in another study (Sheare, 1978) measuring the self-concepts of learning disabled students before and at the end of one year of attendance in a resource room, the LD students evidenced lower self-concepts than their nonhandicapped classmates at the beginning of the year, and there were no changes for either group at the end of the year. When Head (1979) compared the self-concepts of visually handicapped students in a residential setting with those receiving resource room or itinerant services, findings showed there were no significant differences in the self-concept scores for the three groups.

It seems that the issue of how placement in a special class or resource room might affect a student's self-concept has been oversimplified; we cannot presume that this experience is necessarily positive or negative. Furthermore the effects of different educational settings may depend on the type of handicap the student evidences. A unique study by Warner, Thrapp and Walsh (1973) queried students about how they liked being in a special class. The personal interviews with 369 randomly selected EMR students indicated 61 percent liked being in a special class and 41 percent had no desire to be in some other class in their school. The reasons for their attitudes toward preference for special placement were primarily related to the academic nature of the class. Clearly there is a need for further research to specify the conditions that promote positive self-attitudes. Whether or not Festinger's theory can be used to predict the self-concepts of handicapped students in the school setting is not yet verified. Omwake (1954) suggested that how a person sees himself will have an effect upon how he perceives others; those with low self-attitudes tend to reject others and view others as rejecting them. Thus, it is important to pursue explanations about the self-concept of handicapped students.

ATTITUDES AND "MAINSTREAMING"

Since treatment of handicapped children had traditionally involved placement in a special classroom situation, the concept of the "least restrictive alternative" mandated by public law 94-142 (resulting in the "mainstreaming" of special-needs children into the regular classroom) generated considerable controversy. After 1975 numerous investigations regarding all aspects of the mainstreaming procedure were undertaken. For example, an early survey of state education department officials was done in 1976 to determine if these officials felt there was significant progress being made toward mainstreaming activities and if school administrators had recognized the need for change: results showed advancements (Wendel, 1977). In surveys during the last decade investigators have: (1) queried teachers, principals, and special educators about their attitudes toward the concept, and asked for opinions about a variety of related issues, including the efficacy of the procedure; (2) examined feelings toward the notion of resource rooms as a service delivery model; (3) sought to determine factors underlying mainstreaming attitudes; and (4) asked for the teachers' assessments of who was responsible for the legislation. Many of the responses from these surveys are presented in greater detail in the following paragraphs in an effort to demonstrate what types of concerns teachers expressed. Although some of these studies were conducted when mainstreaming was first undertaken, differences for later surveys do not seem to indicate that teachers have become more positive toward the procedure in spite of a greater familiarity with the approach.

It will become apparent that the findings from these surveys support the recommendations that although teacher training programs preparing regular classroom teachers have made some changes in their programs in order to prepare teachers for working with mainstreamed handicapped students, further adjustments in the content of coursework seem necessary (Byford, 1979; Middleton, Morsink, & Cohen, 1979).

Professional Attitudes Toward "Mainstreaming"

Some surveys have indicated that teachers may have negative feelings toward many aspects of mainstreaming. Barngrover (1971) interviewed teachers, administrators and school psychologists prior to the legislation and found over half the sample felt that even mildly handicapped students should be retained in the special class. Ten years later Childs's (1981) survey of primary through high school regular classroom teachers, who had mainstreamed EMR students in their classes, indicated generally negative attitudes toward mainstreaming. Only 38 percent of the teachers supported the concept; approximately 50 percent felt they were inadequately prepared, lacked coursework, and did not have the resource materials or necessary consultant services to teach EMR students. Furthermore the teachers did not feel the educable mentally handicapped students should be in their classes since these students could not master the regular class curriculum and regular students did not want to socialize with them.

The results were similar in another survey (Horne, 1983). Elementary teachers indicated that they did not understand the legislation and questioned the efficacy of classroom instruction for special-needs children, the adequacy of the resource-room teacher's training for teaching the handicapped, and classroom teachers' willingness to make curriculum or instructional alterations. Over 80 percent did not think they had adequate training and approximately 70 percent felt that mainstreaming handicapped students would require significant changes in classroom procedures.

Ringlaben and Price's (1981) study of regular classroom teachers of grades kindergarten through high school showed: (1) approximately 50 percent of the teachers felt they knew very little about the laws related to mainstreaming; (2) over 75 percent said they agreed with the philosophy of mainstreaming; (3) approximately 50 percent did not feel they had the preparation to implement the procedure; (4) over 75 percent said they were willing to accept a mainstreamed student into their class; (5) approximately 30 percent felt mainstreaming was not working well in their class; (6) 25 percent felt mainstreamed students had a negative effect on other students; (7) 14 percent felt the regular students had a negative effect on mainstreamed students; (8) 30 percent felt mainstreamed students had a negative effect on teaching performance; (9) 23 percent felt mainstreaming had a negative effect on their attitudes toward teaching; and (10) 22 percent felt mainstreaming had a negative effect on the mainstreamed students.

Hudson, Graham, & Warner (1979) surveyed elementary teachers and found: (1) 47 percent did not support mainstreaming; (2) 83 percent did not think they had time to teach exceptional students in their classes; (3) 38 percent did not feel they had adequate materials; (4) 58 percent did not think they had the necessary support services; (5) 68 percent felt training would help them; and (6) 64 percent felt they had the necessary skills in identification, individualized instruction, and parent conferencing.

Guerin (1979) asked regular classroom teachers who had educable mentally retarded, educationally handicapped and emotionally disturbed children in their classes how much "comfort" or "discomfort" they experienced in working with these students. Teachers were most comfortable supervising (lunch, playground, etc.); less comfortable planning academic work for these pupils; and least comfortable about the verbal, social and leadership competence of the educable mentally retarded and educationally handicapped students.

Schultz (1982) used open-ended survey questions to find out what questions or concerns regular classroom teachers had about educating handicapped students. The categorized responses showed that the teachers were especially concerned about having to plan for individual differences and were not sure about what their role or responsibility is when they have a handicapped student in their class. Other concerns related to working with specialists, screening and identification, inservice training, behavior management techniques, their own feelings of acceptance and student acceptance of mainstreamed students, and instructional materials.

Some surveys have asked special educators as well as regular classroom teachers how they feel about mainstreaming. Graham, Hudson, Burdg, & Carpenter (1980) surprisingly found that resource-room teachers did not feel mainstreaming was effective, but that regular classroom teachers did. Furthermore, regular classroom teachers felt that handicapped students gained more academically by staying in the mainstream; resource teachers did not agree. Both groups agreed that placing a handicapped student in the mainstream would restrict the progress of other class members and that regular classroom teachers did not have adequate skills to work with mainstreamed children.

In another study (Moore & Fine, 1978), teachers of retarded and learning disabled students were more positive about mainstreaming these children than were regular classroom teachers; all three groups supported mainstreaming children with learning disabilities more than the retarded student.

The findings of two surveys demonstrate somewhat more supportive teacher attitudes toward mainstreaming. One study (Warger & Trippe, 1982) surveyed undergraduate students who had completed student teaching in an elementary or secondary class and had some experience with special education and mainstreaming about their opinions toward mainstreaming emotionally disturbed children. The findings were generally positive, although the respondents expressed concerns about dealing with the behaviors typical of an emotionally disturbed child. Even though they perceived themselves as having been generally adequately prepared for mainstreaming, they felt inadequately prepared in professional knowledge of main streaming, assessment procedures, and consultation skills. It seems likely that some experience with special education, as well as exposure to a training program which had presumably been modified somewhat as a result of the mainstreaming legislation (most states require that students take at least one introductory special education course) contributed to these teachers expressing more positive attitudes. (See Chapter 6 for a discussion of the effects of education and experience on attitudes.)

In another study, Schmelkin (1981) compared the mainstreaming attitudes of experienced special education teachers, experienced regular classroom teachers and a nonteacher group comprised of nurses, counselors, and school psychologists, all of whom were graduate students. Results showed that all three groups thought that mainstreaming would not negatively effect academics in the regular classroom (e.g., routines, teacher time, the academic progress of nonhandicapped students), or the social and emotional development of handicapped students. However, the special educator group thought the academic effects of mainstreaming on the regular classroom would be less negative than the other two groups. These findings might indicate that teachers are becoming more accepting of the concept of mainstreaming, perhaps because of their experiences. On the other hand, it may be that as graduate student enrollees, these teachers could also be a positively biased sample.

Some studies have asked principals about which handicapped students they think can be mainstreamed. These findings have shown that principals share some of the reservations teachers have about mainstreaming. Payne and Murray (1974) found that only 40 percent of urban principals had positive attitudes about mainstreaming, although 71 percent of suburban principals favored the procedure. Both groups evidenced similar rankings for handicapped groups they thought could be mainstreamed (from most to least "mainstreamable" were visually handicapped, hard of hearing, physically handicapped, educable mentally retarded, and trainable mentally retarded).

Smith, Flexer, & Sigelman (1980) found principals rated the learning disabled student significantly less positively than the "normal person;" but they were perceived more favorably than mentally retarded students.

In another study (Davis, 1980), school principals were asked how successful they thought mainstreaming would be for different groups of handicapped students. As shown in Table 4.6, 89.9 percent of the principals thought children with mild learning disabilities could be successfully mainstreamed, but the figure for mild emotional disturbance is only 50.1 and even less for mild mental retardation (46.4 percent).

Cline (1981) compared the attitudes of principals in an urban school district with the attitudes of experts used in the standardization of the *Rucker-Gable Educational Programming Scale* (Rucker & Gable, 1974).[1] Results indicated the experts were more positive about mainstream placements for mildly learning disabled and emotionally distrubed students; but curiously the principals were more positive about placing the severely learning disabled, emotionally disturbed and mentally retarded students, as well as mildly retarded students, closer to the mainstream.

Resource Rooms

Resource rooms were conceptualized as being an instructional alternative to special class placement particularly for mentally retarded, learning disabled, and emotionally disturbed children. When this service plan is used, the handicapped student spends as much time as is instructionally suitable or profitable (this is determined by the evaluation team) in the regular classroom or mainstream and goes to a resource room for specialized instruction. A few surveys have endeavored to assess teacher perceptions of this model. In one of the earlier studies published (DiSipio, Nake, & Perney, 1978), classroom teachers were asked about their views of resource rooms which had been established as a result of legislation passed in Massachusetts one year prior to P.L. 94-142. The results showed that teachers were generally positive about the resource room model; however, the teachers thought resource rooms should focus on learning disabled students and not students with behavior disorders. The teachers also indicated that there should be considerable communication between the regular classroom teacher and resource room teacher for the approach to work (i.e., approximately 40 percent of respondents felt communication between the regular classroom teacher and resource room teacher should occur once a day; another approximately 40 percent felt communication should occur no more than twice a week). Kavale & Rossi (1980) queried teachers about their attitudes toward resource rooms established for educable mentally retarded students in California. The

---

[1]See Chapter 3 for a discussion of this instrument.

TABLE 4.6

Rank Order of Principals' Perception of Successful Mainstreaming
According to Type and Degree of Handicapping Condition

(Responses in Combined Excellent and Good Categories)

Rank	Handicapping Condition	Number	(%)
1	Mild Learning Disability	310	89.9
2	Mild Speech/Language Disability	277	80.3
3	Mild Vision Impairment	270	78.3
4	Mild Auditory Impairment	262	75.9
5	Mild Physical/Motor Disability	260	75.4
6	Moderate Learning Disability	237	68.7
7	Moderate Speech/Language Disability	217	62.9
8	Moderate Vision Impairment	197	57.1
9	Moderate Auditory Impairment	191	55.4
10	Mild Emotional Disturbance/Behavior Disorder	173	50.1
11	Moderate Physical Motor Disability	171	49.6
12	Mild Mental Retardation	160	46.4
13	Moderate Mental Retardation	92	26.7
14	Moderate Emotional Disturbance/Behavior Disorder	86	24.9
15	Severe and Profound Speech/Language Disability	74	21.4
16	Severe and Profound Physical/Motor Disability	63	18.3
17	Severe and Profound Vision Impairment	60	17.4
18	Severe and Profound Auditory Impairment	46	13.3
19	Severe and Profound Learning Disability	41	11.9
20	Severe and Profound Emotional Disturbance/Behavior Disorder	19	5.5
21	Severe and Profound Mental Retardation	13	3.8

From Davis (1980). Public school principals' attitudes toward mainstreaming retarded pupils.
Education and Training of the Mentally Retarded, 15, 174-178.

teachers were generally positive about the program, resource room teacher functions, and student progress in these programs; lower elementary and secondary teachers were more positive than middle-school teachers. These findings are in contrast to a previous report by MacMillan, Meyers and Yoshida (1978) wherein California teachers indicated their dissatisfaction with resource room services for mentally retarded students. In another study (Speece & Mandell, 1980), Ohio teachers reported of which 26 resource-room teacher services they thought helped them mainstream learning disabled students. Those services rated as most important or vital by over 50 percent of the teachers were:

1. attends parent conferences (74.2 percent);
2. arranges for informal meetings with the classroom teacher to discuss the student's progress (74.2 percent);
3. gives instruction in the resource room (67.0 percent);
4. provides information on the behavioral characteristics of the child (54.5 percent);
5. provides academic assessment data (53.9 percent);
6. schedules meetings to evaluate student progress (52.7 percent);
7. provides materials the classroom teacher can use (52.1 percent);
8. suggests materials the classroom teacher can use (52.1 percent); and
9. provides written reports of the student's activities and progress (51.5 percent).

The perception teachers have about resource rooms may vary from state to state, maybe even from school to school, and they may have different expectations for the services provided which differ for various handicapped student groups. Perhaps this is because there are differences in the way the model is applied and variations in the nature of the population served. It appears that the services a classroom teacher receives from resource room specialists will influence their attitudes about the model and about mainstreaming handicapped students. Consequently, comprehensive explorations of teacher perceptions about all aspects of the service delivery model seem justified.

Factors Underlying Mainstreaming Attitudes

As discussed in the preceding section, perceptions teachers have about resource-room programming may contribute to their attitudes toward mainstreaming, but some researchers have sought to determine what factors might underlie teachers' attitudes toward mainstreaming. Stephens and Braun (1980) found the following to be effective predictors of a positive attitude by regular classroom teachers toward mainstreaming: the confidence teachers had in themselves about their ability to teach the handicapped; a belief that handicapped persons can become useful societal members; and a belief that handicapped students should be educated in public schools. Teachers of lower grades and those who had some special education coursework were also more positive toward mainstreaming students. Somewhat similarly Larrivee (1982) concluded that regular classroom teachers' attitudes toward mainstreaming were related to five underlying dimensions: (1) the teachers' general philosophy about mainstreaming and its impact on the affective and emotional development of the handicapped and nonhandicapped students; (2) the classroom behavior of the handicapped student; (3) the perceptions teachers have of their own ability to teach handicapped children; (4) the impact the handicapped student had on classroom management; and (5) the impact mainstreaming had on the academic and social growth of the handicapped child. Larrivee and Cook (1979) reported that the teacher's perception of the degree of success they had in dealing with the special-needs child was probably the most important variable. In this study, teacher attitudes toward mainstreaming were not found to be influenced by class size, school size, or type of community (urban, suburban, or rural); elementary teachers were more positive toward the philosophy of mainstreaming than secondary teachers. There was also a stong relationship between teachers' attitudes and the level of administrative support and availability of supportive services (e.g., resource room, resource room teacher, counselor).

Even if effects of the grade level the teacher is working at and special education coursework do have a relationship to mainstreaming attitudes (see Chapter 5 for a discussion of several factors relating to attitude including age, sex, socioeconomic status), it appears that classroom teachers must be given assistance in working with handicapped students to enable them to have success experiences when working with these students.

Teacher's Assessment of Responsibility for the Mainstreaming Legislation

The attitudes of special educators, principals, and classroom teachers toward mainstreaming may be interrelated. Although Mandell and Strain (1978) did not find a relationship among the attitudes of principals, special educators, and classroom teachers, Guerin & Szatlocky (1974) reported marked agreement between the feelings of special educators and regular classroom teachers. If, according to Guerin and Szatlocky, the special educator with whom the teacher worked had a positive or negative attitude, then the regular classroom teacher tended to have the same attitude about mainstreaming. Thus, it is important to undertand how classroom teachers assess other group members' feelings toward the mainstreaming concept. Only two studies have queried teachers about their perceptions of how they think others feel about the procedure. In the first (Harasymiw & Horne, 1976), elementary classroom teachers enrolled in an inservice program designed to modify their attitudes toward handicapped students and a comparable control group were tested. In the second study (Horne, 1983) teachers enrolled in an introductory special education course completed the same inventory. Table 4.7 shows the rankings of the mean scores obtained using a

TABLE 4.7
Rankings of Mean Scores for Classroom Teacher Evaluations for Professional Peer and Parent Attitudes Toward Mainstreaming

Group Members	Ranking		
	Harasymiw & Horne, 1976 Inservice Teachers (N=191)	Harasymiw & Horne, 1976 Control Group (N=161)	Horne, 1983 Enrollees (N=139)
College of Professor of Special Education	2	1	1
Educational Researchers	1	2	2
School Psychologists	3	4	3
Professors of Elementary Education	5	5	4
Parents of Children with Special Needs	6	8	5
Children with Special Needs	9	9	6
Resource Room Teachers	4	6	7
Student Teachers	8	7	8
State Legislators	7	3	9
School Administrators	–	–	10
Children Without Special Needs	11	10	11
Parents of Children Without Special Needs	10	11	13
Regular Classroom Teachers	12	12	12

From Harasymiw and Horne (1976). Teacher attitudes toward handicapped children and regular class integration. *The Journal of Special Education, 4,* 393-401.

From Horne (1983). Elementary classroom teacher attitudes toward mainstreaming. *The Exceptional Child, 30,* 93-98.

Likert-type scale which asked the participants to rate the positivity of a variety of groups toward mainstreaming. All three groups of respondents agreed that educational researchers and college professors of special education had the most positive feelings toward the mainstreaming legislation; all three groups also believed that children without special needs, parents of children without special needs, and regular classroom teachers had the most negative feelings. If the respondents were accurate in their assessments about the negative attitudes of students, parents, and teachers (also administrators in the 1983 study) toward the legislation, their feelings may be subject to reinforcement from colleagues, and may be even students, on a day-to-day basis. Even if they are inaccurate, their belief system may nonetheless operate in determining the attitude they have toward carrying out mainstreaming. Since mainstreaming was thrust upon teachers without their having been consulted, and, at the same time, the approach required them to work with children that theretofore had been acknowledged as requiring the services of a specialist, it is not surprising to find that teachers are not strongly supportive of the procedure.

COMMUNITY MEMBERS ATTITUDES TOWARD HANDICAPPED PERSONS

Research has shown that community members express negative attitudes toward handicapped populations. Most of the studies have focused specifically on how community members feel about the mentally ill (Phillips, 1963; Rootman & LaFave, 1969) or retarded individuals (Kastner, Reppucci, & Pezzoli, 1979), and have reported that these groups are rejected. This may be because these groups are perceived as being more seriously handicapped by societal members than, for example, the blind or deaf and have been more traditionally placed in some type of segregated setting.

At the same time, a Gallup survey in 1976 indicated generally positive community attitudes toward mentally retarded individuals. According to Kastner, Reppucci, and Pezzoli (1979) however, these findings may reflect a positive response bias toward mental retardation on the part of the participants. Using some of the same questions posed in the Gallup survey, Kastner, Reppucci and Pezzoli found that participants responded differently and somewhat more negatively when they thought their responses might have an impact on whether or not a group home was going to be established in their neighborhood.

Indeed the resistance encountered by developers of group homes for retarded persons (Berdiansky & Parker, 1977; Sigelman, Spanhel, & Lorensen, 1979) may be more indicative of the actual feelings held toward handicapped people. It has been shown (Berdiansky & Parker, 1977) that community residents were concerned about retarded individuals as being dangerous to their family, sexually deviant, and criminal. They were also worried about the effect a community residential facility or group home would have on their property values, despite evidence that property values do not decrease in such situations (Dear,1977; Weiner, Anderson, & Nietupski, 1982). Another study (O'Connor & Sitkei, 1975) rank ordered the twelve most serious problems involved in establishing a group residence for mentally retarded or developmentally disabled persons. The attitude of community members toward residents ranked sixth; funding, finding staff, developing individualized client programs, a lack of community support services, and problems with certification and/or licensure were ranked higher.

There are far fewer published studies having to do with how community members feel about handicapped children. In one such study (Meyers, Sitkei, and Watts, 1966) household interviews of a random sample indicated large percentages of the respondents felt mentally retarded children should not be provided with special programming in the public school but should instead be institutionalized. But similar household interviews of families who had had a retarded child in a public school class for the mentally retarded showed they were more favorable about public school placements. Gottlieb and Corman (1975) administered questionnaires to community members and found that those who had school-aged children were more often opposed to integrating retarded children into regular classrooms. Older respondents, and those without previous contact with a retarded person were also in favor of segregated education placements. Somewhat in contrast, Hollinger and Jones (1970) used a structured interview to determine community members' attitudes toward the slow learner and mentally retarded student and found that, although there was some misunderstanding of both terms, there was greater acceptance than rejection of both groups.

Although the research has been largely limited to an examination of how community members perceive mentally retarded and mentally ill individuals, it appears that adults and/or children having some type of handicap will likely experience some degree of rejection on the part of the general public, with the degree of rejection dependent on the perceived severity of the handicap by the community member.

The Media and Attitudes

As evidenced by the presence of commercials and advertisements, the mass media influences public attitudes. Very few studies, however, have considered the possible effects of television, radio, or print media on the attitudes that societal members form toward handicapped individuals. In one of the few existing studies, Donaldson (1981) randomly selected 85 half-hour segments of prime-time television which were then viewed and analyzed by observers. Results indicated that handicapped persons are not highly visible in television programs, and when they are included, they are more often cast in negative role portrayals; for example, appearing as handicapped criminals. An analysis of comic books

(Weinberg & Santana, 1978) revealed that 63 to 290 characters were in some way deformed (physical deformity, sensory impairments, skin abnormalities, head distortion, limb deformities). All of the 290 characters were rated as being evil, neutral, or good depending upon their actions in the stories; results indicated that 57 percent of those with a physical deformity were "evil" characters, as compared to only 20 percent of those without some type of deformity. According to Weinberg and Santana:

> It may well be that if the media continue to present the disabled as different from the nondisabled, as either exceptionally good or exceptionally evil, but never of ordinary status, the stereotype will long endure and equal acceptance of the disabled will never triumph (p. 311).

SUMMARY

Although there is variability in the rankings assigned disabilities by seemingly disparate groups, a hierarchy of preference is supported. It appears that the more severe the handicap, the more negative the attitude. This commonality may indicate that stereotypes are well established in our society and may not be subject to simplistic modification.

Teachers are not unique in their attitudes toward handicapped groups and tend to have negative attitudes. That the results for studies done prior to the 1975 legislation mandating "mainstreaming" are not markedly different from later findings supports the conclusion drawn by researchers focusing on attitude modification procedures. They stress that just placing handicapped students in regular classrooms will not result in more positive classroom teacher attitudes (See Chapter 6). Professional awareness of the hierarchy phenomenon and knowledge of the relative position on the acceptance continuum of various disabilities might enhance efforts directed toward facilitating their acceptance. For example, qualitatively and quantitatively different types of attitude modification procedures may need to be developed in accordance with the degree of expressed preference for particular handicaps.

Research that seeks to understand truly teacher attitudes toward handicapped students needs to be continued and expanded. Clearly, a major problem with interpreting the extant data has to do with the various response modes used in different studies. For example, asking respondents to rank disability groups in terms of "acceptability," "severity," or "manageability" may make a difference in the findings. Future research designs should give careful consideration not only to response modes but also consider the multifaceted nature of attitudes. Furthermore, what factors might underlie the expressed attitude? Teacher attitudes toward mainstreamed children seem to be influenced by perceptions of their competency to work with these children, availability of support services, previous training or experiences, or their own educational philosophy.

Research suggests peers also hold negative attitudes toward handicapped students. It does not seem to make any difference whether or not handicapped students are placed in a regular classroom with or without resource room services, in an open-space school, or in a setting where they are not necessarily members of a minority group. There are very few studies in which the rejected status of handicapped students by peers is not clearly evidenced, a trend that has been demonstrated over a 30-year period.

Are classmates more positive toward some handicaps? It is not clear if mentally retarded students are more likely to be rejected by classmates than learning disabled or emotionally disturbed students. Future research should be directed toward clarifying preferences since these data will be useful for school personnel concerned with modifying the status of a particular handicapped student in the classroom; the information will assist in predictions of the degree of peer rejection which must be anticipated and considered in developing the overall educational program (within and outside of the regular classroom). Information about peer preferences for handicaps will also facilitate the development of attitude modification procedures. Methodologies for change (for example, content, procedures, and duration) can be more directly responsive to the level of negativity or preference students express toward particular handicaps.

It is also important for future research to determine more specifically the reasons why peers reject handicapped students. Handicapped students might then be provided with instruction designed to develop those behaviors predictive of peer acceptance and eliminate those related to rejection. The relative contribution of other variables such as race, sex, and physical attributes also require further study as they relate to handicapped student status. Chapter 5 discusses these factors in more depth as well as many other variables salient to the perceptions an individual has about handicapped persons.

There are also many unanswered questions surrounding the issue of the self-attitudes of handicapped students and the effect of specialized versus regular class instructional settings. Indeed it may be that specialized or segregated instruction is essential as an effective educational treatment for some students, at least until such time as their interactions in the regular or mainstreamed situations become more positive.

Finally, since most studies done on the classroom status of handicapped students have utilized a sociometric rating procedureto demonstrate rejection, future research should aim toward clarifying the relationship of expressed rejection on these measures and the actual numbers of interactions that occur among handicapped and nonhandicapped students in the classroom. There is some evidence that sociometric findings do not accurately reflect the extent of these interactions (Dunlop, Stoneman, & Cantrell, 1980; Schumaker,Wildgen, & Sherman, 1982).

Research on classmates' attitudes toward handicapped peers supports the need for school personnel to design interventions for handicapped students that not only consider the educational deficits exhibited by the child, but also attempt to enhance the attitudes and interactions among the exceptional students and classmates.

REFERENCES

Abroms, K. I., & Kodera, T. L. (1979). Acceptance hierarchy of handicaps: Validation of Kirk's statement, "Special education often begins where medicine stops." *Journal of Learning Disabilities, 12,* 24–29.

Ackerman, P. T., Elardo, P. T., & Dykman, R. A. (1979). A psychosocial study of hyperactive and learning disabled boys. *Journal of Abnormal Child Psychology, 7,* 91–99.

Affleck, G. G. (1975). Role-taking ability and the interpersonal competencies of retarded children. *American Journal of Mental Deficiency, 80,* 312–316.

Aloia, G. F., Knutson, R., Minner, S. H., & Von Seggern, M. (1980) Physical education teachers' initial perceptions of handicapped children. *Mental Retardation, 18,* 85–87.

Antonak, R. F. (1980). A hierarchy of attitudes toward exceptionality. *Journal of Special Education, 14,* 231–241.

Axelrod, L. (1982). Social perception in learning disabled adolescents. *Journal of Learning Disabilities, 15,* 610–613.

Bachara, G. H. (1976). Empathy in learning disabled children. *Perceptual and Motor Skills, 43,* 541–542.

Baldwin, W. K. (1958). The social position of the educable mentally retarded child in the regular grades. *Exceptional Children, 25,* 106–108, 112.

Barksdale, M. W. (1961). Social problems of mentally retarded children. *Mental Hygiene, 45,* 509–512.

Barngrover, E. (1971). A study of educators' preferences in special education programs. *Exceptional Children, 37,* 754–755.

Barsch, R. H. (1964). The handicapped ranking scale among parents of handicapped children. *American Journal of Public Health, 54,* 1560–1567.

Battle, J., & Blowers, T. (1982). A longitudinal comparative study of the self-esteem of students in regular and special education classes. *Journal of Learning Disabilities, 15,* 100–102.

Bell, A. H. (1962). Attitudes of selected rehabilitation workers and other hospital employees toward the physically disabled. *Psychological Reports, 10,* 183–186.

Berdiansky, H. A., & Parker, R. (1977). Establishing a group home for the adult mentally retarded in North Carolina. *Mental Retardation, 15,* 8–11.

Billings, H. K. (1963). An exploratory study of the attitudes of non-crippled children toward crippled children in three selected elementary schools. *Journal of Experimental Education, 31,* 381–387.

Bloom, R. B., Shea, R. J., & Eun, B. (1979). The Piers-Harris Self-Concept Scale: Norms for behaviorally disordered children. *Psychology in the Schools, 16,* 483–487.

Bruck, M., & Hebert, M. (1982). Correlates of learning disabled students' peer interaction patterns. *Learning Disability Quarterly, 5,* 353–362.

Bruininks, V. L. (1978). Actual and perceived peer status of learning disabled students in mainstream programs. *Journal of Special Education, 12,* 51–58.

Bryan, T. (1974). Peer popularity of learning disabled children. *Journal of Learning Disabilities, 7,* 621–625.

Bryan, T. (1976). Peer popularity of learning disabled children: A replication. *Journal of Learning Disabilities, 9,* 307–311.

Bryan, T. (1977). Learning disabled children's comprehension of nonverbal communication. *Journal of Learning Disabilities, 10,* 36–41.

Bryan, T., Donahue, M., & Pearl, R. (1981). Learning disabled children's peer interactions during a small-group problem-solving task. *Learning Disability Quarterly, 4,* 13–22.

Bryan, T., Donahue, M., Pearl, R., & Sturm, C. (1981). Learning disabled childrens' conversational skills–The "tv talk show." *Learning Disability Quarterly, 4,* 250–259.

Bryan, T., Wheeler, R., Felcan, J., & Henek, T. (1976). "Come on Dummy": An observational study of children's communications. *Journal of Learning Disabilities, 9,* 661–669.

Byford, E. M. (1979). Mainstreaming: The effect on regular teacher training programs. *Journal of Teacher Education, 30,* 23–24.

Centers, L., & Centers, R. (1963). Peer group attitudes toward the amputee child. *The Journal of Social Psychology, 61,* 127–132.

Cermak, S. A., Coster, W., & Drake, C. (1980). Representational and nonrepresentational gestures in boys with learning disabilities. *The American Journal of Occupational Therapy, 34,* 1–19.

Chigier, E., & Chigier, M. (1968). Attitudes to disability of children in the multi-cultural society of Israel. *Journal of Health and Social Behavior, 9,* 310–317.

Childs, R. E. (1981). Perceptions of mainstreaming by regular classroom teachers who teach mainstreamed educable mentally retarded students in the public schools. *Education and Training of the Mentally Retarded, 16,* 225–227.

Cline, R. (1981). Principals' attitudes and knowledge about handicapped children. *Exceptional Children, 48,* 172–174.

Coie, J. D., & Pennington, B. F. (1976). Children's perceptions of deviance and disorder. *Child Development, 47,* 407–413.

Coker, G. (1979). A comparison of self-concepts and academic achievement of visually handicapped children enrolled in a regular school and in a residential school. *Education of the Visually Handicapped, 11,* 67–74.

Coleman, J. M. (1983). Handicapped labels and instructional segregation: Influences on children's self-concepts versus the perceptions of others. *Learning Disability Quarterly, 6,* 3–11.

Conine, T. A. (1969). Acceptance or rejection of disabled persons by teachers. *Journal of School Health, 39,* 278–281.

Davids, A., & Parenti, A. N. (1958). Personality, social choice, and adults' perceptions of these factors in groups of disturbed and normal children. *Sociometry, 12,* 212–224.

Davis, W. E. (1980). Public school principals' attitudes toward mainstreaming retarded pupils. *Education and Training of the Mentally Retarded, 15,* 174–178.

Dear, M. (1977). Impact of mental health facilities on property values. *Community Mental Health Journal, 13,* 150–157.

Dentler, R. A., & Mackler, B. (1964). Effects on sociometric status of institutional pressure to adjust among retarded children. *British Journal of Social and Clinical Psychology, 3,* 81–89.

Dickstein, E. B., & Warren, D. R. (1980). Role-taking deficits in learning disabled children. *Journal of Learning Disabilities, 13,* 378–382.

Di Sipio, Z., Nake, J., & Perney, J. (1978). How teachers view the resource room-Part I. *Journal for Special Educators of the Mentally Retarded, 14,* 164–172.

Donaldson, J. (1981). The visibility and image of handicapped people on television. *Exeptional Children, 47,* 413–416.

Dunlop, K. H., Stoneman, Z., & Cantrell, N. H. (1980). Social interaction of exceptional and other children in a mainstreamed preschool. classroom. *Exceptional Children, 47,* 132–141.

Elser, R. (1959). The social position of handicapped children in regular grades. *Exceptional Children, 25,* 305–309.

Enright, R. D., & Lapsley, D. K. (1980). Social role-taking: A review of the constructs, measures, and measurement-properties. *Review of Educational Research, 50,* 647–674.

Festinger, L. (1954). A theory of social comparison processes. *Human Relations, 7,* 117–140.

Fincham, F. (1978). Recipient characteristics and sharing behavior in the learning disabled. *Journal of Genetic Psychology,133,* 143–144.

Force, D. (1956). Social status of physically handicapped children. *Exceptional Children, 23,* 132–134.

Freeman, G. G., & Sonnega, J. A. (1956). Peer evaluation of children in speech corrections class. *Journal of Speech and Hearing Disorders, 21,* 179–182.

Gallup Organization Report for the President's Committee on Mental Retardation. Public attitudes regarding mental retardation. In R. Nathan (Ed.), *Mental retardation: Century of decision* (No. 040-000-00343-6). Washington, DC: U.S. Government Printing Office, 1976.

Garrison, W. M., & Tesch, S. (1978). Self-concept and deafness: A review of research literature. *Volta Review, 80,* 457–466.

Gerber, P. J., & Zinkgraf, S. A. (1982). A comparative study of social perceptual ability in learning disabled and nonhandicapped students. *Learning Disability Quarterly, 5,* 374–378.

Goodman, H., Gottlieb, J., & Harrison, R. H. (1972). Social acceptance of emrs integrated into a non-graded elementary school. *American Journal of Mental Deficiency, 76,* 412–417.

Goodman, N., Dornbusch, S. M., Richardson, S. A., & Hastorf, A. H. (1963). Variant reactions to physical disabilities. *American Sociological Review, 28,* 429–435.

Gottlieb, J., & Budoff, M. (1973). Social acceptability of retarded children in nongraded schools differing in architecture. *American Journal of Mental Deficiency, 78,* 15–19.

Gottlieb, J., & Corman, L. (1975). Public attitudes toward mentally retarded children. *American Journal of Mental Deficiency, 80,* 72–80.

Gottlieb, J., & Davis, J. E. (1973). Social acceptance of emr children during overt behavioral interactions. *American Journal of Mental Deficiency, 78,* 141–143.

Gottlieb, J., Semmel, M. I., & Veldman, D. J. (1978). Correlates of social status among main-streamed mentally retarded. *Journal of Educational Psychology, 70,* 396–405.

Graham, S., Hudson, F., Burdg, N. B., & Carpenter, D. (1980). Educational personnel's percep-tions of mainstreaming and resource from effectiveness. *Psychology in the Schools, 17,* 128–134.

Grand, S. A., Bernier, J. E., & Strohmer, D. C. (1982). Attitudes toward disabled persons as a function of social context and specific disability. *Rehabilitation Psychology, 27,* 165–174.

Greenbaum, J. J., & Wang, D. D. (1965). A semantic-differential study of the concepts of mental retardation. *The Journal of General Psychology, 73,* 257–272.

Guerin, G. R. (1979). Regular teacher concerns with mainstreamed learning handicapped children. *Psychology in the Schools, 16,* 543–545.

Guerin, G. R., & Szatlocky, K. (1974). Integration programsfor the mildly retarded. *Exceptional Children, 40,* 173–179.

Harasymiw, S. J., & Horne, M. D. (1976). Teacher attitudes toward handicapped children and regular class integration. *Journal of Special Education, 10,* 393–400.

Harasymiw, S. J., Horne, M. D., & Lewis, S. C. (1976). Disability social distance hierarchy for population subgroups. *Scandinavian Journal of Rehabilitation Medicine, 8,* 33–36.

Hays, W. (1951). Mental level and friend selection among institutionalized defective girls. *American Journal of Mental Deficiency, 56,* 198–203.

Head, D. N. (1979). A comparison of self-concept scores for visually impaired adolescents in several class settings. *Education of the Visually Handicapped, 11,* 51–55.

Hirshoren, A., & Burton, T. (1979). Willingness of regular teachers to participate in mainstreaming handicapped children. *Journal of Research and Development in Education, 12,* 93–100.

Hoffman, E., Marsden, G., & Kalter, N. (1977). Children's understanding of their emotionally disturbed peers: A replication. *Journal of Clinical Psychology, 33,* 949–953.

Holdaway, S. L., & Jensen, L. C. (1983). Self-, teachers',and mothers' perceptions of the behav-iorally disordered child. *Psychology in the Schools, 20,* 388–394.

Hollinger, C. S., & Jones, R. L. (1970). Community attitudes toward slow learners and mental retardates: What's in a name? *Mental Retardation, 8,* 19–23.

Horne, M. D. (1983). Elementary classroom teacher attitudes toward mainstreaming. *The Exceptional Child, 30,* 93–98.

Horowitz, E. C. (1981). Popularity, decentering ability and role-taking skills in learning disabled and normal childen. *Learning Disability Quarterly, 2,* 23–30.

Hudson, F., Graham, S., & Warner, M. (1979). Mainstreaming: An examination of the needs of regular classroom teachers. *Learning Disability Quarterly, 2,* 58–62.

Hus, Y. (1979). The socialization process of hearing-impaired children in a summer day camp. *Volta Review, 81,* 146–156.

Hutton, J. B., & Polo, L. (1976). A sociometric study of learning disability children and type of teaching strategy. *Group Psychotherapy and Psychodrama, 29,* 113–120.

Hutton, J. B., & Roberts, T. G. (1982). Relationships of sociometric status and characteristics of emotional disturbance. *Behavioral Disorders, 1,* 19–24.

Iano, R. P., Ayers, D., Hellern, H. B., McGettingan, J. F., & Walker, V.S. (1974). Sociometric status of retarded children in integrative program. *Exceptional Children, 40,* 267–271.

Jaffe, J. (1967). ''What's in a name''—Attitudes toward disabled persons. *Personnel and Guidance Journal, 45,* 557–560.

Johnson, G. O. (1950). A study of the social position of mentally-handicapped children in regular grades. *American Journal of Mental Deficiency, 55,* 60–89.

Johnson, G. O., & Kirk, S. A. (1950). Are mentally handicapped children segregated in the regular grades? *Exceptional Children, 17,* 65–68, 87–88.

Jones, R. L., Lavine, K., & Shell, J. (1972). Blind children integrated into classrooms with sighted children: A sociometric study. *The New Outlook for the Blind, 66,* 75–80.

Kang, Y. W., & Masoodi, B. A. (1977). Attitudes toward blind people among theological and education students. *Visual Impairment and Blindness, 71,* 394–400.

Kastner, L. S., Reppucci, N. D., & Pezzoli, J. J. (1979). Assessing community attitudes toward mentally retarded persons. *American Journal of Mental Deficiency, 83,* 137–144.

Kavale, K., & Rossi, C. (1980). Regular class teachers attitudes and perceptions of the resource specialist program foreducable mentally retarded pupils. *Education and Training of the Mentally Retarded, 15,* 195–198.

Kennedy, P., & Bruininks, R. H. (1974). Social status of hearing impaired children in regular classrooms. *Exceptional Children, 40,* 336–342.

Kern, W. H., & Pfaeffle, H. (1963). A comparison of social adjustment of mentally retarded children in various educational settings. *American Journal of Mental Deficiency, 67,* 407–413.

Kvaraceus, W. C. (1956). Acceptance—rejection and exceptionality. *Exceptional Children, 22,* 328–331.

Lapp, E. R. (1957). A study of the social adjustment of slow -learning children who were assigned part-time to regular classes. *American Journal of Mental Deficiency, 62,* 254–262.

Larrivee, B. (1982). Factors underlying regular classroom teachers' attitudes toward mainstreaming. *Psychology in the Schools, 19,* 374–379.

Larrivee, B., & Cook, L. (1979). Mainstreaming: A study of the variables affecting teacher attitude. *Journal of Special Education, 13,* 315–324.

MacMillan, D. L., Meyers, C. E., & Yoshida, R. K. (1978). Regular class teachers' perceptions of transition programs for emr students and their impact on the students. *Psychology in the Schools, 15,* 99–103.

MacMillan, D. L., & Morrison, G. M. (1980). Correlates of social status among mildly handicapped learners in self-contained special classes. *Journal of Educational Psychology, 72,* 437–444.

Maheady, L., & Maitland, G. E. (1982). Assessing social perception abilities in learning disabled students. *Learning Disability Quarterly, 5,* 363–370.

Mandell, C. J., & Strain, P. S. (1978). An analysis of factors related to the attitudes of regular classroom teachers toward mainstreaming mildly handicapped children. *Contemporary Educational Psychology, 3,* 154–162.

Marden, P. W., & Farber, B. (1961). High-brow versus low-grade status among institutionalized mentally retarded boys. *Social Problems, 8,* 300–312.

Marge, D. K. (1966). The social status of speech-handicapped children. *Journal of Speech and Hearing Research, 9,* 165–177.

Marsden, G., & Kalter, N. (1976). Children's understanding of their emotionally disturbed peers. *Psychiatry, 39,* 227–238.

Matthews, V., & Westie, C. (1966). A preferred method for obtaining rankings: Reactions to physical handicaps. *American Sociological Review, 31,* 851–854.

McCorkle, L. W., Elias, A., & Bixby, F. L. (1958). *The Highfields Story: An experimental treatment project of youthful offenders.* New York: Holt.

Meyerowitz, J. H. (1962). Self-derogation in young retardates and special class placement. *Child Development, 33,* 443–451.

Meyers, C. E., Sitkei, E. C., & Watts, C. A. (1966). Attitudes toward special education and the handicapped in two community groups. *American Journal of Mental Deficiency, 71,* 78–84.

Middleton, E. J., Morsink, C., & Cohen, S. (1979). Program graduates' perception of need for training in mainstreaming. *Exceptional Children, 45,* 256–261.

Miller, M., Richey, D. D., & Lammers, C. A. (1983). Analysis of gifted students' attitudes toward the handicapped. *Journal for Special Educators, 19,* 14–21.

Miller, R. V. (1956). Social status and sociometric differences among mentally superior, mentally typical, and mentally retarded children. *Exceptional Children, 23,* 114–119.

Moore, J., & Fine, M. J. (1978). Regular and special class teachers' perceptions of normal and exceptional children and their attitudes toward mainstreaming. *Psychology in the Schools, 15,* 253–259.

Morgan, S. R. (1978). A descriptive analysis of maladjusted behavior in socially rejected children. *Behavioral Disorders, 4,* 23–30.

O'Connor, G., & Sitkei, E. G. (1975). Study of a new frontier in community services: Residential facilities for the developmentally disabled. *Mental Retardation, 13,* 35–39.

Omwake, K. T. (1954). The relation between acceptance of self and acceptance of others shown by three personality inventories. *Journal of Consulting Psychology, 18,* 443–446.

Pandy, C. (1971). Popularity, rebelliousness, and happiness among institutionalized retarded males. *American Journal of Mental Deficiency, 76,* 325–331.

Parish, T. S., Dyck, N., & Kappes, B. M. (1979). Stereotypes concerning normal and handicapped children. *Journal of Psychology, 102,* 63–70.

Parish, T. S., Eads, G. M., Reece, N. H., & Piscitello, M. A. (1977). Assessment and attempted modification of future teachers' attitudes toward handicapped children. *Perceptual and Motor Skills, 44,* 540–542.

Parish, T. S., Ohlsen, R. L., & Parish, J. G. (1978). A look at mainstreaming in light of children's attitudes toward the handicapped. *Perceptual and Motor Skills, 46,* 1019–1021.

Parker, L. G., & Stodden, R. L. (1977). Attitudes towards the handicapped. *Journal for Special Education of the Mentally Retarded, 14,* 24–28.

Paulauskas, S. L., & Campbell, S. B. G. (1979). Social perspective-taking and teacher ratings of peer interaction in hyperactive boys. *Journal of Abnormal Child Psychology, 7,* 483–493.

Payne, R., & Murray, C. (1974). Principals' attitudes toward integration of the handicapped. *Exceptional Children, 40,* 123–125.

Pearl, R., & Cosden, M. (1982). Sizing up a situation: LD children's understanding of social interactions. *Learning Disability Quarterly, 5,* 371–373.

Perlmutter, B. F., Crocker, J., Cordray, D., & Garstecki, D. (1983). Sociometric status and related personality characteristics of mainstreamed learning disabled adolescents. *Learning Disability Quarterly, 6,* 20–30.

Perrin, E. H. (1954). The social position of the speech defective child. *Journal of Speech and Hearing Disorders, 19,* 250–252.

Phillips, D. L. (1963). Rejection: A possible consequence of seeking help for mental disorders. *American Sociological Review, 28*, 963–972.

Prillaman, D. (1981). Acceptance of learning disabled students in the mainstream environment: A failure to replicate. *Journal of Learning Disabilities, 14*, 344–368.

Purkey, W. (1970). *Self-concept and school achievement*. Englewood Cliffs, NJ: Prentice Hall.

Randolph, A. H., & Harrington, R. M. (1981). Fifth graders' projected responses to a physically handicapped classmate. *Elementary School Guidance Counseling, 16*, 31–35.

Raskind, M. H., Drew, D. E., & Regan, J. O. (1983). Nonverbal communication signals in behavior-disordered and non-disordered ld boys and nld boys. *Learning Disability Quarterly, 6*, 12–19.

Reese-Dukes, J. L., & Stokes, E. H. (1978). Social acceptance of elementary educable mentally retarded students in the regular classroom. *Education and Training of the Mentally Retarded, 13*, 356–361.

Renz, P., & Simensen, R. J. (1969). The social perception of normals toward their emr grade-mates. *American Journal of Mental Deficiency, 74*, 405–408.

Richardson, S. A., Goodman, N., Hastorf, A. H., & Dornbusch, S. M. (1961). Cultural uniformity in reaction to physical disabilities. *American Sociological Review, 26*, 241–247.

Richardson, S. A., Ronald, L., & Kleck, R. E. (1974). The social status of handicapped and nonhandicapped boys in a camp setting. *The Journal of Special Education, 8*, 143–152.

Richardson, S. A., & Royce, J. (1968). Race and physical handicap in children's preference for other children. *Child Development, 39*, 467–480.

Ringlaben, R. P., & Price, J. R. (1981). Regular classroom teachers' perceptions of mainstreaming effects. *Exceptional Children, 47*, 302–304.

Rootman, I., & LaFave, H. G. (1969). Are popular attitudes towards the mentally ill changing? *American Journal of Psychiatry, 126*, 147–151.

Rucker, C. N., & Gable, R. K. (1974). *Rucker-Gable educational programming scale manual*. Storrs, CT: Rucker-Gable Associates.

Rucker, C. N., Howe, C. E., & Snider, B. (1969). The participation of retarded children in junior high academic and nonacademic regular classes. *Exceptional Children, 35*, 617–623.

Schmelkin, L. P. (1981). Teachers' and nonteachers' attitudes toward mainstreaming. *Exceptional Children, 48*, 42–47.

Schneider, C. R., & Anderson, W. (1980). Attitudes toward the stigmatized: Some insights from recent research. *Rehabilitation Counseling Bulletin, 23*, 299–313.

Schultz, L. R. (1982). Educating the special needs student in the regular classroom. *Exceptional Children, 48*, 366–368.

Schumaker, J. B., Hazel, J. S., Sherman, J. A., & Sheldon, J. (1982). Social skill performances of learning disabled, non-learning disabled, and delinquent adolescents. *Learning Disability Quarterly, 5*, 388–397.

Schumaker, J. B., Wildgen, J. S., & Sherman, J. A. (1982). Social interaction of learning disabled junior high students in their regular classrooms: An observational analysis. *Journal of Learning Disabilities, 15*, 355–358.

Schurr, K. T., Towne, R. C., & Joiner, L. M. (1972). Trends in self-concept of ability over 2 years of special-class placement. *The Journal of Special Education, 6*, 161–166.

Scranton, R. R., & Ryckman, D. B. (1979). Sociometric status of learning disabled children in an integrative program. *Journal of Learning Disabilities, 12*, 49–54.

Serafica, F. C., & Harway, N. I. (1979). Social relations and self-esteem of children with learning disabilities. *Journal of Clinical Child Psychology, 8*, 227–233.

Sheare, J. B. (1978). The impact of resource room programs upon the self-concept and peer acceptance of learning disabled students. *Psychology in the Schools, 15*, 406–412.

Shears, L. M., & Jensema, C. J. (1969). Social acceptability of anomalous persons. *Exceptional Children, 36*, 91–96.

Shotel, J. R., Iano, R. P., & McGettigan, J. B. (1972). Teacher attitudes associated with the integration of handicapped children. *Exceptional Children, 38,* 677–683.

Sigelman, C., Spanhel, C., & Lorensen, C. (1979). Community reactions to deinstitutionalization. *Journal of Rehabilitation, 45,* 52–54, 60.

Siller, J. (1960). Psychological concomitants of amputation in children. *Child Development, 31,* 109–120.

Siperstein, G. N., Bopp, N. J., & Bak, J. J. (1978). The social status of learning disabled children. *Journal of Learning Disabilities, 11,* 49–53.

Smith, D. H., & Olson, J. T. (1970). Sociometric status in a psychiatrically deviant adolescent collectivity. *Psychological Reports, 27,* 483–497.

Smith, T. E. C., Flexer, R. W., & Sigelman, C. K. (1980). Attitudes of secondary principals toward the learning disabled, the mentally retarded and work-study programs. *Journal of Learning Disabilities, 13,* 62–64.

Soldwedel, B., & Terrill, I. (1957). Physically handicapped and non-handicapped children in the same elementary school. *Exceptional Children, 23,* 371–383.

Speece, D. L., & Mandell, C. J. (1980). Resource room support services for regular teachers. *Learning Disability Quarterly, 3,* 49–53.

Stephens, T. M., & Braun, B. L. (1980). Measures of regular classroom teachers' attitudes toward handicapped children. *Exceptional Children, 46,* 292–294.

Strang, L., Smith, M. D., & Rogers, C. M. (1978). Social comparison, multiple reference groups, and the self-concepts of academically handicapped children before and after mainstreaming. *Journal of Educational Psychology, 70,* 487–497.

Tringo, J. L. (1970). The hierarchy of preference toward disability groups. *Journal of Special Education, 4,* 295–306.

Vandivier, P. L., & Vandivier, S. C. (1981). Teacher attitudes toward mainstreaming exceptional students. *Journal for Special Education, 17,* 381–388.

Van Putte, A. W. (1979). Relationship of school setting to self-concept in physically disabled children. *Journal of School Health, 49,* 576–578.

Vidoni, D. O., Fleming, N. J., & Mintz, S. (1983). Behavior problems of children as perceived by teachers, mental health professionals, and children. *Psychology in the Schools, 20,* 93–98.

Warger, C. L., & Trippe, M. (1982). Preservice teacher attitudes toward mainstreamed students with emotional impairments. *Exceptional Children, 49,* 246–252.

Warner, F., Thrapp, R., & Walsh, S. (1973). Attitudes of children toward their special class placement. *Exceptional Children, 40,* 37–38.

Warren, S. A., & Turner, D. R. (1966). Attitudes to professionals and students toward exceptional children. *Training School Bulletin, 62,* 136–144.

Warren, S. A., Turner, D. R., & Brody, D. S. (1964). Can education students' attitudes toward the retarded be changed? *Mental Retardation, 12,* 235–242.

Weinberg, N., & Santana, R. (1978) Comic books: Champions of the disabled stereotype. *Rehabilitation Literature, 39,* 327–331.

Weiner, D., Anderson, R. J., & Nietupski, J. (1982). Impact of community-based residential facilities for mentally retarded adults on surrounding property values using realtor analysis methods. *Education and Training of the Mentally Retarded, 17,* 278–281.

Wendel, F. C. (1977). Progress in mainstreaming. *Phi Delta Kappan, 59,* 58.

Wiig, E. H., & Harris, S. P. (1974). Perception on interpretation of nonverbally expressed emotions by adolescents with learning disabilities. *Perceptual and Motor Skills, 38,* 239–245.

Williams, R. J., & Algozzine, B. (1977). Differential attitudes toward mainstreaming: An investigation. *Alberta Journal of Educational Research, 23*(3), 207–212.

Wylie, R. (1974). *The self-concept,* (Vol. 1). Lincoln, NB: University of Nebraska Press.

5

Factors Affecting the Development and Maintenance of Attitudes

The previous chapter presented evidence of the negative attitudes professionals and peers may express toward handicapped students. The purpose of this chapter is to examine other factors that may affect the development and maintenance of attitudes toward handicapped and nonhandicapped students. There are many student characteristics, in addition to a handicapping condition, that may be associated with the attitudes teachers and peers develop toward students in their classes. At the same time, different personal and background characteristics of teachers and peers themselves may be determinants of the formation and development of their attitudes.

The chapter opens with a summary of what has been a controversial issue—teacher expectations and the potential influence these expectations may have on student performance; next, models for communicating expectations to students are presented. The following section examines a variety of student characteristics that may influence a teacher's attitude toward a student. Next, personal and background characteristics of the teacher are discussed as they may relate to the attitudes they develop toward students.

The final section of the chapter is devoted to a discussion of student characteristics that may influence classmates' perceptions about them; and in turn, personal and background characteristics of students which may be related to the attitudes they develop toward their peers.

TEACHER EXPECTATIONS

Interestingly it was the findings for animal studies that led to the exploration of classroom teacher expectations. In one such investigation (Rosenthal & Lawson,

1964), rats were randomly assigned to several learning tasks. Half of the research assistants were led to believe their rats were particularly intelligent; the other group was told they had low caliber rats. When the analysis of the rats' performance indicated that the supposedly more intelligent rats had made greater progress, it was concluded that the expectations of the research assistants affected how the rats performed.

In *Pygmalion in the Classroom,* the seminal study on teacher expectations for classroom students, Rosenthal and Jacobson (1968) detailed their study of the effects of teachers' expectations on students' performance. Teachers were told that some of their students were late developers and could be expected to improve. It was indeed found that this group of ''late bloomers'' made greater academic gains than the children in the control group who had the same learning potential but who were not identified as ''likely to make great gains.'' It was concluded that the teachers' expectancy for the childrens' improvement affected interactions the teachers had with them, which in turn influenced the students' achievement.

Numerous critical commentaries followed the publication of the report (Barber & Silver, 1968; Elashoff & Snow, 1971; Gephart & Antonoplos, 1969; Snow, 1969; Thorndike, 1968) and a surge of interest in replicating the effect followed. Some researchers were successful, others were not. Descriptions of some early attempts to replicate the Rosenthal and Jacobson findings clarify the nature of the research.

Beez (1968) conducted a laboratory study in which kindergarten children were randomly assigned a high or low ability rating. The teachers (graduate students) were given reports on the 60 pupils which described all as having average intelligence; however, the interpretation for each group differed. Reports for the low group interpreted the IQ information negatively, while the IQ information for the high ability group was positively interpreted. The teachers were given ten minutes to teach as many words to the pupils as they could. Results showed the two groups differed significantly in performance; the ''high ability'' group learned more words. It was also found that the teachers in the ''high ability'' group tried to teach additional information. Significant differences were noted in the number of words taught to the ''high'' and ''low ability'' groups, and teachers of the ''low groups'' explained words significantly more often to their pupils. The teachers also differed significantly in their ratings of the ''high'' and ''low ability'' groups on achievement, social competency, intellectual ability, and on the evaluations they made of the difficulty of the task for the students.

In a study in a natural classroom setting, Kester and Letchworth (1972) found that labeling students as bright influenced the behaviors of the teachers but did not alter the attitudes or achievement of 150 average seventh graders. During the first week of school students were administered the *Otis-Lennon Mental Abilities Test,* the *Stanford Achievement Test,* and a semantic differential to assess their attitudes toward themselves and school. Some average students were designated as bright and their names were given to the teachers. Observers then recorded teacher-student interaction for 50 minutes during the second, fourth, sixth, and eighth weeks of school with posttesting conducted during the ninth week. Teachers were more responsive to the "bright" students than to their classmates; however, there were no significant differences in student attitude or achievement.

The effects of teacher expectancy on the performance of severely retarded students in a state school setting was studied by Soule (1972). Twelve experimental and 12 control subjects, who were aged 8 to 16, were included in the study. Pre-testing included the administration of the *Peabody Picture Vocabulary Test, Slosson Intelligence Test,* and the *Behavior Maturity Check List* (a locally used behavior inventory). Cottage parents of the experimental group were told that the selected subjects were expected to show greater gains in the future. During the following 6-month period, members of the research team made weekly visits to ask the cottage parents how each experimental student was progressing and to reinforce the expectation for future gains. Post-testing, which included readministration of tests given initially as well as additional measures and observations, indicated no differences between the groups of students. Cottage parent bias did not influence the performance of the subjects.

Numerous other studies also failed to support the effect of teacher expectations on, for example, second grade student IQ scores (Fleming & Anttonen, 1971); first grade students' IQ's and teacher behavior (Claiborn, 1969); second and third grade student IQ scores, achievement, and teacher behavior (José & Cody, 1971); and retarded students' achievement (Schwarz & Cook, 1972). But some studies showed teacher expectations could affect performance. In one study, for example, second and fourth graders' academic performance was found related to teacher rankings (Dusek & O'Connell, 1973), and, in another, adolescent offenders' test scores and interactions with teachers were related to teacher expectations (Meichenbaum, Bowers, & Ross, 1969).

There are several excellent reviews of the research on teacher expectations (Braun, 1976; Brophy & Good; 1974; Cooper, 1979; Dusek, 1975), which the reader should consult for a more detailed discussion of investigations related to the expectancy effect. An apt summary of the literature is that it appears that teachers do not bias childrens' learning as a result of correct or incorrect knowledge they have about them, but teachers do form expectations that may result in their according differential treatment to students, which may in turn influence student performance (Dusek, 1975).

Dusek (1975) distinguished between "teacher bias" and "teacher expectancy":

"teacher bias will refer to significant effects due to the teacher's differential expectations for student's performance in the case where expectancies have been induced by a principal investigator. That is, teacher bias refers to a manipulation of the teacher's expectancies by a principal investigator. Such effects are analogous to those reported by Rosenthal and Jacobson (1968) and are biased in the sense that the teacher has differential expectations regarding the performance of children who are equivalent on some objective measure. The term "teacher expectancy" will refer to significant effects due to the teachers' own, self-generated expectations regarding students' performance. In this case, it is the teachers' own expectancy, formed however teachers form it, which is related to student's performance (p. 679).

Dusek suggested future research be directed toward understanding student characteristics that may determine teacher expectations.

Models for Communicating Expectancies

It is not entirely clear how the expectations teachers have for students are communicated; nor is it apparent how expectations may influence student performance. Causal models drawing from extant research, however, provide a frame of reference for beginning to understand the variables that may influence the teachers' attitudes or expectations.

Cooper (1979) proposed a model to explain how teacher expectations can influence student achievement as shown in Fig. 5.1. According to this model, student ability and background (these variables are not specified) cause teachers to form differential expectations for students; in turn these expectations influence the perceptions the teacher has about their personal control over interactions with the student in the classroom. That is, classroom teachers have control over (1) the content (what the interaction is about) of their interactions with students; (2) when the interaction occurs; and (3) how long the interaction lasts. Although control may differ somewhat depending on whether the teacher or child initiates the interaction, teacher initiated interaction gives the teacher more control since the teacher has chosen the topic or content, selected a student to respond (control over when the interaction occurs), and will be able to determine the length of the interaction. Student initiated interactions give the pupil control over the content and timing or when an interaction occurs, but teachers will still control the duration of the interaction. The interaction context, or whether interactions take place during a time when the teacher is interacting with the class as a whole, or speaking to the student in private while other children are working will also influence interactions.

Interactions with low expectation students are perceived by teachers as less controllable (in the sense that low expectation students may not know much about the topic, not know the answer, respond inappropriately, and may take more or less time to respond) and less likely successful. The teachers' perception of control influences classroom climate and feedback choices. Teachers increase the control they have over low expectation students by developing a negative climate and feedback pattern. The negative climate causes low expectation stu-

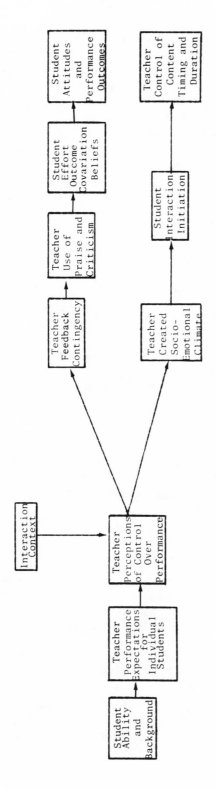

FIG. 5.1. A model for expectation communication and behavior influence

From Cooper, H. M. Pygmalion grows up: a model for teacher expectation communication and performance influence. *Review of Educational Research*, 1979, *49*, 389–410.

dents to engage in fewer initiations; at the same time low expectation students are praised and criticized more often for control purposes rather than for their effort in school work. The end result is a belief on the part of low expectation students that reinforcements are the result of external teacher control rather than their own personal effort that may influence their future performance. In contrast, teachers perceive high-expectation students as more controllable, and expect that interaction with them will be more successful. The feedback given to high expectation students is therefore less likely to be based on control and more frequently based upon the students' performance. The high expectation students are led to believe that their effort influences their academic performance; consequently they are motivated to continue to exert an effort to achieve.

From Braun's (1976) perspective, teacher expectations influence the expectations a student has about himself, which in turn influence performance. The cycle is perpetuated: "If the learner thinks of himself as inferior his actions will tend to be those of an inferior person and will confirm to his teacher and peers the reasonableness of treating him as inferior" (p. 205). Braun proposed a model, shown in Fig. 5.2, which illustrated input variables (intelligence test results, sex, name of child, cumulative folders, ethnic background, knowledge of siblings, physical attractiveness, previous achievement, socioeconomic status) that contribute to teacher expectations. In turn, teacher expectations influence their "output" or actions toward students in terms of grouping, interactions, and activities with students. These behaviors are input into the pupil's self-expectation, which in turn influence the student's behavior which may confirm (as input) the teacher's expectations.

Good (1980) reviewed the steps in a model of how teachers' expectations are realized in the classroom:

Step 1. The teacher expects specific behavior and achievement from particular students.

Step 2. Because of these different expectations, the teacher behaves differently toward students.

Step 3. This treatment tells the student what behavior and achievement the teacher expects from them, and affects their self-concepts, achievment motivation, and levels of aspiration.

Step 4. If this treatment is consistent over time, and if the students do not resist or change it in some way, it will shape their achievement and behavior. High-expectation students will be led to achieve at high levels, whereas the achievement of low expectation students will decline.

Step 5. With time, students' achievement and behavior will conform more and more closely to the behavior originally expected of them (p. 84).

As the model indicates, expectations are not always self-fulfilling because teachers: (1) do not necessarily have expectations for each student, (2) expectations can change; and (3) may not be consistent in their communication. Furthermore

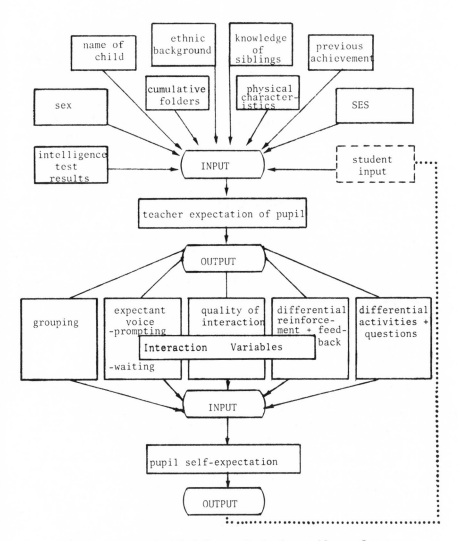

FIG. 5.2.   The Behavioral Cycle Between Teacher Input and Learner Output

From Braun, C. Teacher expectation: Sociopsychological dynamics. *Review of Educational Research,* 1976, *46,* 185–213.

students can resist or overcome the effect of teacher expectations. Good noted that the steps are not necessarily sequential; thus, behavior at Step 2 can be followed directly by Step 5.

The models proposed by Cooper, Braun, and Good advance our understanding of how teacher attitudes and expectations may contribute to student performance. There is, however, a need to continue to build sequential models. Efforts should be directed toward the development of models to account for all of the variables related to teacher expectations, their communication to students, and the differential effect these variables may have on student performance. At the same time, professionals need to be aware of existing models because these models can help them to recognize they may have different expectations for students and that these perceptions may be communicated to students. Ideally, professionals could then begin to monitor their interactions with students.

TEACHER ATTITUDES AND STUDENT CHARACTERISTICS

Teacher attitudes toward students may be influenced by a number of student characteristics. These include the student's: (1) label; (2) achievement; (3) gender; (4) attractiveness; (5) race; (6) socioeconomic status; (7) conduct; (8) personality characteristics; (9) first name; and (10) sibling characteristics. Foremost in the literature on handicapped students is the effect of the handicap label (e.g., learning disabled, mentally retarded, or emotionally disturbed) on teacher attitudes. Because this issue has engendered so much controversy, and is still open to question, the topic of labeling will be discussed first.

The Issue of the Handicap Label

Since the late sixties, the issue of labeling has received considerable attention in the literature. The beginnings of "heavy" debate, particularly in the field of special education, can be traced at least in part back to Dunn (1968). He reviewed Rosenthal and Jacobson's (1968) findings for the effect of teacher expectations and concluded that, ". . . we must expect that labeling a child 'handicapped' reduces the teacher's expectancy for him to succeed" (p. 9). Just a year earlier Combs and Harper (1967) showed that some labels had a negative effect on the perception of classroom teachers and suggested:

> . . . professionals should be extremely careful, if not reluctant to use clinical labels in describing a child to teachers (p. 402).

At a time when the learning disability category was just emerging, Towne and Joiner (1968) were concerned about the labeling and special classroom placement of this new group of students and remarked:

> The meaning of the label 'learning disabled' . . . will expand beyond the set of diagnostic behaviors that define the category so that the child is now thought of as being personally defective rather than as a child deficient in specific learning skills.

Thus, whatever the label means to others, regardless of its accuracy or connection with the child's immediate behavior, each person's expectations of the child's behavior will be affected by his definition of what this kind of person is supposed to be like (pp. 219–220).

Numerous studies were designed to explore the effects of labeling students.

Negative Effects of Labels.   There is some evidence that supports the negative effects labels may have on professional attitudes. Labels may affect teacher expectations for achievement as well as recommendations for program placements.

Foster and Ysseldyke (1976) conducted a two-phase experiment to study teacher expectations for normal and labeled students in the elementary school. In the expectancy phase of the study, the teachers were randomly assigned to one of four label groups (normal, mentally retarded, learning disabled, or emotionally disturbed) and asked to complete a referral form containing personality and behavioral items according to how they expected it might appear for that label. In the second (halo) phase of the study, teachers were shown a videotape of a normal child under the four label conditions after which they were asked to complete the referral form again; but this time, based upon the student behaviors they observed. Results showed that labeled students received significantly lower personality and behavioral ratings in both the expectancy and halo phases of the experiment, thus confirming that teachers do have negative expectations for labeled students and that the biasing effect of a label may be sustained even when teachers are presented with contradictory information (i.e., a film of a normal but labeled child). In a similarly designed investigation, Ysseldyke and Foster (1978) demonstrated the biasing effects the labels (emotionally disturbed and learning disabled) had on teacher's behavioral ratings. Once again, the teachers completed a behavioral checklist based on their observations. The biasing effects of the label were sustained. The findings for these two experiments confirmed evidence obtained in a similar and earlier experiment (Foster, Ysseldyke, & Reese, 1975) wherein the biasing effect of the label "emotionally disturbed" was noted in the behavioral ratings assigned a normal student by graduate and undergraduate students enrolled in a special education course.

Carroll and Reppucci (1978) examined the responses of teachers and mental health workers to unlabeled and labeled (mentally retarded, emotionally disturbed, and juvenile delinquent) case studies. Results showed that the labels influenced the ratings both groups made; for example, the likelihood of the student completing high school, motivation for learning, and the need for different kinds of treatment. Teachers were more influenced by the labels than were mental health workers. The differential responses of the teachers and social workers suggest that different professional groups may attach different meanings to labels.

Schloss and Miller (1982) found differences the labels ''in a residential facility'' versus ''in a public school self-contained classroom'' included in identical psychological reports on an adolescent labeled behavior disordered had on the expectations and recommendations of primary and secondary school teachers.

In a report examining the effect that labels may have on placement decisions, Gillung and Rucker (1977) found that when teachers were presented with identically labeled and unlabeled descriptions of children, labeled children were placed in more restrictive educational settings.

Some studies on labeling have paired labels with student characteristics. For example, Taylor, Smiley, and Ziegler (1983) tested the effects of associating positive and negative behavioral and social attributes with the label ''mentally retarded.'' Findings showed that the label significantly altered teacher perceptions of a normal child presented in a videotape; furthermore, the assignment of positive attributes did not alter special or regular classroom teachers' negative perceptions. Similarly Minner (1982) gave high school vocational education teachers descriptions of unlabeled students and students labeled as ''learning disabled'' and ''mentally retarded'' described positively and negatively. The labels lowered expectations, regardless of the positive descriptions.

Labels May Not Always Be Detrimental.   There is some evidence to suggest that the negative effect a label may have on a teacher's initial attitudes toward a student may be overcome by the behaviors the child displays in the classroom.

Reschly and Lamprecht (1979) tested teacher expectations for students labeled ''normal,'' ''educable mentally retarded,'' and ''gifted.'' First, teachers were presented with a case description of a student in one of the labeled conditions and asked to make predictions about the child's behavior on cognitive tasks. Next they were provided with increasing amounts of videotape exposure to a normal child in the labeled condition (i.e., first teachers viewed a 10-minute videotape, then two 10-minute videotapes, and finally three 10-minute videotapes). The analysis of the teachers' predictions about the student's behavior after viewing each tape indicated a significant effect for the labels. There was, however, also a significant interaction effect beween the label and amount of exposure. The effect of the label diminished with each exposure to the child; with the final viewing of the tape, the effect of the label was entirely eliminated. Thus, the results of this study suggest that if teachers observe behaviors in children that are inconsistent with the expectations engendered by the label, the effect of the label will not be sustained.

In another experiment (Pfeiffer, 1980), two groups of child-study team members (e.g., school psychologists, special educators, counselors) were asked to read descriptions of typical behaviors of unlabeled mentally retarded, emotionally disturbed, and learning disabled students. One group was asked to assign the described student an educational placement (e.g., regular classroom, consultation, resource room); and the other to assign a label and placement to the description. Results showed that the act of labeling did not result in the child study team members selecting more restrictive placements. Thus, labels may not necessarily convey a meaning that will influence a placement decision.

There is also evidence that labels to not influence the goal setting or programming decisions that teachers make for learning disabled and emotionally disturbed students (Boucher & Deno, 1979).

Studies on the effects descriptive information have on teacher attitudes suggest that labels are indeed not the only source of information contributing to the formation of teacher expectations. Boucher (1981), for example, found that when teachers are presented with behavioral characteristics in an unlabeled condition, teachers attribute the problem to a handicap category. Javel & Greenspan (1983) demonstrated that descriptive information had more influence than did an assigned label on the placement decisions schools psychologists made for handicapped students.

Labels and Attribution Theory.   Attribution theory (Weiner, Frieze, Kukla, Reed, Rest, & Rosenbaum, 1971) proposes that an individual's affective and cognitive reactions to a success or failure experience (his own or other's) are a function of the causal attributions the person arrives at as to why an event occurred. Four causes are proposed: ability, effort, task difficulty, and luck. For example, a student may attribute his failure on a mathematics test to a lack of ability for the subject matter, not enough studying, a high level of test difficulty, or bad luck. Similarly classroom teachers form explanations or attributions about the "why" of student performance; they may also attribute a student's achievement on a task to ability, effort, task difficulty, or luck. According to the theory, the causal attributions made about an event determine the expectations for future success or failure experiences, and these expectations affect future behavior.

Some studies have explored the effects of labels on attributions for success and failure. Severance and Gasstrom (1977) found that undergraduate students made differential attributions for unlabeled and labeled (mentally retarded) descriptions of task outcomes.

In another investigation, Palmer (1979) studied the causal attributions and instructional prescriptions elementary classroom teachers provided for normally achieving, educationally handicapped and educable mentally retarded students performing at or below grade level. Hypothetical case reports presented in a labeled or unlabeled condition indicated that teacher attributions for failure were related to labels and achievement information; furthermore, labels and achievement information affected instructional-prescription ratings.

Results of an experiment conducted by Stoller, Algozzine, and Ysseldyke (1981) showed that the labels "learning disabled" and "emotionally disturbed" did not affect special education teacher expectations for the students future performance but work samples did. That is, teachers expected future performance would be similar to current performance. Results for attributional ratings showed that attributions for students were a function of the competence the student exhibited in work samples and not labels.

In his review of the findings of attributional investigations, Palmer (1983) considered the implications of the findings for labeling effects. Palmer concluded that although labels as antecedents may affect teacher attributions, and that perceived causes or attributions in turn affect the teacher's behavior toward the student, other variables may be as important as a label on the development of attributions. The model posited by Palmer, shown in Table 5.1 illustrates the point of view that teacher attributions about student behaviors may be influenced by many types of background information and that attributions are the variable of concern.

When Brophy and Rohrkemper (1981) studied teacher attributions about students with twelve different types of behavior problems described in vignettes (e.g., defiant, underachiever, hyperactive, withdrawn), results demonstrated that teacher attributions for the student were not only affected by their knowledge about the type of student problem, but also by the attributions the teachers made about their ability to cope with the problem. The teachers' attributions about the students and their coping ability resulted in cognitive and affective reactions to the attributions, which, in turn, determined the goals set for students and the teaching strategies the teachers selected.

Summary of the Labeling Controversy

Findings of the effects of the handicapped label on teacher expectations are mixed. Unfortunately, much of the research represents an effort to study the effect under artificial conditions; that is, teachers provide ratings for contrived or artificial reports and/or videotapes of students in labeled or unlabeled conditions. Although these procedures allow researchers the opportunity to control for the type and amount of information given to the teacher, evidence obtained under these contrived circumstances precludes making any definitive conclusions about teacher attitudes toward labeled students in the actual classroom situation.

Observational studies of classroom teacher interactions with handicapped versus nonhandicapped students have not commonly been undertaken. Although studies of teacher interactions with high and low ability students, discussed in the next section, suggest the likelihood that classroom teacher interactions with handicapped students will reflect negative attitudes toward this population, there is some, albeit limited, evidence of the fallacy of reaching such a conclusion. For example, when Kurtz, Harrison, Neisworth, & Jones (1977) examined undergraduate student's nonverbal behavior toward unlabeled and labeled mentally retarded students in a contrived laboratory experiment, results indicated that the "teachers" reacted more positively to the labeled students. Thompson, White, and Morgan (1982) compared the interaction third-grade teachers had with high-achieving nonhandicapped students, low-achieving nonhandicapped students,

TABLE 5.1

Attributional Analysis of Formal and Informal Labels

Antecedent Cues ⟶	Attributions ⟶ (May be expressed through informal labels)	Behavioral Consequences (Domain of Labeling Effects)
Current Performance	Ability (smart, gifted/stupid, neurologically impaired)	Expectancy for Future Performance
History of Performance	Effort (motivated, industrious/ doesn't try, lazy)	Persistence
–Formal Labels	Task (easy/difficult)	Achievement Outcomes
–Special Education Placement	Chance (lucky/unlucky)	Reward-Punishment Feedback
–Teacher Observation and Report		
–Psychometric Test Results		
– Parental Report		
Pattern of Performance		
Performance of Others		
Social Attraction & Rejection		
Nature of the Task or Setting		

From Palmer (1983). An attributional perspective on labeling. *Exceptional Children, 49,* 423-429.

learning disabled students, and behaviorally disordered students. Observations of teacher interactions (using a modified version of the Teacher-Child Dyadic Interaction System developed by Brophy & Good, 1969) showed there were some differences in the patterns of interaction but there was "... no strong evidence that general preferential treatment or treatment likely to result in better educational gains or a more effective learning environment is consistently provided to any one group of students" (p. 233).

It may also be that the effects of the handicap label are somehow diminished because handicapped students receive special services. One study (Quinn & Wilson, 1977) suggested that special services provided for learning disabled children mitigated against the negative effects of the label.

MacMillan, Jones, and Aloia (1974) undertook a critical analysis of the mentally retarded label. They concluded that, "While many accept as fact that labeling children mentally retarded has detrimental effects, conclusive empirical evidence of these effects was not found" (p. 257). It appears that this is still true, and furthermore accurate for many other handicapped student groups as well.

Student Achievement

Teacher attitudes toward students are very much related to achievement behaviors. According to Solomon and Kendall (1977), "Teachers' perceptions of students' academic ability and performance are primary and influence perceptions of all other attributes" (p. 412). Numerous studies have shown that teachers prefer high achievers.

Reports on observations (using a variety of classroom observation systems) of teacher–student interactions in the classrooms are reasonably consistent and demonstrate that high versus low ability students are favored. Good (1970) found teachers gave first-grade students they had ranked as high achievers more opportunity to speak in class than low achievers. Brophy and Good (1970) also studied first-grade classrooms and found that the students ranked by teachers as high achievers received more praise, and support; furthermore, teachers demanded better performance from the high achievers. Good, Cooper, & Blakey (1980) found teacher interactions with third, fourth, & fifth graders they had ranked as high achievers were more favorable across the school year. Another study (Sherry, Armstrong, & Algozzine, 1980) showed that teachers reacted more positively toward fourth, fifth, and sixth graders they had rated as bright versus dull. When Heller and White (1975) observed junior high school high and low ability social studies and mathematics classes, findings showed teachers exhibited more disapproving statements in the low ability classes.

Some studies have examined the behaviors teachers displayed toward students in their classes for whom they had provided attitudinal ratings of attachment ("If you could keep one student for the sheer joy of it, whom would you pick?"), concern ("If you could devote all your attention to a child who concerns you a great deal, whom would you pick?), indifference ("If a parent were to drop in unannounced for a conference whose child would you least be prepared to talk about?"), and rejection ("If your class was to be reduced by one child whom would you be relieved to have removed?") in an interview situation. Silberman (1969) observed, for 20 hours, third-grade teachers' behavior toward the four children she named in response to the above questions and two additional controls. In addition, these six children were asked about the teacher's behavior toward them and toward the five other pupils. The analysis of the data revealed significant differences in teacher behaviors toward particular children and that some teacher attitudes were more clearly expressed than others; that is, teachers were more open in their expression of concern, for example, than indifference. The rejected students had about as much contact with teachers as the others but they were both praised and criticized more frequently. An important finding was that students were aware of the behaviors expressed towards them and could predict the teachers' behavior toward classmates.

Good and Brophy (1972) attempted to replicate the above findings. They observed 9 first-grade teachers' behavior toward 270 children for a total of 40 hours over a 3-month period. Teachers were first asked to rank children according to achievement, then they were observed, and finally interviewed by the investigators. Basically, the same questions used by Silberman were asked to determine attitudes of attachment, concern, indifference, and rejection. The results indicated that achievement was related to all four attitudes. For the most part the attachment group was made up of high achievers, while low achievers were mostly in the rejected or concerned category. Teachers were found to avoid contact with rejected students, failed to provide these students with a follow-up to their work, and were more critical of them.

When reading groups have been observed the results have been somewhat less consistent. Martin, Veldman and Anderson (1980) studied the ways teachers interacted with first-grade students, and their findings supported more positive interactions with high achievers in the classroom situation. Results also showed that a student's relative performance within the reading group made a difference in teacher interactions and once again favored the better student. However, when Weinstein (1976) observed first grade reading groups during the first five months of the school year, teacher-child interactions did not favor the highest reading group; rather the lowest group received more praise despite poorer performance. In another study, Alpert (1974) found that second-grade teachers treated high and low groups the same. However, there was some limited evidence of a small amount of preferential treatment toward the low group which may have been a function of size; the group was smaller and teachers had more time to make positive statements. Eder (1981) videotaped first-grade reading group instruction. An analysis of the tapes showed that the social content of the low group was different from that of the high group and was characterized by student inattentiveness and by disruption. Although only one class was studied, it may be that the characteristics of students in low groups combine to create a poor learning environment.

Student Gender

Teachers may express a preference toward male or female students. Although numerous studies have explored gender preferences in nonhandicapped populations, the results have been inconsistent. There is some limited evidence that teachers have more positive attitudes toward female students (Brown & Macdougall, 1973; Kehle, Bramble, & Mason, 1974) but sometimes the gender variable has not been a significant factor in teacher judgments (Mertens, 1976). There is also evidence that gender may contribute to teacher attitudes but is a less influential factor when compared to student conduct (LaVoie & Adams, 1974), personality characteristics (Helton & Oakland, 1977), or ability and achievement (Prawat & Jarvis, 1980).

Classroom observations have demonstrated that male students receive more positive and negative communication from their teachers. For example, Simpson and Erickson (1983) found white first-grade teachers provided black and white male students with more positive and negative verbal and nonverbal communication than they did with female students. Davis (1967) also showed first-grade teachers made more disapproving comments to male students during reading instruction. Stake and Katz (1982) observed elementary teachers and reported that males were reprimanded more often than females; they were also reprimanded for behaviors which observers had classified as achievement behaviors.

Good, Sikes, and Brophy (1973), however, observed teachers and students in seventh- and eighth-grade classrooms and concluded that male and female teachers behave differently in their classrooms but do not evidence any preference toward male or female students. Good et al. concluded that the data suggested teacher behaviors are "reactive" to: (1) the differential behaviors exhibited by males and females; and (2) the teacher's role as an authority figure responsible for getting students to conform to their role of a student as defined by the school.

As pointed out by Good et al., it may be that teachers are more likely to be more reactive to male student behaviors because of the higher rate of behavior problems traditionally reported for males in the literature. However when Martin (1972) observed second-grade teachers' responses to male and female students matched on behavior problems, results indicated behavior problem males had more contact and interaction (e.g., response opportunity, reading recitation, work contact, behavior contact) with teachers than did behavior problem female students and students who were not behavior problems. Martin suggested that school psychologists could help teachers to overcome seemingly "anxious overvigilant" behavior toward male students using classroom observation procedures; by giving teachers feedback about their interactions with students a more balanced distribution of teacher attention could be achieved.

Student Attractiveness

The physical appearance of a student has also been shown to influence teacher attitudes. In one of the earlier studies Dion, Berscheid, and Walster (1972) confirmed their hypothesis that "what is beautiful is good." Psychology student ratings of the personality characteristics and expected lifetime success of photographed attractive individuals were higher than ratings assigned average or unattractive persons. Findings for teacher populations have been similar.

Clifford and Walster (1973) accompanied student reports with photos of students which had previously been rated high and low in attractiveness. They found fifth-grade teachers attributed attractive children with higher IQ's, educational potential, and parents who were more interested in their child's education.

Kehle, Bramble, and Mason (1974) studied the effects of student attractiveness on fifth-grade teachers' ratings of a student's psychological stability and performance on a written essay. Results showed attractive females were rated higher on their essay performance than unattractive females and that unattractive students were rated as relatively more unstable.

In another study (Adams & Cohen, 1976), elementary-grade teachers reviewed cumulative folders of hypothetical students (i.e., containing information on the child's ability, a statement by their former teacher, and home background) accompanied by a photo. Attractive students were judged as more creative and intelligent. Teachers also expected attractive students to achieve higher levels of educational training. The teachers indicated, however, that they did not think attractiveness of the student would influence the quality of teacher-student communications in the classroom.

However, Adams, and Cohen (1974) examined the effects of facial attractiveness, personal appearance, verbal ability, and disruptive behavior on the frequency of interactions between teachers and students. Only facial attractiveness was significantly related to teacher interaction; results showed the relationship was stronger for older children. It was also found that children of average attractiveness received significantly more neutral interactions from teachers. The authors speculated that this reflected a compensatory effort on the part of teachers who recognized the biases they had toward more attractive children.

Marwit, Marwit, and Walker (1978) found that teacher ratings of students' misbehavior described in reports accompanied by photographs were more severe for attractive than unattractive children; they concluded that this finding is probably due to the fact that teachers expect attractive students to be good.

Indeed even the likelihood of special class placement may be greater for physically unattractive students. Ross and Salvia (1975) found that elementary teachers presented with a fictitious psychological report accompanied by a photo of an attractive or unattractive child consistently rated unattractive children less favorably. Special classroom placements were considered more appropriate for the unattractive children. The teachers also indicated that further evaluation of the unattractive students would identify more problems, and that unattractive students would have more difficulties in peer relationships as well as academic work.

In a similarly designed study, Elovitz and Salvia (1982) mailed photographs and case studies to a nationally representative sample of school psychologists. Findings indicated the school psychologists provided more negative behavioral and academic evaluations and recommended more serious classifications for unattractive students than for attractive students. Attractive students were more often classified as learning disabled or socially-emotionally disturbed; but unattractive students were more often considered as mentally retarded.

It appears that student attractiveness influences teacher ratings for student performance in a variety of areas, as well as predictions professionals make about future attainments. Furthermore, the behaviors teachers exhibit toward attractive students may be more favorable. One study (LaVoie & Adams, 1974) did show academic ability, aspirations, and leadership potential were influenced more by the conduct report than attractiveness.

Student Race

Some studies have demonstrated that teacher attitudes are influenced by the student's racial background.

In an observation of first grade teacher behaviors toward students Simpson and Erikson (1983) found white teachers administered most nonverbal criticism to black males and more nonverbal criticism to black females than they administered to white males or females. Rubovits and Maehr (1973) also observed classroom interactions and found white teachers gave black students less attention and praise than they gave white students. In this study the ''gifted'' white students received the most attention and praise and the ''gifted'' black students the least. The ''gifted'' black students were also criticized the most.

Teacher ratings of students presented in fictitious case reports have shown students labeled ''mentally retarded Mexican-American'' rather than ''mentally retarded White'' were more likely to be recommended for special class placement by special education teachers (Zucker & Prieto, 1977) and regular classroom teachers (Zucker, Prieto, & Rutherford, 1980). Similarly, students labeled ''emotionally disturbed'' and ''Mexican-American'' versus ''White'' were recommended significantly more often for special class placement by regular and special class teachers (Prieto & Zucker, 1981).

In another study (DeMeis & Turner, 1978), white elementary teachers were presented with a picture of attractive or unattractive black and white students and a taped response of a student speaking Black English or Standard English (controlled for qualitative differences). After listening to the tapes paired with pictures, teachers provided ratings on the speaker's personality, quality of response, current and future academic abilities. Black students, Black-English-speaking students and unattractive students received lower ratings than white Standard English speaking attractive students.

Adams (1978) examined the effects of gender, physical attractiveness, and race on preschool teachers. A general description of a student was prepared and accompanied by a picture of a black or white student previously rated as attractive or unattractive. Results showed that white teachers predicted the highest academic achievement for attractive white males and females and the lowest achievement for black students regardless of their sex or attractiveness. Black teachers predicted the highest academic achievement for white males, and gave the next highest rating to attractive and unattractive white females. Unattractive black males and females were rated least likely to achieve academically.

Although practitioners in school psychology and special education attest to the unimportance of race in educational placement decisions (Knoff, 1983), studies have pointed out that a disproportionate number of black students have been placed in classes for mentally retarded students (Mercer, 1973). Furthermore, with the emergence of the learning disabilities category, the trend to label more black students as learning disabled has been evidenced (Tucker, 1980). Stevens (1981) found teachers' and school psychologists' ratings of hyperkinetic behavior were influenced by a student's ethnic group membership; the differential findings for the ratings of Mexican-American and Afro-American students led Stevens to conclude that there may be differences in the expectations these professionals have for students based upon their ethnicity.

It has also been shown that white teachers rate more black students emotionally disturbed than do black teachers (Kelly, Bullock, & Dykes, 1977) and made differential recommendations for academic assistance depending upon whether the child is black or white (Giesbrecht & Routh, 1979). Another study showed that the severity ratings assigned by white teachers to misbehaviors (tantrum behavior or stealing lunch money) were significantly higher for black than white students (Marwit, Marwit, & Walker, 1978).

Teacher preferences for white students have had considerable documentation, but there is some limited evidence that Asian-American students may be more favored. Wong (1980) found elementary and secondary teachers rated Asian-American students more emotionally stable and academically competent than white students.

The effect ethnicity may have on teacher expectations has also been demonstrated among Israeli teachers by Guttman and Bar-Tal (1982). Their findings showed teacher evaluations and expectations were higher for descriptions of students with European-American surnames than for students with Asian-African surnames.

Student Socioeconomic Status

Several studies have demonstrated differential teacher attitudes based on the socioeconomic background of students. Rist (1970) observed a class of ghetto children during kindergarten, first, and second grade and found that students were placed in reading groups according to the perceptions teachers had about the socioeconomic status of the students over the three year period. Those children perceived as having a higher socioeconomic status background (as a result of parental interviews, reports of the family's financial status, whether or not they received public welfare, and the appearance, behavior, and language of the child) were placed in the high reading group. Furthermore, teacher behaviors toward the students reflected the status the students had been assigned by the teacher; high group students received more attention, praise, and support but low group members were more frequently ignored, belittled, or punished.

Although a more recent study (Haller & Davis, 1981) did not show that student socioeconomic status biased elementary teacher decisions about reading group placement, it appears that socioeconomic status, a characteristic which should, seemingly, not have anything to do with teacher ratings, indeed does impact upon teacher attitudes and behaviors toward students. When Friedman (1976) observed the frequencies of reinforcement delivered by teachers in first- and third-grade classrooms to lower- and middle-class students, results showed that there were differences in the types of reinforcement given to low versus middle class children and that middle class students received more reinforcement.

Studies in which researchers have used hypothetical case histories or descriptions of students identified as being from high or low socioeconomic status backgrounds to determine the potential influence of the socioeconomic status factor on attitudes have supported the potency of this variable. Brown and Macdougall (1973) found teacher ratings of students' effectiveness on academic tasks, peer social acceptance, and school adjustment were influenced by the student's socioeconomic status. Similarly, Miller McLaughlin, Haddon, & Chansky (1968) found preservice teachers rated students described with lower- versus middle-class origins significantly less favorably in the areas of achievement and social behavior.

In another study (Adams & Cohen, 1976), social class information was the strongest factor (in terms of estimated experimental variance) (others were sex of the teacher and student, student ability, and student attractiveness) in elementary teacher predictions for the academic success of students described in fictitional reports. Middle class students were not only expected to achieve greater academic success than were lower class children, but to also have more supportive interactions with teachers.

Stevens (1981) showed school psychologists and elementary teachers a silent film of students from different ethnic backgrounds (Anglo-American, Afro-American and Mexican-American) about whom they had read fictitious biographies which described lower or middle socioeconomic backgrounds. Then these professionals were asked to provide ratings of the amount of hyperkinetic behavior students exhibited in the film (there were no actual differences) "as compared to all other children you have ever known'' (p. 101). Results indicated that the school psychologists consistently gave students with lower class backgrounds higher ratings on hyperkinetic behavior. Classroom teachers similarly rated lower class children as more hyperkinetic but their ratings were also influenced by student ethnicity; Mexican-Americans were rated lowest, middle class Afro-American and Anglo-Americans were rated similarly, but lower socioeconomic status Afro-Americans were attributed as displaying the highest rate of hyperactive behavior.

Lenkowsky & Blackman (1968) developed hypothetical student reports and found mentally retarded students with lower class backgrounds were rated lower on a scale of social acceptability than were middle class mentally retarded students by white graduate students in education, but the children's race (white versus black), however, did not influence the ratings.

Smith, Zingale, and Coleman (1978) studied elementary school students with normal or "near normal" intellectual ability who had severe academic deficiencies. Students from high SES backgrounds evidenced low self-concept scores, but those from low SES backgrounds did not demonstrate lowered self-concepts. The authors interpreted their study as evidence of the differential expectations parents and teachers have for high SES students. That is, high SES students are expected to do well; when they do not, a lower self-concept results.

Student Classroom Conduct

Surprisingly, only a few studies have looked at the effects of student conduct on teacher attitudes. A study by Natriello and Dornbush (1983) indicated that secondary teachers' ratings of students are influenced most by the immediate behaviors (academic or behavioral) exhibited by students, followed by the student's achievement and social behavior record. Ethnicity and gender were related least to teacher assessments.

LaVoie and Adams (1974) examined the effects of students' conduct, gender, and physical attractiveness on elementary grade teacher ratings of academic ability, aspirations, and leadership potential. The reported conduct level of the child influenced teacher ratings more than did physical attractiveness or sex.

Student Personality Characteristics

The student's personality also may influence teacher attitudes. Feshbach (1969) found preservice teacher ratings of the academic and social competence of students were influenced by the personality traits included in descriptive reports. Higher ratings were assigned to the conforming, rigid, and dependent, passive student than to the flexible, nonconforming and independent, assertive student.

In another investigation, Helton and Oakland (1977) explored the relationship of teacher attitudes of attachment, rejection, concern, and indifference to student academic ability, sex, and personality characteristics. Findings indicated that student personality characteristics had the strongest influence on teacher attitudes. Teacher feelings of attachment were: (1) higher for rigid-conforming-orderly and passive-dependent-acquiescent students than for active-independent-assertive or flexible-nonconforming-untidy students; and (2) were more rejecting of flexible-nonconforming-untidy or active-independent-assertive students that passive-dependent-acquiescent and rigid-conforming-orderly students. Teachers showed more concern for passive-dependent-acquiescent students than active-independent-assertive students. They were more indifferent toward active-independent-assertive students and least indifferent toward rigid-conforming-orderly students. Teachers also evidenced higher feelings of attachment, less concern, and less indifference toward high ability students. Feelings of concern were highest for low-ability females, and lowest for high-ability females.

Student First Name

There is some literature which suggests that first names may influence teacher attitudes toward a student. Harari and McDavid (1973) studied the possible effect of students' first names on teachers' evaluation of a student's performance. Findings showed that essays supposedly written by fifth grade students with rare, unpopular, or unattractive names were given significantly lower ratings than were those of students with common, popular, and attractive names.

The results of another study (Garwood, 1976) suggested that names could influence teacher interactions which in turn might affect students. Garwood reported male sixth graders who possessed first names that teachers rated as desirable had higher achievement and self-concept scores than comparable students with names rated as undesirable.

Nelson (1977) explored the relationship of first names to academic achievement among college students. It was hypothesized that stereotypes may affect the expected academic achievement. A list of college students in the honors group and those of students rated in the bottom 10 percent of the college on achievement were ranked by a group of students and teachers. Indeed, the names of the honors students had received significantly more positive ratings.

It has also been reported that boys with peculiar first names attending a child guidance clinic were more disturbed than boys with common names (Ellis & Beechley, 1954); that more males with unusual first names failed in college and demonstrated personality or neurotic disorders (Savage & Wells, 1948); and that female college students with uncommon names were more neurotic (Houston & Sumner, 1948). However, it is not clear why males and females with unusual names evidenced significantly more psychological disturbance. Hartman, Nicolay, & Hurley (1968), who reported a higher rate of psychoses in 17- to 60-year old males with peculiar names, hypothesized that ". . . unique names interfere with normal social interaction and that this produces disturbed adjustment" (p. 109).

Not all studies indicated more pathology among those with unusual first names. Schonberg and Murphy (1974) found that college males with common, as opposed to uncommon first names, evidenced significantly more guilt, inferiority, and timidity.

Student Sibling Characteristics

Seaver (1973) hypothesized that teacher expectations would be different for students who had the same teacher as their "bright" or "dull" sibling and that these expectations would result in higher achievement. Findings showed that the siblings of bright students did indeed have higher achievement scores. There is also some limited evidence that the results of recommendations for a special education placement for a student are influenced by whether or not the student has a handicapped sibling (Sydney & Minner, 1983).

Teacher Attitudes and Student Characteristics—A Summary

It is difficult to interpret the data regarding the effect of different student characteristics on teacher attitudes let alone to generalize from the diverse studies for several reasons: (1) different studies have included different student characteristics as variables; (2) some studies have used classroom observations but most have relied on teacher responses to contrived case reports, cumulative folder data, and/or exposure to videotapes of children; (3) measurement devices have varied from study to study; and (4) the samples of teachers have varied in composition. For example in the latter case, older elementary school female teachers may react differently to the same student characteristics than younger male high-school teachers. It seems that the salience of the handicapped label may also be enhanced or diminished as a result of other characteristics displayed by the student.

Programmatic research that considers a systematic inclusion of student characteristics as independent variables seems essential to achieve an understanding of the potency of the individual student characteristics as they relate to teacher attitude and furthermore how these differential student characteristics not only interact with one another but also with those of the teacher.

Teacher Attitudes and Teacher Characteristics

A number of factors may be related to the attitudes teachers display toward handicapped and nonhandicapped pupils. Contact and experience with handicapped students show a strong relationship to attitudes (see Chapter 6 for a discussion of the effects). However, teacher attitudes toward students may also reflect a number of other personal and background characteristics. These include the teacher's: (1) gender; (2) race; (3) age; (4) grade level; (5) amount of experience; and (6) socioeconomic status. Other variables that may influence teacher attitudes include the size of the class and whether the teacher is in an urban or suburban district. Each of these factors are discussed in the following section.

Teacher Gender.   There is some evidence that, in general, teachers demonstrate a preference for students of the same sex (Goebes & Shore, 1975). At the same time, data on teacher attitudes toward handicapped students suggest males and females may have different attitudes toward handicapped students. Generally, findings indicate that females may be more positive toward handicapped groups. When Conine (1969) administered the *Attitudes Toward Disabled Persons Checklist* to elementary classroom teachers, results indicated female teachers were significantly more accepting of handicapped persons.

Ranking or hierarchy studies (see Chapter 4) suggest there is agreement among the sexes from the standpoint of the most preferred to least preferred disability (see for example Janicki, 1970; Tringo, 1970). However from the perspective of social distance, females are more positive. For example male and female teachers may agree on a relative preference ranking for learning disabled students as being preferred over mentally retarded students and least prefer emotionally disturbed pupils. But, from the standpoint of social distance, female teachers may be accepting of handicaps; that is they are more willing to work with, talk to, play with, etc., a handicapped person. Tringo (1970) evidenced the similarity of preference rankings for 21 disability groups by males and females, and at the same time showed the significant difference for the sexes on social distance for 12 of the disability groups indicating females were more accepting of disability groups. Similarly, Harasymiw, Horne, & Lewis (1978) found that females demonstrated less social distance toward 10 out of 20 disability groups.

Numerous studies have explored professional attitudes toward mainstreaming (see Chapter 4): yet very few of the investigations have undertaken an examination of attitudinal differences in male and female professionals toward this concept. The relationship of teacher gender to attitudes toward mainstreaming thus has not been clarified. Some studies have reported that the gender of the teacher was not related to mainstreaming attitudes (Ringlaben & Price, 1981; Stephens & Braun, 1980). However, Aloia, Knutson, Minner, & Von Seggern (1980) reported female physical education teachers were more positive about mainstreaming handicapped students into physical education classes than were male physical education teachers. In another study (Parish, Dyck, & Kappes, 1979), female teachers demonstrated more positive attitudes toward mentally retarded students than did male teachers; but there were no differences in male and female teacher attitudes toward learning disabled, physically handicapped, emotionally disturbed, gifted, and normal students.

Taken together, the results of investigations suggest that female teachers may have more positive attitudes toward handicapped students. Whether or not they will be more positive toward handicapped females than handicapped males is not clear.

Teacher Race.   There are not many studies on the differential behaviors of teachers based on their racial background. Although it appears that differences may exist, the effect of teacher race is not clear. In one study, Brown, Payne, Lankewich, & Cornell (1970) observed female white and black elementary teachers who were teaching children with similar or different racial backgrounds. The results indicated that teachers provided more praise and less criticism when children were from a different racial background. Results of another study were in agreement. Byalick and Bersoff (1974) found that although black and white female elementary teachers did not differ in the amount and kind of reinforcers they used in the classroom, opposite-raced students were reinforced more. Black teachers reinforced white children more often and white teachers reinforced black students more frequently.

On the other hand, Feldman and Donohoe (1978) found black and white undergraduate students acting as teachers were more positive toward students with their own racial background. Two experiments were undertaken to observe the nonverbal behaviors directed toward white and black students by high and low racially prejudiced "teachers" (identified using the *Multifactor Racial Attitude Inventory*). Results indicated that the "teachers" directed more positive nonverbal behavior toward students of their own racial background. When Eaves (1975) studied black and white teachers' behavior ratings of black and white 4th and 5th grade males, results showed black teachers did not rate black or white students differently; however, white teachers rated black students as deviant more often than they did white students.

But when Simpson and Erickson (1983) studied white and black female teacher behaviors toward white and black students, there was little evidence of the teacher's race as a significant factor in pupil interactions. However, interaction effects with student race, student sex, and teacher race showed that white teachers behaved differently toward male and female students and black teachers did not. White teachers were also noted to direct more nonverbal criticism toward black males. Of the thirteen different verbal behaviors observed, only one showed a difference in treatment by black teachers (they directed more verbal neutral with nonverbal praise to female students than did white female teachers).

The effects of the teacher's race on interactions with students is not clear. Yet when the available data are considered in relationship to teacher attitudes toward handicapped children, it appears that the racial backgrounds of the handicapped students and the teachers may result in different interactions. The nature of these interactions must be studied. Are handicapped children whose racial background differs from that of their teacher in double jeopardy? Does the sex of the child and teacher make a difference? These are only a few of the questions that need to be answered.

Teacher Age.   It is difficult to understand the relationship between age and attitudes toward handicapped persons because the age variable may be confounded by experience and/or education. When the relationship has been studied, results have been inconclusive. Tringo (1970) posited that a curvilinear relationship may exist; attitudes of societal members become more positive toward handicaps until college age and then begin to decrease. But when Greenbaum and Wang (1965) studied the attitudes of adult professionals, paraprofessionals, and parents toward retarded individuals, the results suggested that older subjects had more positive attitudes. As opposed to either of the previous two studies, Bell's (1962) study of rehabilitation workers and hospital employees showed there was no relationship between age and scores on the *Attitudes Toward Disabled Persons Scale* (this scale groups all forms of disability into a single category called physical disability, see Chapter 3). Nor did Parish, Dyck, and Kappes (1979) find any relationship between age and teachers' attitudes toward mentally retarded, learning disabled, and emotionally disturbed students.

The existing evidence is insufficient to support an attitude-age relationship. On the one hand, it may be speculated that younger professionals may exhibit more positive attitudes toward handicapped students because training programs for school related professions (i.e., regular classroom teachers, school psychologists, administrators) have recently begun to incorporate information about working with handicapped students as a result of legislation (P.L. 94-142). On the other hand, older professionals may be more positive by virtue of past experiences with children.

Teacher Grade Level. There is some evidence that elementary classroom teachers have more positive attitudes toward handicapped students, but the results are inconclusive. Hirshoren and Burton (1979) examined elementary, junior, and senior high school teachers' willingness to mainstream handicapped students and found no significant differences in the attitudes expressed toward mainstreaming orthopedically, hearing, and visually handicapped students. But elementary teachers were more positive about mainstreaming mentally handicapped and emotionally disturbed students. Another study (Morris & McCauley, 1977) showed that elementary teachers were more positive than secondary teachers about less restrictive placements for handicapped students. Larrivee and Cook (1979) reported that first through third grade teachers had the most positive attitudes toward mainstreaming and junior high school teachers were the most negative; teachers of grades 4 to 6 ranked second in positivity followed by high school teachers. Similarly Kavale and Rossi (1980) found that kindergarten through third grade teachers and high school teachers were more positive about resource room programs for mentally retarded students than were upper elementary school teachers or seventh and eighth grade teachers.

Teacher Experience. Although Jordan and Proctor (1969) failed to find a relationship between the amount of teaching experience and teacher attitudes toward regular classroom placement for handicapped students, another study (Mandell & Strain, 1978) showed that more experienced teachers had more positive attitudes toward mainstreaming. This relationship merits further study. Experienced teachers have had an opportunity to become more confident about their ability to manage a classroom containing a range of students. Over the years it is likely they have learned to cope successfully with students displaying a range of academic and/or behavioral problems. Consequently, many of the problems presented by the handicapped student may not be new to the teacher; therefore, the possibility exists that these teachers will have more positive attitudes toward handicapped children placed in their classrooms. At the same time, as Jordan and Proctor (1969) pointed out, experience can increase knowledge, but the result is not necessarily a positive attitude.

Teacher Socioeconomic Status.   Very few studies have been undertaken to explore the relationship of teachers' socioeconomic status to attitudes. One study (Greenbaum & Wang, 1965) showed that low socioeconomic status persons had more positive attitudes toward mental retardation. In another study Dohrenwend and Chin-Shong (1967) concluded low socioeconomic status persons were less tolerant of mental illness. When Harasymiw, Horne, and Lewis (1978) studied the attitudes of approximately 1,000 subjects from the general population toward 20 disability groups, results showed that participants with higher educational levels demonstrated significantly more positive attitudes toward all disability categories.

Other Factors.   There is limited evidence that class size may be related to teacher attitudes (Mandell & Strain, 1978) but the results have not always been consistent (Larrivee & Cook, 1979). Teachers in urban schools may have more favorable attitudes toward handicapped students because of the greater likelihood of contact, but some results are contrary (Larrivee & Cook, 1979). Findings for one study (Smart, Wilton, & Keeling, 1980) suggested that married teachers may be more positive toward mentally retarded students.

PEER ATTITUDES AND STUDENT CHARACTERISTICS

Peer attitudes were discussed in the preceding chapter. There is substantial evidence that handicapped students are rejected by their classmates. In this chapter, attention is devoted to gaining understanding of what other student characteristics, in addition to the handicapping condition, may be related to peer attitudes. The section opens with a discussion of labeling, and then considers the student characteristics of: (1) achievement; (2) gender; (3) attractiveness; (4) race; (5) socioeconomic status; (6) classroom conduct; (7) first name; and (8) athletic or motor ability. Following this discussion is a presentation of the personal or background characteristics of classmates that may influence the attitudes they express toward students in their classes.

Peer Reactions Toward Labeled Students

The effect of the handicapped label on peer attitudes toward a classmate does not seem as potent as the behavioral characteristics demonstrated by the labeled student. For example, the importance of the behavior of handicapped persons as opposed to the label they had been assigned was evidenced in high school student ratings of descriptions of handicapped persons in comparison to labels; when the students read about how the handicapped person functioned they were more positive (Jaffe, 1966, 1967).

Gottlieb (1974) found that fourth grade students' attitudinal ratings toward students labeled mentally retarded were influenced more by academic competence than by the label. In another study (Gottlieb, 1975), third-grade students' attitudes toward a student labeled mentally retarded were influenced by the label but also by whether or not the child displayed aggressive, acting out behaviors. The significant interaction effect between the label and behavior indicated that the students were more negative toward the mentally retarded aggressive student than toward aggressive behavior by unlabeled students.

An investigation by Freeman and Algozzine (1980) examined the effects of the labels "learning disabled," "emotionally disturbed," "mentally retarded," and "normal" when they were associated with positive and negative behavioral attribute statements. Results showed fourth-grade students assigned social acceptance scores based on behavioral attributes rather than assigned labels.

Sutherland, Algozzine, Ysseldyke, and Freeman (1983) did not find any effect for the label "learning disabled" versus "normal" on peer acceptance ratings of fourth graders before or after positive attribute assignments were provided (e.g., this child tells funny stories). However, ratings were lower after the students were given neutral attributes (e.g., the child was similar to other students in the class); thus the findings supported the importance of positive student behaviors for peer acceptance in the classroom.

Even when educable mentally retarded special-class students have been asked to provide attitudinal ratings of a child unlabeled or labeled as mentally retarded and academically competent or incompetent, results have indicated that behavior is the more potent factor in determining their attitudes. Results showed the students were most negative toward the child labeled as mentally retarded and incompetent. Furthermore, ratings evidenced that students were increasingly more positive toward the incompetent unlabeled, competent retarded, and competent unlabeled student (Budoff & Siperstein, 1982).

In another experiment, Siperstein, Budoff, and Bak (1980) demonstrated fifth and sixth graders' attitudinal ratings of students labeled "retard" versus "mentally retarded" were more negative. Findings also showed the students' attitudes toward normally appearing (versus having Down's Syndrome features) and academically competent, or incompetent mentally retarded students were not more negative in the labeled condition. Siperstein and associates speculated that the handicapped label may actually have a positive effect because the label may help students understand and accept the lower academic performance of the handicapped student.

The teacher's attitude toward the student also may be more potent than the label. Foley (1979) showed fourth graders videotapes of students labeled normal, mentally retarded, or learning disabled, exhibiting the same academic deficiencies, whom teachers reacted to either positvely or negatively. Across all labeling conditions, students' peer acceptance scores were higher when teachers reacted positively toward the labeled student.

All of the studies in this area have been artificially contrived (e.g., using sketches, descriptions, pictures and/or videotapes of students). Consequently the generalizability of the findings to real life situations must be questioned. The relationship between peer attitudes and the effect of labels in the actual classroom setting remains to be verified.

Student Achievement

Although there are many correlates to peer acceptance in the classroom, academic achievement is probably one of the primary determinants of the status a student will achieve among his/her peers. High achievers are accorded high acceptance. Investigations designed to study the relationship between school achievement and peer acceptance have often focused on the relationship between reading achievement and peer acceptance in elementary school populations (Cassel & Martin, 1964; Porterfield & Schlichting, 1961; St. John & Lewis, 1975; Stevens, 1971); but the relationship between arithmetic and language arts achievement to peer status has also been evidenced (Buswell, 1953; Green, Forehand, Beck, & Vosk, 1980).

One study (McGinley & McGinley, 1970) showed that even first grade students' preferences for work partners were related to reading achievement. In this investigation of high, middle, and low reading group members an analysis of peer preference choices showed that high-reading-group students chose members of their own reading group significantly more often than would be expected, and made significantly fewer choices than would be expected from the low and middle groups. On the other hand, the low group children showed a low preference for members of their own group and made significantly more choices from the top group than was expected; similarly the middle reading group students chose significantly more high group members and significantly fewer low group members.

Academically successful junior and senior high school students are also more accepted (Muma, 1965). And even achievement in nonacademic areas (e.g., band, shop, chorus, physical education, and driver education) appeared to affect a student's status with his/her peers (Muma, 1968).

Student Gender

The gender of the handicapped student may make a difference in the attitudes peers express toward him/her. Although the results of one study (Gottlieb & Gottlieb, 1977) did not show any differences in the attitudinal ratings junior high school students assigned mentally retarded and physically handicapped males and females described in vignettes, the results of other investigations suggest that students may respond differently depending upon the gender of the handicapped student.

Scranton and Ryckman (1979) and Bryan (1974) found that learning disabled females are more rejected by classmates than learning disabled males and posited that differential gender expectations (i.e., females are usually better achievers at the elementary grade level) could account for the findings. Phillips (1964), who tested an adult sample and found that mentally ill males were more rejected than mentally ill females exhibiting the same behaviors, suggested that society assigns sex roles and that the negative attitudes expressed toward mentally ill males reflects a societal point of view that it is more acceptable for females to have mental health problems. Future research should consider the influence gender expectations may have on peer attitudes toward those with a handicap.

Student Attractiveness

Physical attractiveness has an important influence on peer attitudes. Kleck, Richardson, & Ronald (1974) found that physical appearance was highly related to sociometric status among 9- to 14-year-old boys. The influence of attractiveness on peer friendship choices has also been noted for younger children. When shown photographs, preschoolers (aged 3- to 6½-years) more often selected attractive students as friends (Dion, 1973); and they had more positive behavioral expectations for attractive students. Also, their ratings of attractiveness were similar to those of adults. In another investigation, Dion and Berscheid (1974) studied the ratings assigned each other by nursery school children. Findings revealed that attractive students were more popular with their 4- to 6-year-old peers. Unattractive students were also perceived by peers to demonstrate more antisocial behaviors even though there was no observational data to corroborate these perceptions.

There have not been many attempts to examine how facial attractiveness might affect peer ratings of handicapped students. But when Siperstein and Gottlieb (1977) showed fourth- and fifth-grade students videotapes of mentally retarded students who appeared normal versus those with Down's Syndrome characteristics, higher acceptance ratings were assigned to the normally appearing students. Consequently, it is likely that other handicapped student groups which are characteristically physically different (e.g., the physically disabled) would be considered physically unattractive and most probably rejected by peers.

This conclusion is substantiated by findings for the influence of body build on peer attitudes. Lerner and Gellert (1969) found kindergarten children evidenced negative attitudes toward photographs of "chubby" children. There is also evidence that peers reject obese classmates (Richardson, Goodman, Hastorf, & Dornbusch, 1961, 1963; Richardson & Royce, 1968).

However, in the case of handicaps not associated with an overt physical symptomatology (e.g., learning disabilities and emotional disturbance) physical as well as facial attractiveness may mediate the influence of the handicap on peer acceptance. And one study (Siperstein, Bopp, & Bak, 1978) suggested that peer acceptance of learning disabled students may be influenced by their physical attractiveness.

Student Race

In general, students have more positive attitudes toward peers from similar racial backgrounds. Durrett and Davy (1970) demonstrated that 4-year-old children are aware of racial differences, can identify their own racial membership, and prefer associations with members of their own race. Indeed in a very early study, Criswell (1939) indicated peers preferred to associate with children of their own race; this tendency has also been recently evidenced (Shaw, 1973).

Few investigators have attempted to determine the relative importance of race and handicap on peer acceptance. Richardson and Royce (1968) showed children, aged 10–12 from low and high income families with different racial backgrounds, drawings of a nonhandicapped child and handicapped children (i.e., child with a leg brace and crutches, child in wheelchair, child with missing forearm, child with facial disfigurement, obese child) who were black or white. Results of preference rankings for all the student groups suggested that presence of a physical handicap was a more potent attitude determinant than race; overall the children preferred the nonhandicapped child. The same results were obtained in a replication study with Southern black females who were expected to evidence more concern for skin color than the physical handicap (Richardson & Emerson, 1970).

But in another study (Katz, Katz, & Cohen, 1976), kindergarten and fourth-grade white students' interactions with a handicapped (i.e. wheelchair bound) versus normal black or white adult were observed. Results indicated that the students demonstrated more positive attitudes toward the white nonhandicapped and handicapped adult. Thus, in contrast to findings for the two former studies, race was demonstrated as the more salient variable in this study. As pointed out by Katz and associates, the differential findings may reflect the differences in: (1) measurement techniques used in the two studies; (2) ages of the students; or (3) the age of the stimulus persons. Katz et al. suggest future research to clarify the relationship of age, race, and handicap to social acceptance wherein, using a single experimental design, evaluative and behavioral data would be collected on variously aged children reacting to handicapped and nonhandicapped black and white adults and children.

Student Socioeconomic Status

There are very few investigations of the possible effects of handicapped students' socioeconomic status on their acceptance by peers. But in one investigation (Monroe & Howe, 1971), findings indicated that classroom peer acceptance was higher for mentally retarded students from higher socioeconomic status backgrounds than for those from low socioeconomic status backgrounds. Thus, as Monroe and Howe concluded, a retarded student from a lower class family is likely to experience greater rejection from peers.

If it follows a pattern similar to that for the nonhandicapped, socioeconomic status may be an influencing factor in the peer acceptance of students exhibiting a variety of disabilities. Studies of nonhandicapped populations have demonstrated that peers are more accepting of students from higher socioeconomic status backgrounds (Bonney, 1944; Grossman & Wrighter, 1948). And Tudor (1971) demonstrated that even first-grade students perceive social class differences and that social class awareness is fairly well developed between grades one and four. By grade six, the development of class awareness is completed.

Student Classroom Conduct

Whether or not a student is accepted by classmates can depend upon the behaviors he/she demonstrates. A summary of the research on correlates of peer status, albeit in nursery school children, presented by Moore (1967) provides a good overview of the social characteristics of those children who achieve a high degree of peer acceptance or popularity:

> He presents a picture of easygoing good will, is cooperative with both adults and peers, and is prone to use a preponderance of positive, friendly behaviors relative to negative aggressive behavior. He is likely to be an active participant in associative play with his companions and is able to give nurturance, approval and deference to them as well as elicit these things from them. He is less likely than his unpopular counterpart to be distracted from peer activities by a preoccupation with adults-either for purposes of defying them or seeking comfort and support from them (pp. 295–296).

There is a growing interest in research on interpersonal strategies associated with peer acceptance. Specific behaviors such as smiling, sharing, giving help, and so on, are now being referred to in the literature as social skills; endeavors are being directed toward identifying social skill deficits associated with peer rejection and providing training to handicapped students in deficit areas so that they will become more accepted by peers. Studies of nonhandicapped children, as well, have indicated that many children lack strategies or behaviors which facilitate peer acceptance; at the same time the possible behaviors related to peer acceptance and the relative potency of particular behaviors for determining the degree of status a student will be accorded among peers is not clear (Gottman, Gonso, & Rasmussen, 1975; Hartup, Glazer, & Charlesworth, 1967; Rubin, 1972). Further complicating efforts to achieve an understanding of student behaviors associated with peer acceptance are findings that the tolerance or desirability of different behaviors may vary depending upon the student's grade level (Gottman, Gonso, & Rasmussen, 1975; Minturn & Lewis, 1968; Tuddenham, 1951), socioeconomic status (Gottman, Gonso, & Rasmussen, 1975); and gender (Victor & Halverson, 1980).

Although achievement is a highly influential factor in peer acceptance, there is some indication that antisocial behaviors can mitigate the relationship. McMichael (1980) found that poor readers who were cooperative and compliant with classroom routines were less accepted by classmates but were not significantly more rejected than good readers; furthermore that when poor readers were rejected it was because of their aberrant behavior and not their reading difficulties.

Student First Name

In 1937 Walton talked about the affective value of first names, and stated that the name which a child is given ". . . may be a determining factor in his development of personality, acquisition of friends, and, in all probability, in his success or failure of life" (p. 396). And, just as teachers have been shown to be influenced by a student's first name, it appears that a student's first name may also affect how he/she is regarded by peers.

McDavid and Harari (1966) studied the possible effect of students' first names on their popularity with peers. Fourth and fifth graders ranked the social desirability of the names of peer group members (i.e., "If you like the name very much and think it is a nice-sounding name, put an X in the first blank;" "If you don't really care one way or the other about the name, put an X in the second blank;" "If you don't like the name, and think it is not a very nice-sounding name, put an X in the third blank" [p. 545]) and other 'filler' names; one month later a sociometric procedure was used to determine peer acceptance by group members. Results showed a significant relationship between the desirability of a student's name and social status. Another study (Busse & Seraydarian, 1979) used a somewhat similar procedure. First name desirability data were collected and two months later sociometric data were obtained from second through sixth grade students. Findings indicated that there was a relationship between the female's first name desirability rating, and male and female peer acceptance. Male student acceptance by females but not males also was influenced by the male's first name. However, there was no relationship between peer rejection and name desirability; this was an aspect which was not explored by McDavid and Harai (1966).

A student's first name may represent yet another factor that may contribute to peer group acceptance. Other studies on the relationship first names have to peer acceptance will have to be done, however, particularly since students' preferences for names appear to change across age groups (Busse & Helfrich, 1975) and may be altered as a result of social interactions (Blain & Ramirez, 1968).

Student Athletic Ability or Motor Skills

The degree to which peers accept a student may even depend on the student's athletic or motor abilities. When McCraw and Tolbert (1953) investigated the relationship between athletic ability, mental maturity, and sociometric status, results indicated that athletic ability, but not mental maturity, was related to peer popularity among junior high school males. Siperstein, Bopp, and Bak (1978) found that elementary-aged learning disabled students were rejected by peers but that their popularity may be affected by athletic ability. Motor ability has been shown to be related to the social status which mentally retarded students assign each other (Smith & Hurst, 1961).

Peer Attitudes and Student Characteristics—A Summary

Many factors may contribute to a student's acceptance by his/her peers. And it is difficult to interpret the data regarding the relative contribution of different student characteristics to peer status in the classroom. Achievement and classroom conduct seem to be the most important factors; at the same time other characteristics may mediate their influence. The student's level of physical attractiveness seems to have a strong association to peer acceptance; but, gender, race, socioeconomic status, and the student's first name must also be taken into account. Possibly athletic ability or motor skills need to be considered. The combined effects different student characteristics have on peer acceptance will have to be studied in handicapped as well as nonhandicapped student groups. A programmatic approach (such as was recommended for understanding the relationship of teacher attitudes to different student characteristics) seems to be a desirable first step toward understanding the relationship of, and interaction among, student characteristics as factors in determining a student's social status in the classroom.

Student Attitudes and Student Characteristics

Several personal or background characteristics may be related to the attitudes students display toward their handicapped as well as nonhandicapped peers.

These are not only contact and experience with handicapped students (a discussion of these effects is presented in Chapter 6); but a number of other student characteristics. These include the student's: (1) gender; (2) age and/or grade level; (3) socioeconomic status; (4) race; and (5) adjustment and social status. Each of these factors are discussed in the following section.

Student Gender.   There is a growing body of evidence that females demonstrate more positive attitudes toward their handicapped peers. This has been a fairly consistent finding in studies of adult attitudes toward handicapped persons; when the attitudes of student groups have been investigated, results have indicated that, even at the elementary school level, females may evidence greater acceptance of handicaps (Sandberg, 1982; Voeltz, 1980; Wilkins & Velicer, 1980). However, it is not clear at what age differences begin to emerge in the degree of acceptance males and females demonstrate toward handicapped groups. There also appears to be some shifting in gender preferences toward disability groups among young students (Richardson, 1970), which would, at least in part, account for inconsistencies in the literature about female versus male student positivity toward handicapped peers.

Attitudes expressed by nonhandicapped males and females may also depend upon the gender of the handicapped student. Some studies have found that females are more negative toward handicapped students of the same gender than males are toward handicapped males (Hutton & Polo, 1976; Novak, 1975).

At the same time, Gronlund (1959) noted that there is a tendency for young students to rate members of the opposite gender lower on sociometric devices; and studies have found that students are more likely to choose peers of the same gender to be friends with (Asher, 1973; Criswell, 1939; St. John & Lewis, 1975). Reese-Dukes and Stokes (1978) demonstrated that when a student is a member of the opposite gender and handicapped, he/she will be rated significantly lower by classmates than opposite-gender nonhandicapped students.

Student Age/Grade.   There is some evidence to indicate younger children have more positive attitudes toward handicapped children. Jones and Sisk (1967) studied nondisabled children between two and six years old and found that at about the age of four the children demonstrated an understanding of the limitations an orthopedic disability imposed upon an individual. Weinberg (1978) also studied young childrens' perceptions of an orthopedic disability. Findings were somewhat similar and showed that between the ages of three and four, children begin to recognize and understand an orthopedic disability; by the age of four or five children begin to show a preference for interacting with the nonhandicapped. Although there is some contrary evidence (Voeltz, 1980; Wilkins & Velicer, 1980) most studies that have compared the attitudes of lower and upper elementary grade level students provide support for the tendency of the students to become increasingly more negative toward disability groups (Billings, 1963; Sandberg, 1982). Richardson (1970) studied the attitudes toward physical handicaps of children in kindergarten through sixth grade, and in a sample of seventh, ninth, and twelfth graders. Excepting the kindergarten children, all subjects evidenced a preference for nonhandicapped individuals on a picture ranking measure. Richardson also demonstrated that, with increasing age, childrens' attitudes toward disabilities become more like those of their parents. By the time a child is in high school, their preferences for disability groups are almost identical to the preferences of their parents.

Student Socioeconomic Status. There is some limited evidence that the socioeconomic background of a student may be related to how accepting the student is toward a handicap. One study (Budoff & Siperstein, 1978) showed that children from low socioeconomic status families were more accepting of academically competent but not incompetent students; but at the same time they were more accepting of labeled versus unlabeled mentally retarded students. Findings for another investigation (Gottlieb, 1974) indicated low-but not middle-class students were more accepting of students who were academically incompetent and that the label "mental retardation" had no effect on either group of students.

Student Race. Some findings indicate that students from different racial backgrounds have different attitudes toward student behaviors. Steinberg and Hall (1981) demonstrated that white males were more likely not to choose friends who exhibited aggressive behaviors but that black males viewed aggressiveness as a less important factor when making friendship choices, or considered aggressive behavior as a positive attribute. Cultural values may also be reflected in the attitudes students display toward handicapped individuals (Chigier & Chigier, 1968; Richardson et al., 1961, 1963). But when Horne (1978) studied bilingual Hebrew, Italian, and Spanish fourth grader's attitudes toward ten disability groups, findings provided only minimal support for a cultural influence on attitudes toward disabilities. The results also suggested there was a reasonably stable hierarchy of preference among the four groups that was similar to monolingual elementary students.

Student Adjustment and Social Status. Berger (1952) reported that for adult samples there was a relationship between self-acceptance and acceptance of others. There is limited evidence that better adjusted or more popular students may have more positive attitudes toward handicapped peers. When Gottlieb (1969) explored the relationship of psychological adjustment (using a discrepancy score between the student's ideal and actual self-concept) to Norwegian students' attitudes toward the retarded, findings showed that better adjusted students in second through ninth grade had more favorable attitudes. But an effort to replicate these findings with elementary-aged students in the United States showed that well adjusted students had more positive attitudes toward their classmates; however, adjustment was not related to attitudes toward retarded students (Gottlieb, Cohen, & Goldstein, 1974). Another study (Siperstein & Gottlieb, 1977) showed that more popular or high social status fourth- and fifth-grade students were more willing to interact with a retarded classmate than were low status students, but that their willingness also depended on how normal appearing the handicapped child was. Billings's (1963) hypothesis that elementary-aged students rated high in social adjustment in the school setting by their teachers would have more positive attitudes toward physically handicapped children was not supported.

SUMMARY

Numerous student characteristics are related to teacher attitudes toward students. Although the data on the topic have limitations, it is nevertheless appropriate to conclude that a label does not necessarily have a negative effect on teacher attitudes toward a student. Other student characteristics that may contribute to the attitude a teacher develops toward a child include the student's level of achievement, gender, degree of attractiveness, and so on. What is not clear, however, is the specific influence of any one variable, or combination of variables, on teacher attitudes. Confounding this issue are the personal and background characteristics of the teacher (such as their age, sex, and experience), which must be considered in understanding the attitudes they form toward students. We have yet to begin to understand the interactions among these factors. Furthermore, there is contradictory and inconclusive evidence about the influence of some student characteristics and teacher background variables on attitudes.

The research also suggests that a number of student characteristics may influence the amount of acceptance achieved by a handicapped student within the classroom. Peer attitudes toward a student may be influenced by a handicap label, but as was the case for teachers, findings do not clearly support its deleterious effect. Peer attitudes may be influenced by many different characteristics of the handicapped student, including the student's academic achievement, classroom conduct, and degree of attractiveness. At the same time the personal and background characteristics of the student rater need to be considered, since these characteristics may influence the perceptions formed about another student in the classroom. Findings for the differential effects of student characteristics on peers are sometimes controversial and inconclusive; this is true for the data on the attitudinal effects of the personal and background variables of students as raters of their classmates.

Unfortunately, it is impossible to draw any definitive conclusions about what happens to students with a given set of characteristics in the classroom situation. To be able to do so would require that factors related to the development and maintenance of attitudes be studied in far greater detail over longer periods of time than has been the case to date.

It is difficult to interpret the meaning and relationships of findings for a number of reasons.

First, it is important to recognize that numerous student and teacher variables can contribute to the social status a handicapped or nonhandicapped child achieves in the classroom. Although these factors have been isolated in the research and in this chapter, they do not operate in isolation in the classroom. Consequently, it is necessary that future research attempt to further an understanding of their probable interactive effects.

Second, some data gathered to study the attitudinal effects of selected teacher and student characteristics have largely been obtained from some type of artificial approach. For instance, most of the research on labeling has required teachers or students to respond to hypothetical reports and/or videotapes of students presented in labeled or unlabeled conditions. Similarly, studies of the influence attractiveness on attitudes have obtained the responses of teachers and students using some type of case report accompanied by a photograph. Many more observational studies in a natural classroom environment need to be undertaken.

Third, data on the effects of a particular student characteristic on teacher and peer attitudes often primarily reflect studies of nonhandicapped populations. Consequently, whatever influence the factor may have on attitudes toward a handicapped student are not known. For example, the effect of student attractiveness has been almost exclusively studied in nonhandicapped populations. Thus, the extent to which being attractive diminishes the negative attitudinal effect of being labeled "learning disabled" is not at all clear.

Lastly, factors related to teacher and peer attitudes have not been given uniform attention by researchers. Consequently, there may be very little information about the contribution of a particular variable to student status. A good example is the racial factor and its potential influence on peer attitudes. Extant research suggests that students are likely to be more positive toward a classmate with a similar racial background, but we do not know if this means that a minority handicapped student enrolled in a predominantly white classroom will be even more rejected than a minority nonhandicapped student. Furthermore, it is not clear if minority or white students exhibit more or less prejudice toward handicapped students; nor if, indeed, the students' race or culture are even influential factors in the attitudes demonstrated toward handicapped students.

One hopes that the body of research on factors contributing to student status will continue to expand, and the research will become more sophisticated and systematic about providing insights into the factors that contribute to a handicapped student's status in the classroom. Until then, awareness of existing literature may help professionals come to an understanding of their own attitudes toward students and those of classmates, and perhaps provoke interest in pursuing processes to modify classroom interaction.

REFERENCES

Adams, G. R. (1978). Racial membership and physical attractiveness effects on preschool teachers' expectations. *Child Study Journal, 8,* 29–41.

Adams, G. R., & Cohen, A. S. (1974). Children's physical and interpersonal characteristics that effect student-teacher interactions. *The Journal of Experimental Education, 43,* 1–5.

Adams, G. R., & Cohen, A. S. (1976). An examination of cumulative folder information used by teachers in making differential judgments of children's abilities. *The Alberta Journal of Educational Research, 22,* 216–225.

Aloia, G. F., Knutson, R., Minner, S. H., & Von Seggern, M. (1980). Physical education teachers' initial perceptions of handicapped children. *Mental Retardation, 18,* 85–87.

Alpert, J. L. (1974). Teacher behavior across ability groups: A consideration of the mediation of pygmalion effects. *Journal of Educational Psychology, 66,* 348–353.

Asher, N. W. (1973). Manipulating attraction toward the disabled: An application of the similarity-attraction model. *Rehabilitation Psychology, 20,* 156–164.

Barber, T. X., & Silver, M. J. (1968). Fact, fiction and the experimenter's bias effect. *Psychological Bulletin Monograph, 70,* 1–29.

Beez, W. V. (1968). Influence of the biased psychological reports on teacher behavior and pupil performance. *Proceeding of the 76th Annual Convention of the American Psychological Association,* 605–606.

Bell, A. H. (1962). Attitudes of selected rehabilitation workers and other hospital employees toward the physically disabled. *Psychological Reports, 10,* 183–186.

Berger, E. M. (1952). The relation between expressed acceptance of self and expressed acceptance of others. *Journal of Abnormal and Social Psychology, 47,* 778–782.

Billings, H. K. (1963). An exploratory study of the attitudes of noncrippled children toward crippled children in three selected elementary schools. *The Journal of Experimental Education, 31,* 381–387.

Blain, M. J., & Ramirez, M. (1968). Increasing sociometric rank, meaningfulness, and discriminability of children's names through reinforcement and interaction. *Child Development, 39,* 949–955.

Bonney, M. E. (1944). Relationships between social success, family size, socio-economic home background, and intelligence among school children in grades III to V. *Sociometry, 7,* 26–39.

Boucher, C. R. (1981). Teacher attributioning in decision making. *Psychology in the Schools, 18,* 115–120.

Boucher, C. R., & Deno, S. L. (1979). Learning disabled and emotionally disturbed: Will the labels affect teacher planning? *Psychology in the Schools, 16,* 395–402.

Braun, C. (1976). Teacher expectation: Sociopsychological dynamics. *Review of Educational Research, 46,* 185–213.

Brophy, J. E., & Good, T. L. (1969). *Teacher-child dyadic interaction: A manual for coding classroom behavior.* Austin: University of Texas Research and Development Center for Teacher Education.

Brophy, J. E., & Good, T. L. (1970). Teachers' communication of differential expectations for children's classroom performance: Some behavior data. *Journal of Educational Psychology, 61,* 365–374.

Brophy, J. E., & Good, T. L. (1974). *Teacher-student relationships: Causes and consequences.* New York: Holt, Rinehart & Winston.

Brophy, J. E., and Rohrkemper, M. M. (1981). The influence of problem ownership on teachers' perceptions of and strategies for coping with problem students. *Journal of Educational Psychology, 73,* 295–311.

Brown, J. A., & Macdougall, M. A. (1973). Teacher consultation for inproved feelings of self-adequacy in children. *Psychology in the Schools, 10,* 320–326.

Brown, W. E., Payne, L. T., Lankewich, C., & Cornell, L. (1970). Praise, criticism, and race. *Elementary School Journal, 70,* 373–377.

Bryan, T. H. (1974). Peer popularity of learning disabled children. *Journal of Learning Disabilities,* *7,* 621–625.

Budoff, M., & Siperstein, G. N. (1978). Low-income children's attitudes toward mentally retarded children: Effects of labeling and academic behavior. *American Journal of Mental Deficiency, 82,* 474–479.

Budoff, M., & Siperstein, G. N. (1982). Judgments of emr students toward their peers: Effects of label and academic competence. *American Journal of Mental Deficiency, 86,* 367–371.

Busse, T. V., & Helfrich, J. (1975). Changes in first name popularity across grades. *Journal of Psychology, 89,* 281–283.

Busse, T. V., & Seraydarian, L. (1979). First names and popularity in grade school children. *Psychology in the Schools, 16,* 149–153.

Buswell, M. M. (1953). The relationship between the social structure of the classroom and the academic success of the pupils. *Journal of Experimental Education, 22,* 37–52.

Byalick, R., & Bersoff, D. (1974). Reinforcement practices of black and white teachers in integrated classrooms. *Journal of Educational Psychology, 66,* 473–480.

Carroll, C. F., & Reppucci, N. D. (1978). Meanings that professionals attach to labels for children. *Journal of Clinical and Consulting Psychology, 46,* 372–374.

Cassell, R., & Martin, G. (1964). Comparing peer status ratings of elementary pupils with their guidance data and learning efficiency indices. *Journal of Genetic Psychology, 105,* 39–42.

Chigier, E., & Chigier, M. (1968). Attitudes to disability of children in the multi-cultural society of Israel. *Journal of Health and Social Behavior, 9,* 310–317.

Claiborn, W. L. (1969). Expectancy effects in the classroom: A failure to replicate. *Journal of Educational Psychology, 60,* 377–383.

Clifford, M. M., & Walster, E. (1973). The effect of physical attractiveness on teacher expectations. *Sociology of Education, 46,* 248–258.

Combs, R. H., & Harper, J. L. (1967). Effects of labels on attitudes of educators toward handicapped children. *Exceptional Children, 33,* 399–403.

Conine, T. A. (1969). Acceptance or rejection of disabled persons by teachers. *Journal of School Health, 39,* 278–281.

Cooper, H. M. (1979). Pygmalion grows up: A model for teacher expectation, communication, and performance influence. *Review of Educational Research, 49,* 389–410.

Criswell, J. H. (1939). A sociometric study of race cleavage in the classroom. *Archives of Psychology,* No. 235, 1–82.

Davis, O. L. (1967). Teacher behavior toward boys and girls during first grade reading instruction. *American Educational Research Journal, 4,* 261–270.

DeMeis, D. K., & Turner, R. R. (1978). Effects of students' race, physical attractiveness, and dialect on teachers' evaluations. *Contemporary Educational Psychology, 3,* 77–86.

Dion, K. K. (1973). Young children's stereotyping of facial attractiveness. *Developmental Psychology, 9,* 183–188.

Dion, K. K., & Berscheid, E. (1974). Physical attractiveness and peer perception among children. *Sociometry, 37,* 1–12.

Dion, K., Berscheid, E., & Walster, E. (1972). What is beautiful is good. *Journal of Personality and Social Psychology, 24,* 285–290.

Dohrenwend, B. P., & Chin-Shong, E. (1967). Social status and attitudes toward psychological disorder: The problem of tolerance of deviance. *American Sociological Review, 32,* 417–433.

Dunn, L. M. (1968). Special education for the mildly retarded-Is much of it justifiable? *Exceptional Children, 35,* 5–22.

Durrett, M. E., & Davy, A. J. (1970). Racial awareness in young Mexican-American, Negro, and Anglo children. *Young Children, 26,* 16–24.

Dusek, J. B. (1975). Do teachers bias children's learning? *Review of Educational Research, 45,* 661–684.

Dusek, J. B., & O'Connell, E. J. (1973). Teacher expectancy effects on the achievement test performance of elementary school children. *Journal of Educational Psychology, 65,* 371–377.

Eaves, R. C. (1975). Teacher race; student race, and the behavior problem checklist. *Journal of Abnormal Child Psychology, 3,* 1–9.

Eder, D. (1981). Ability grouping as a self-fulfilling prophecy: A micro-analysis of teacher-student interaction. *Sociology of Education, 54,* 151–162.

Elashoff, J. D., & Snow, R. E. (1971). *Pygmalion reconsidered.* Worthington, OH: Charles A. Jones Publishing Co.

Ellis, A., & Beechley, R. M. (1954). Emotional disturbance in children with peculiar given names. *Journal of Genetic Psychology, 85,* 337–339.

Elovitz, G. P., & Salvia, J. (1982). Attractiveness as a biasing factor in the judgments of school psychologists. *Journal of School Psychology, 20,* 339–345.

Feldman, R., & Donohoe, L. (1978). Nonverbal communication of affect in interracial dyads. *Journal of Educational Psychology, 70,* 979–987.

Feshbach, N. D. (1969). Student teacher preferences for elementary school pupils varying in personality characteristics; *Journal of Educational Psychology, 60,* 126–132.

Fleming, E. S., & Anttonen, R. G. (1971). Teacher expectancy or my fair lady. *American Educational Research Journal, 8,* 241–252.

Foley, J. M. (1979). Effect of labeling and teacher behavior on children's attitudes. *American Journal of Mental Deficiency, 83,* 380–384.

Foster, G., & Ysseldyke, J. (1976). Expectancy and halo effects as a result of artiticially induced teacher bias. *Contemporary Educational Psychology, 1,* 37–45.

Foster, G. G., Ysseldyke, J. E., & Reese, J. H. (1975). I wouldn't have seen it if I hadn't believed it. *Exceptional Children, 41,* 469–473.

Freeman, S., & Algozzine, B. (1980). Social acceptability as a function of labels and assigned attributes. *American Journal of Mental Deficiency, 84,* 589–595.

Friedman, P. (1976). Comparisons of teacher reinforcement schedules for students with different social class backgrounds. *Journal of Educational Psychology, 68,* 286–292.

Garwood, S. G. (1976). First-name stereotypes as a factor in self-concept and school achievement. *Journal of Educational Psychology, 68,* 482–487.

Gephart, W. J., & Antonoplos, D. P. (1969). The effects of expectancy and other research biasing factors. *Phi Delta Kappan, 50,* 579–583.

Giesbrecht, M. L., & Routh, D. K. (1979). The influence of categories of cumulative folder information on teacher referrals of low-achieving children for special educational services. *American Educational Research Journal, 16,* 181–187.

Gillung, T. B., & Rucker, C. N. (1977). Labels and teacher expectations. *Exceptional Children, 43,* 464–465.

Goebes, D. D., & Shore, M. F. (1975). Behavioral expectations of students as related to the sex of the teacher. *Psychology in the Schools, 12,* 222–224.

Good, T. L. (1970). Which pupils do teachers call on? *Elementary School Journal, 70,* 190–198.

Good, T. L. (1980). Classroom expectations: Teacher-pupil interactions. In J. H. MacMillan (Ed.), *The social psychology of school learning.* New York: Academic Press.

Good, T. L., & Brophy, J. E. (1972). Behavioral expression of teacher attitudes. *Journal of Educational Psychology, 63,* 617–624.

Good, T. L., Cooper, H. M., & Blakey, S. L. (1980). Classroom interaction as a function of teacher expectations, student sex, and time of year. *Journal of Educational Psychology, 72,* 378–385.

Good, T. L., Sikes, J. N., & Brophy, J. E. (1973). Effects of teacher sex and student sex on classroom interaction. *Journal of Educational Psychology, 65,* 74–87.

Gottlieb, J. (1969). Attitudes toward retarded children: Effects of evaluator's psychological adjustment and age. *Scandinavian Journal of Educational Research, 13,* 170–182.

Gottlieb, J. (1974). Attitudes toward retarded children: Effects of labeling and academic performance. *American Journal of Mental Deficiency, 79*, 268–273.

Gottlieb, J. (1975). Attitudes toward retarded children: Effects of labeling and behavioral aggressiveness. *Journal of Educational Psychology, 67*, 581–585.

Gottlieb, J., Cohen, L., & Goldstein, L. (1974). Social contact and personal adjustment as variables relating to attitudes toward emr children. *Training School Bulletin, 71*, 9–16.

Gottlieb, J., & Gottlieb, B. W. (1977). Stereotypic attitudes and behavioral intentions toward handicapped children. *American Journal of Mental Deficiency, 82*, 65–71.

Gottman, J., Gonso, J., & Rasmussen, B. (1975). Social interaction, social competence, and friendship in children. *Child Development, 46*, 709–718.

Green, K. D., Forehand, R., Beck, S. J., & Vosk, B. (1980). An assessment of the relationship among measures of children's social competence and children's academic achievement. *Child Development, 51*, 1150–1156.

Greenbaum, J. J., & Wang, D. D. (1965). A semantic-differential study of the concepts of mental retardation. *Journal of Genetic Psychology, 73*, 257–272.

Gronlund, N. E. (1959). *Sociometry in the classroom.* New York: Harper.

Grossman, B., & Wrighter, J. (1948). The relationship between selection-rejection and intelligence, social status, and personality amongst sixth grade children. *Sociometry, 11*, 346–355.

Guttmann, J., & Bar-Tal, D. (1982). Stereotypic perceptions of teachers. *American Educational Research Journal, 19*, 519–528.

Haller, E. J., & Davis, S. A. (1981). Teacher perceptions, parental social status and grouping for reading instruction. *Sociology of Education, 54*, 162–174.

Harari, H., & McDavid, J. W. (1973). Name stereotypes and teachers' expectations. *Journal of Educational Psychology, 65*, 222–225.

Harasymiw, S. J., Horne, M. D., & Lewis, S. C. (1978). Age, sex, and education as factors in acceptance of disability groups. *Rehabilitation Psychology, 25*, 201–208.

Hartman, A. A., and Nicolay, R. C., & Hurley, J. (1968). Unique personal names as social adjustment factor. *Journal of Social Psychology, 75*, 107–110.

Hartup, W. W., Glazer, J. A., & Charlesworth, R. (1967). Peer reinforcement and sociometric status. *Child Development, 38*, 1017–1024.

Heller, M. S., & White, M. A. (1975). Rates of teacher verbal approval and disapproval to higher and lower ability classes. *Journal of Educational Psychology, 67*, 796–800.

Helton, G. B., & Oakland, T. D. (1977). Teachers' attitudinal responses to differing characteristics of elementary school students. *Journal of Educational Psychology, 69*, 261–265.

Hirshoren, A., & Burton, T. (1979). Willingness of regular teachers to participate in mainstreaming handicapped children. *Journal of Research and Development in Education, 12*, 93–100.

Horne, M. D. (1978). Cultural effect on attitudes toward labels. *Psychological Reports, 43*, 1051–1058.

Houston, T. J., & Sumner, F. C. (1948). Measurement of neurotic tendency in women with uncommon given names. *Journal of General Psychology, 39*, 289–292.

Hutton, J. B., & Polo, L. (1976). A sociometric study of learning disability children and type of teaching strategy. *Group Psychotherapy, Psychodrama and Sociometry, 29*, 113–120.

Jaffe, J. (1966). Attitudes of adolescents toward the mentally retarded. *American Journal of Mental Deficiency, 70*, 907–912.

Jaffe, J. (1967). "What's in a name"—Attitudes toward disabled persons. *Personnel and Guidance Journal, 45*, 557–560.

Janicki, M. P. (1970). Attitudes of health professionals toward twelve disabilities. *Perceptual and Motor Skills, 30*, 77–78.

Javel, M. E., & Greenspan, S. (1983). Influence of personal competence profiles on mainstreaming recommendations of school psychologists. *Psychology in the Schools, 20*, 459–465.

Jones, R. L., & Sisk, D. A. (1967). Early perceptions of orthopedic disability. *Exceptional Children, 34*, 42–43.

Jordan, J. E., & Proctor, D. I. (1969). Relationships between knowledge of exceptional children, kind and amount of experience with them, and teacher attitudes toward their classroom integration. *Journal of Special Education, 3*, 433–439.

José, J., & Cody, J. J. (1971). Teacher pupil interaction as it relates to attempted changes in teacher expectancy of academic ability and achievement. *American Educational Research Journal, 8*, 39–49.

Katz, P. A., Katz, I., & Cohen, S. (1976). White children's attitudes toward blacks and the physically handicapped: A developmental study. *Journal of Educational Psychology, 68*, 20–24.

Kavale, K., & Rossi, C. (1980). Regular class teachers' attitudes and perceptions of the resource specialist program for educable mentally retarded pupils. *Education and Training of the Mentally Retarded, 15*, 195–198.

Kehle, T. J., Bramble, W. J., & Mason, E. J. (1974). Teachers' expectations: Ratings of student performance as biased by student characteristics. *The Journal of Experimental Education, 43*, 54–60.

Kelly, T. J., Bullock, L. M., & Dykes, M. K. (1977). Behavioral disorders: Teachers' perceptions. *Exceptional Children, 43*, 316–318.

Kester, S. W., & Letchworth, G. P. (1972). Communication of teacher expectations and their effects on achievement and attitude of secondary school students. *Journal of Educational Research, 66*, 51–55.

Kleck, R. E., Richardson, S. A., & Ronald, L. (1974). Physical appearance cues and interpersonal attraction in children. *Child Development, 45*, 305–310.

Knoff, H. M. (1983). Effect of diagnostic information on special education placement decisions. *Exceptional Children, 49*, 440–444.

Kurtz, P. D., Harrison, M., Neisworth, J. T. & Jones, R. T. (1977). Influence of "Mentally Retarded" label on teachers' nonverbal behavior toward preschool children. *American Journal of Mental Deficiency, 82*, 204–206.

Larrivee, B., & Cook, L. (1979). Mainstreaming: A study of the variables affecting teacher attitude. *Journal of Special Education, 13*, 315–324.

LaVoie, J. C., & Adams, G. R. (1974). Teacher expectancy and its relation to physical and interpersonal characteristics of the child. *The Alberta Journal of Educational Research, 20*, 122–132.

Lenkowsky, R. S., & Blackman, L. S. (1968). The effect of teacher knowledge of race and social class on their judgments of children's academic competence and social acceptability. *Mental Retardation, 6*, 15–17.

Lerner, R. M., & Gellert, E. (1969). Body build identification, preference, and aversion in children. *Developmental Psychology, 1*, 456–462.

MacMillan, D. L., Jones, R. L., & Aloia, G. F. (1974). The mentally retarded label: A theoretical analysis and review of the research. *American Journal of Mental Deficiency, 79*, 241–261.

Mandell, C. J., & Strain, P. S. (1978). An analysis of factors related to the attitudes of regular classroom teachers toward mainstreaming mildly handicapped children. *Contemporary Educational Psychology, 3*, 154–162.

Martin, J., Veldman, D. J., & Anderson, L. M. (1980). Within class relationships between student achievement and teacher behaviors. *American Educational Research Journal, 17*, 479–490.

Martin, R. (1972). Student sex and behavior as determinants of the type and frequency of teacher-student contacts. *Journal of School Psychology, 10*, 339–347.

Marwit, K. L., Marwit, S. J., & Walker, E. (1978). Effects of student race and physical attractiveness on teachers' judgments of transgressions. *Journal of Educational Psychology, 70*, 911–915.

McCraw, L. W., & Tolbert, J. W. (1953). Sociometric status and athletic ability of junior high school boys. *Research Quarterly, 24*, 72–80.

McDavid, J. W., & Harari, H. (1966). Stereotyping of names and popularity in grade-school children. *Child Development, 37*, 453–459.

McGinley, P., & McGinley, H. (1970). Reading groups as psychological groups. *Journal of Experimental Education, 39,* 35–42.

McMichael, P. (1980). Reading difficulties, behavior, and social status. *Journal of Educational Psychology, 72,* 76–86.

Meichenbaum, D., Bowers, K., & Ross, R. A. (1969). A behavioral analysis of teacher expectancy effect. *Journal of Personality and Social Psychology, 13,* 306–316.

Mercer, J. R. (1973). *Labeling the mentally retarded.* Berkeley, CA: University of California Press.

Mertens, D. M. (1976). Expectations of teachers-in-training: The influence of a student's sex and a behavioral vs. descriptive approach in a biased psychological report. *Journal of School Psychology, 14,* 222–229.

Miller, C. K., McLaughlin, J. A., Haddon, J., & Chansky, N. M. (1968). Socioeconomic class and teacher bias. *Psychological Reports, 23,* 806.

Minner, S. (1982). Expectations of vocational teachers for handicapped students. *Exceptional Children, 48,* 451–453.

Minturn, L., & Lewis, M. (1968). Age differences in peer ratings so socially desirable and socially undesirable behavior. *Psychological Reports, 23,* 783–791.

Monroe, J. D., & Howe, C. E. (1971). The effects of integration and social class on the acceptance of retarded adolescents.*Education and Training of the Mentally Retarded, 6,* 20–24.

Moore, S. G. (1967). Correlates of peer acceptance in nursery school children. *Young Children, 22,* 281–297.

Morris, P. S., & McCauley, R. W. (1977). *Placement of handicapped children by Canadian mainstream administrators and teachers: A Rucker-Gable survey.* Paper presented at the Annual International Convention, the Council for Exceptional Children, Atlanta, GA. (ERIC Document Reproduction Service No. ED 139 139).

Muma, J. R. (1965). Peer evaluation and academic performance. *Personnel and Guidance Journal, 44,* 405–409.

Muma, J. R. (1968). Peer evaluation and academic achievement in performance classes. *Personnel and Guidance Journal, 46,* 580–585.

Natriello, G., & Dornbusch, S. M. (1983). Bringing behavior back in: The effects of student characteristics and behavior on the classroom behavior of teachers. *American Educational Research Journal, 20,* 29–43.

Nelson, S. D. (1977). First-name stereotypes and expected academic achievement of students. *Psychological Reports, 41,* 1343–1344.

Novak, D. W. (1975). Children's responses to imaginary peers labelled as emotionally disturbed. *Psychology in the Schools, 12,* 103–106.

Palmer, D. J. (1979). Regular-classroom teachers' attributions and instructional prescriptions for handicapped and nonhandicapped pupils. *Journal of Special Education, 13,* 325–337.

Palmer, D. J. (1983). An attributional perspective on labeling. *Exceptional Children, 49,* 423–429.

Parish, T. S., Dyck, N., & Kappes, B. M. (1979). Stereotypes concerning normal and handicapped children. *Journal of Psychology, 102,* 63–70.

Pfeiffer, S. I. (1980). The influence of diagnostic labeling on special education placement decisions. *Psychology in the Schools, 17,* 346–350.

Phillips, D. L. (1964). Rejection of the mentally ill: The influence of behavior and sex. *American Sociological Review, 29,* 679–687.

Porterfield, Q. V., & Schlichting, H. F. (1961). Peer status and reading achievement. *Journal of Educational Research, 54,* 292–297.

Prawat, R. S., & Jarvis, R. (1980). Gender difference as a factor in teachers' perceptions of students. *Journal of Educational Psychology, 72,* 743–749.

Prieto, A. G., & Zucker, S. H. (1981). Teacher perception of race as a factor in the placement of behaviorally disordered children. *Behavioral Disorders, 7,* 34–38.

Quinn, J. A., & Wilson, B. (1977). Programming effects on learning disabled children: Performance and affect. *Psychology in the Schools, 14,* 196–199.

Reese-Dukes, J. L., & Stokes, E. H. (1978). Social acceptance of elementary educable mentally retarded pupils in the regular classroom. *Education and Training of the Mentally Retarded, 13,* 356–361.

Reschly, D. J., & Lamprecht, M. J. (1979). Expectancy effects of labels: Fact or artifact? *Exceptional Children, 46,* 55–58.

Richardson, S. A. (1970). Age and sex differences in values toward physical handicaps. *Journal of Health and Social Behavior, 11,* 207–214.

Richardson, S. A., & Emerson, P. (1970). Race and physical handicap in children's preferences for other children: A replication in a Southern city. *Human Relations, 23,* 31–36.

Richardson, S. A., Goodman, N., Dornbusch, S. M., & Hastorf, A. H. (1963). Variant reactions to physical disabilities. *American Sociological Review, 28,* 429–435.

Richardson, S. A., Goodman, N., Hastorf, A. H., & Dornbusch, S. M. (1961). Cultural uniformity in reaction to physical disabilities. *American Sociological Review, 26,* 241–247.

Richardson, S. A., Royce, J. (1968). Race and physical handicap in children's preference for other children. *Child Development, 39,* 467–480.

Ringlaben, R. P., & Price, J. R. (1981). Regular classroom teachers' perceptions of mainstreaming effects. *Exceptional Children, 47,* 302–304.

Rist, R. C. (1970). Student social class and teacher expectations: The self-fulfilling prophecy in ghetto education. *Harvard Educational Review, 40,* 411–451.

Rosenthal, R., & Jacobson, L. (1968). *Pygmalion in the classroom.* New York: Holt, Rinehart & Winston.

Rosenthal, R., & Lawson, R. A. (1964). A longitudinal study of the effects of experimenter bias on the operant learning of laboratory rats. *Journal of Psychiatric Research, 2,* 61–72.

Ross, M. B., & Salvia, J. (1975). Attractiveness as a biasing factor in teacher judgments. *American Journal of Mental Deficiency, 80,* 96–98.

Rubin, K. H. (1972). Relationship between egocentric communication and popularity among peers. *Developmental Psychology, 7,* 364.

Rubovits, P., & Maehr, M. (1973). Pygmalion black and white. *Journal of Personality and Social Psychology, 25,* 210–218.

Sandberg, L. D. (1982). Attitudes of nonhandicapped elementary school students toward school-aged trainable mentally retarded students. *Education and Training of the Mentally Retarded, 17,* 30–34.

Savage, B. M., & Wells, F. L. (1948). A note on singularity in given names. *Journal of Social Psychology, 27,* 271–272.

Schloss, P., & Miller, S. R. (1982). Effects of the label ''institutionalized'' vs. ''regular school student'' on teacher expectations. *Exceptional Children, 48,* 363–364.

Schonberg, W. B., & Murphy, D. M. (1974). The relationship between the uniqueness of a given name and personality. *Journal of Social Psychology, 93,* 147–148.

Schwarz, R. H., & Cook, J. J. (1972). Teacher expectancy as it relates to academic achievement of emr students. *Journal of Educational Research, 65,* 393–396.

Scranton, T. R., & Ryckman, D. B. (1979). Sociometric status of learning disabled children in an integrative program. *Journal of Learning Disabilities, 12,* 402–407.

Seaver, W. B. (1973). Effects of naturally induced teacher expectancies. *Journal of Personality and Social Psychology, 28,* 333–342.

Severance, L. J., & Gasstrom, L. L. (1977). Effects of the label ''mentally retarded'' on causal explanations for success and failure outcomes. *American Journal of Mental Deficiency, 81,* 547–555.

Shaw, M. E. (1973). Changes in sociometric choices following forced integration of an elementary school. *Journal of Social Issues, 29,* 143–157.

Sherry, L. S., Armstrong, S. W., Algozzine, B. (1980). Teachers' perceptions and classroom interactions. *Psychological Reports, 46,* 535–540.

Silberman, M. L. (1969). Behavioral expression of teachers' attitudes toward elementary school students. *Journal of Educational Psychology, 60,* 402–407.

Simpson, A. W., & Erickson, M. T. (1983). Teachers' verbal and nonverbal communication patterns as a function of teacher race, student gender, and student race. *American Educational Research Journal, 20,* 183–198.

Siperstein, G. N., Bopp, N. J., & Bak, J. J. (1978). The social status of learning disabled children. *Journal of Learning Disabilities, 11,* 49–53.

Siperstein, G. N., Budoff, M., & Bak, J. J. (1980). Effects of the labels "mentally retarded" and "retard" on the social acceptability of mentally retarded children. *American Journal of Mental Deficiency, 84,* 596–601.

Siperstein, G. N., & Gottlieb, J. (1977). Physical stigma and academic performance as factors affecting children's first impressions of handicapped peers. *American Journal of Mental Deficiency, 81,* 455–462.

Smart, R., Wilton, K., & Keeling, B. (1980). Teacher factors and special class placement. *Journal of Special Education, 14,* 217–229.

Smith, M. D., Zingale, S. A., & Coleman, J. M. (1978). The influence of adult expectancy/child performance discrepancies upon children's self-concepts. *American Educational Research Journal, 15,* 259–265.

Smith, J. R., & Hurst, J. G. (1961). The relationship of motor abilities and peer acceptance of mentally retarded children. *American Journal of Mental Deficiency, 66,* 81–85.

Snow, R. E. (1969). Unfinished pygmalion. *Contemporary Psychology, 14,* 197–199.

Solomon, D., & Kendall, A. (1977). Dimensions of children's classroom behavior as perceived by teachers. *American Educational Research Journal, 14,* 411–421.

Soule, D. (1972). Teacher bias effects with severely retarded children. *American Journal of Mental Deficiency, 77,* 208–211.

Stake, J. E., & Katz, J. F. (1982). Teacher-pupil relationships in the elementary school classroom: Teacher-gender and pupil-gender differences. *American Educational Research Journal, 19,* 465–471.

Steinberg, J. A., & Hall, V. C. (1981). Effects of social behavior on interracial acceptance. *Journal of Educational Psychology, 73,* 51–56.

Stephens, T. M., & Braun, B. L. (1980). Measures of regular classroom teachers' attitudes toward handicapped children. *Exceptional Children, 46,* 292–294.

Stevens, D. O. (1971). Reading difficulty and classroom acceptance. *The Reading Teacher, 25,* 52–55.

Stevens, G. (1981). Bias in the attribution of hyperkinetic behavior as a function of ethnic identification and socioeconomic status. *Psychology in the Schools, 18,* 99–106.

St. John, N. H., & Lewis, R. G. (1975). Race and the social structure of the elementary classroom. *Sociology of Education, 48,* 346–368.

Stoller, L., Algozzine, B., Ysseldyke, J. (1981). Expectations and attributions for a handicapped child: Teachers pay attention to classroom performance. *Educational Research Quarterly, 6,* 53–59.

Sutherland, J. H., Algozzine, B., Ysseldyke, J. E., & Freeman, S. (1983). Changing peer perceptions: Effects of labels and assigned attributes. *Journal of Learning Disabilities, 16,* 217–220.

Sydney, J., & Minner, S. (1983). The influence of sibling information on the placement recommendation of special class teachers. *Behavioral Disorders, 9,* 43–45.

Taylor, R. L., Smiley, L. R., Ziegler, E. W. (1983). The effects of labels and assigned attributes on teacher perceptions of academic and social behavior. *Education and Training of the Mentally Retarded, 18,* 45–51.

Thompson, R. H., White, K. R., & Morgan, D. P. (1982). Teacher-student interaction patterns in classrooms with mainstreamed mildly handicapped students. *American Educational Research Journal 19*, 220–236.

Thorndike, R. L., (1968). Review of R. Rosenthal and L. Jacobson, pygmalion in the classroom. *American Educational Research Journal, 5*, 708–711.

Towne, R. C., & Joiner, L. M. (1968). Some negative implications of special placement for children with learning disabilities, *Journal of Special Education, 2*, 217–222.

Tringo, J. L. (1970). The hierarchy of preference toward disability groups. *Journal of Special Education, 4*, 295–306.

Tucker, J. A. (1980). Ethnic proportions in classes for the learning disabled: Issues in nonbiased assessment. *Journal of Special Education, 14*, 93–105.

Tuddenham, R. D. (1951). Studies in reputation III. Correlates of popularity among elementary-school children. *Journal of Educational Psychology, 42*, 257–276.

Tudor, J. F. (1971). The development of class awareness in children. *Social Forces, 49*, 470–476.

Victor, J. B., & Halverson, C. F. (1980). Children's friendship choices: Effects of school behavior. *Psychology in the Schools, 17*, 409–414.

Voeltz, L. M. (1980). Children's attitudes toward handicapped peers. *American Journal of Mental Deficiency, 84*, 455–464.

Walton, W. E. (1937). The affective value of first names. *Journal of Applied Psychology, 21*, 396–409.

Weinberg, N. (1978). Preschool children's perceptions of orthopedic disability. *Rehabilitation Counseling Bulletin, 21*, 183–189.

Weiner, B., Frieze, I., Kukla, A., Reed, L., Rest, S., & Rosenbaum, R. M. (1971). *Perceiving the causes of success and failure*. New York: General Learning Press.

Weinstein, R. S. (1976). Reading group membership in first grade: Teacher behaviors and pupil experience over time. *Journal of Educational Psychology, 68*, 103–116.

Wilkins, J. E., & Velicer, W. F. (1980). A semantic differential investigation of children's attitudes toward three stigmatized groups. *Psychology in the Schools, 17*, 364–371.

Wong, M. G. (1980). Model students? Teachers' perceptions and expectations of their Asian and white students. *Sociology of Education, 53*, 236–246.

Ysseldyke, J. E., & Foster, G. G. (1978). Bias in teachers' observations of emotionally disturbed and learning disabled children. *Exceptional Children, 44*, 613–615.

Zucker, S. H., & Prieto, A. G. (1977). Ethnicity and teacher bias in educational decisions. *Instructional Psychology, 4*, 2–5.

Zucker, S. H., Prieto, A. G., & Rutherford, R. B. (1980). Racial determinants of teachers' perceptions of placement of the educable mentally retarded. *Exceptional Child Education Resources, 11*, 909.

6

Modifying Professional and Peer Attitudes Toward Handicapped Students

There is considerable empirical support for the position that positive attitudes can be facilitated through some type of intervention. Procedures that have been used to modify professional and peer attitudes toward handicapped students are reviewed in this chapter. The presentation begins with a discussion of attempts to modify professional attitudes and closes with a consideration of efforts to promote peer acceptance.

ATTEMPTS TO CHANGE PROFESSIONAL ATTITUDES

This section opens with a summary of a controversial issue: the relative importance of personal contact with handicapped students versus knowledge about their handicapping conditions in promoting change. Then, attempts to modify the attitudes of classroom teachers, pre-service teachers, and teacher trainers are considered.

The Experience-Information Issue

There is considerable controversy about how to modify teacher attitudes toward handicapped children. One major point of contention has been the extent to which the "treatment" should involve personal contact with handicapped children as opposed to knowledge about them. Some studies show that contact changes attitudes; others suggest that both components of contact and knowledge are needed.

The results of studies in which contact alone was employed are inconclusive. On one hand studies by Efron and Efron (1967) and Frith and Edwards (1981) revealed that personal contact with handicapped pupils promoted positive attitudinal changes. Kuhn (1971), however, did not find this to be the case. Given the limited number of studies in this area, differences in the treatments, methodology, and types of handicapped involved, it is impossible to draw any firm conclusions. About all that can be said is that at times personal contact alone does appear to have a positive impact on attitudes; but at other times it does not.

Shaw and Gillung (1975) demonstrated that coursework (knowledge) alone can modify teachers attitudes. In this investigation the attitudinal gains that regular classroom teachers evidenced after completing an introductory course about teaching mildly handicapped students in regular classrooms were also evidenced on post posttesting 3 months later. No conclusion can be based on a single study, however.

Some authors (Anthony, 1972; Higgs, 1975) take the point of view that both components are necessary to produce an attitudinal shift. Indeed, studies employing training programs that have included both contact and knowledge have more consistently demonstrated success than when either component is employed by itself. But even then the results have not been consistent. For example, when Jordan and Proctor (1969) compared the effects of the two variables, only coursework was found to be significantly related to teacher attitudes. Panda and Bartel (1972) found that teachers who had both experience teaching handicapped children as well as specialized training were no more positive toward exceptional students than were teachers without either experience teaching handicapped children or training in the area. But another study (Johnson & Cartwright, 1979) in which each component alone and both combined were compared revealed that the combination of knowledge and supervised work experience and just knowledge were equally effective, and more effective than experience alone, in improving teachers' attitudes toward mainstreaming.

Despite the rhetoric and studies, however, the argument over the relative merits of contact vs. knowledge or some combination thereof is actually an oversimplification of the issue. The complexities of the attitude construct and established attitude change theories have generally been ignored in educational research (see Greenwald, Brock, & Ostrom, 1968).

Attitudes are difficult to alter. As shown in Chapter 1, any attitude change that occurs as a result of participation in an attitude modification project may be dependent upon (according to one's theoretical orientation) a variety of interpersonal or situational factors. Individuals remain remarkably fixed in their beliefs, and regardless of the persuasiveness of the approach used, attitudes may change very slowly; a person may also become more or less accepting of an attitude object.

Programs to Modify Classroom Teacher Attitudes

The results for some programs designed to modify teachers attitudes toward handicapped students demonstrate how hard it can be to produce an attitudinal shift. For example, the effects of some projects on teacher attitudes have been very minimal (Jaffe, 1972). Differences in the amount or degree of change in attitudes toward different exceptionality groups may also occur. For example, in one study (Shotel, Iano, & McGettigan, 1972) after classroom teachers had contact with educable mentally, emotionally disturbed, and learning disabled students in their classes, they evidenced less favorable attitudes toward placing the educable mentally retarded student in the regular classroom and were less positive about their potential for social adjustment; at the same time they became more positive about the potential adjustment of emotionally disturbed children but no changes were evidenced in their attitudes toward learning disabled students. Sometimes changes have even occurred in negative directions (Bradfield, Brown, Kaplan, Rickert, & Stannard, 1973; Warren, Turner, & Brody, 1964; Sellin & Mulchahay, 1965).

There is no one correct approach to modifying teachers' attitudes. It appears that when both components of contact and knowledge are included, the likelihood for change is increased; but the format used to represent these elements has varied from project to project. Three programs are described in greater detail in the following paragraphs in order to illustrate the different types of activities (representational of contact and knowledge) that have been incorporated into projects.

In one summer workshop (Glass & Meckler, 1972) designed to enhance the ability of classroom teachers to work with mildly handicapped children in the classroom, the teacher participated in instructional sessions and in planning sessions, taught handicapped students, and attended parent meetings. Post-testing using an attitudinal instrument showed that the teachers were more positive toward regular classroom placement and saw themselves as more able to teach mildly handicapped children.

In another summer workshop, administrators and classroom teachers were involved in: (1) a practicum placement working with handicapped children for 3 hours per week; (2) two additional hours of observation; (3) enrollment for 9 hours of graduate credit; and (4) weekly sensitivity sessions. Post-testing using a semantic differential showed significant and positive attitudinal changes (Brooks & Bransford, 1971).

Larrivee (1981) examined the effects of monthly inservice meetings in contrast to "intensive" inservice. Both groups of regular classroom teachers attended the monthly inservice meetings and were given instruction in such areas as behavior management, diagnostic-prescriptive teaching, and methods of individualizing instruction. However, the "intensive" inservice group also attended a 6-week summer workshop and during the school year participated in weekly meetings with a trainer wherein specific instruction was provided to the teacher in how to manage the total class, and provide for the needs of specific students who had been identified (by the trainer and teacher using a variety of assessment devices) as in need of special help. Classroom observations by the trainer and demonstration activities were also incorporated into the program. Attitude scores indicated the "intensive" group was more positive toward mainstreaming than the monthly meeting group.

Keep in mind that the relative contribution of contact and knowledge in the attitude modification projects described in the preceding paragraphs is not known. Furthermore, there is no evidence about whether the attitudinal gains the teachers demonstrated on posttesting are maintained over time; nor do we know how their interactions with handicapped students in their classrooms might have changed (see Chapter 1 for a discussion of the relationship between attitudes and behavior).

What Information and Experience Do Teachers Need?

The available research seems to support the need for intervention strategies which involve the elements or components of experience with handicapped children and knowledge or information about exceptionalities. However, the findings do not provide any real indication of what the specific characteristics of an attitude modification project should be. Some authors (e.g., Alexander & Strain, 1978) have suggested that a great deal of study will be necessary before we can determine what kinds of skills or information should be presented to teachers, in what manner, and for what time period.

Teacher Survey Results

It seems that planners of attitude modification projects might get some idea about what kinds of information would be appropriately included in an attitude modification project by reviewing how teachers have responded to mainstreaming surveys. These surveys have queried teachers about their knowledge and feelings relative to the legislation, the skills they think they have or need for working with handicapped students, and the kind of assistance they perceive necessary to teach exceptional children. For example, classroom teachers do not seem to: understand the legislation regarding handicapped children (Saunders & Sultana, 1980); know very much about the concept of special education or how schools and agencies have been providing for handicapped children; or be familiar with the rationale for IEPs (Individualized Educational Programs) (Carpenter & Robson, 1979; Gickling & Theobald, 1975; Semmel, 1979) (see Chapter 4 for a more detailed presentation of survey findings).

There is also evidence that teacher attitudes toward mainstreaming exceptional students into their classes depend on the number of handicapped students mainstreamed into their class (Buttery, 1978), and type of handicap the student exhibits (Harasymiw & Horne, 1976; Horne, 1983). Teachers may actually fear a particular exceptionality group (Vacc & Kirst, 1977). Acceptance may also vary with grade level, elementary grade level teachers generally being more accepting (Morris & McCauley, 1977). (See Chapter 5 for a further discussion of factors which may effect attitudes toward handicapped individuals.)

Modifying Preservice Teacher Attitudes

Most states have mandated that undergraduate education majors complete an introductory or survey course in special education; indeed former teachers reentering the profession must enroll in this type of course in order to be recertified. Although one study showed that teachers in the field respond negatively about the usefulness of a survey course in special education (Alberto, Castricone, & Cohen, 1978), teachers are undoubtedly exposed to a great deal of information about handicaps in an introductory class. However, in light of the results for research on the effects of information on attitudes, there is really no sound basis for assuming a positive attitudinal effect. The error in making such an assumption is underscored by the findings of some studies. For example, Buttery (1981) found preservice teachers (undergraduate majors in early childhood, elementary, and middle school education) enrolled in a required course on exceptional children were more negative toward mainstreaming exceptional children into the regular classroom at the end of the course. In another investigation (Parish, Eads, Reece, & Piscitello, 1977) there were no differences in the pre- and posttesting attitudes of preservice teachers who took an introductory special education course.

At the same time, introductory survey courses present an excellent opportunity for attempting to develop more positive attitudes toward handicapped children among prospective regular classroom teachers. Consequently, attempts to describe methodologies for special education coursework which would facilitate positive attitudinal shifts are an important task; but not an easy one. For example, Naor and Milgram (1980) studied the effect of an experiential teaching procedure (wherein teachers attended lectures but also observed special education programs) on preservice teacher attitudes as compared to the results for using the traditional lecture method. Findings indicated preservice teachers in the experiential group had more positive attitudes but those participating in the traditional lecture approach had higher knowledge gain scores. Actually, the mean scores for the two groups on each of the variables (attitude and knowledge gain) were so minimal that impressive evidence of the advantages or disadvantages of either method was lacking. However, since the responses on a two question measure of behavioral intentions (wherein the preservice teachers were asked about their willingness to do volunteer work with handicapped students or accept employment in a summer camp for handicapped individuals) showed students in the experiential group were more positive, it seems that the experiential procedure deserves further exploration.

In another study, Orlansky (1979) explored active learning (including role playing, simulations of handicaps, and discussion) as a mechanism to increase the positivity of preservice teachers' attitudes. Findings indicated that the active learning method may be more effective than lectures but the results depended upon the particular handicapped group in question; that is, preservice teachers may become more positive toward some handicaps and more negative toward others. Results of this study also showed that preservice teachers' perceptions of the importance of special education services for handicapped students (which groups are most to least in need) are more easily modified than are the preferences they have for teaching students with different types of handicaps. Active learning seems to be a potentially effective method; but caution is in order since negative changes may be produced. The approach should be subjected to further examination.

Two recent reports about modifying preservice teacher attitudes provided participants with contact experiences with handicapped students and information about them. Neither study tested participants on how much information they had acquired, but both looked for an attitudinal effect.

In the first, Leyser, Abrams, and Lipscomb (1982) compared the effects of an experimental preservice program that included a course on the handicapped child in the regular classroom, a practicum experience that exposed the participants to a variety of special educational settings and handicapped children, and discussions with guest speakers (i.e., a school psychologist, lawyer) about aspects of mainstreaming. Results of attitudinal testing indicated that the regular elementary education majors enrolled in the program were more positive toward mainstreaming than control groups of regular elementary majors and special education majors who had not attended the class. A second study (Stainback & Stainback, 1982) compared the effect of two methods of presentation of information about severely retarded children on attitudes of undergraduate elementary education majors enrolled in a survey of exceptional children course. The experimental group participated in a lecture/discussion about the pros and cons of mainstreaming severely retarded students and observed and interacted with severely retarded individuals in special classes. The control group students only participated in lecture/discussion sessions which provided information about the definitions and characteristics of mentally retarded students, the concept of normalization, and information about P.L. 94-142 as it relates to severely retarded persons. Results on an attitude survey indicated the experimental group was significantly more positive toward mainstreaming severely retarded students.

As yet, there is no clear cut methodology for insuring the development of positive attitudes among perservice teachers. What is evidenced is the need to continue to search for alternative instructional designs. Classes might involve an informational as well as an experiential component, role playing, discussion, and simulations in some combination. The findings for media presentations discussed in the next section suggest videotape presentations might also be a helpful procedure in preservice as well as inservice education programs.

Effects of Media Presentations on Attitudes

Media presentations about handicapped individuals may be a useful tool for changing attitudes. In an effort to identify possible new methodologies for attitude change, the effects of live versus videotape presentations have been considered in some studies. It has been suggested that live presenters are more likely to elicit an attitude change in observers than are videotaped presentations because the speakers credibility or "expertness" can be more clearly established by the audience as a result of their interactions with the speakers (Croft, Stimpson, Ross, Bray, & Breglio, 1969; Hovland & Weiss, 1952).

In order to clarify whether or not it is more effective to use live presenters Donaldson and Martinson (1977) conducted an experiment with college students enrolled in an introductory psychology class. A live panel discussion, a videotape of the same discussion, and only the audio tape recording of the discussion were presented to groups of students. The speakers were three male and three female adults with physical disabilities (cerebral palsy, blindness, quadraplegia). A nondisabled male and female moderator asked panel members to respond to questions about their disability, their perceptions of the attitudes nonhandicapped had toward them, their social lives, and goals. Although no interaction was allowed because of the comparative nature of the experiment, significant positive changes were demonstrated on an attitudinal measure administered after the presentation for both the live and videotape groups; the largest change occurred for the live discussion group, and no changes were demonstrated for the audiotape group. In this study, credibility of the speakers may have been established because the panel members were disabled; this merits further investigation since the implications for teacher training programs are important. For example, from a practical standpoint, it would be easier for instructors (recognizing that the attitudinal effect may be somewhat lessened) to use videotapes in preservice and inservice programs as an alternative to having to locate in vivo handicapped speakers.

In another study Dailey and Halpin (1981) tried to modify the attitudes of undergraduates enrolled in an introductory special education course using videotapes of handicapped children. Students were majoring in special as well as regular education and the course was a certification requirement for both groups. Results indicated that using videotapes was more effective in modifying the attitudes of non-special education majors, but participation in the course without videotapes was more effective for special education majors. The authors did not offer any reasons for this curious differential effect.

It seems that the effectiveness of videotapes will require further study. The research is not sufficient to conclude that live versus videotaped discussions are more effective in changing attitudes, and the effect they may have on different student groups is not clear. It may also be that a single handicapped presenter is as effective as a group panel. Indeed Austin, Powell, and Martin (1981) found when they exposed a group of undergraduates to one handicapped presenter (a person who used a wheelchair) and a speaker who was non-handicapped, without any opportunity for verbal interaction, an attitude change was demonstrated for both groups, and there was no significant difference in the magnitude of the change.

Teacher Educator Attitudes

It has been suggested (Weisenstein & Gall, 1978) that the attitudes of those who educate teachers also need to be modified in order to affect differences in preservice teachers' acceptance of mainstreaming and working with special students. Programs designed to increase acceptance of the concept of mainstreaming by college and university faculty are becoming more prevalent particularly because of "Dean's Grants" (competitive awards supported by the Office of Special Education and Rehabilitative Services). Results for a few of these projects have been presented in the literature. For example, in one report (Lombardi, Meadowcroft, & Strasburger, 1982) a group of faculty responsible for teaching the courses in the professional education foundation sequence received inservice training designed to modify their attitudes about mainstreaming, and to provide them with knowledge about P.L. 94-142 and the characteristics of handicapped students. The results indicated that the professors who participated in the project became more positive about mainstreaming: however, there was no difference between the inservice participants and a control group on the variables of information about the law or the learning characteristics of handicapped children. It seems that comprehensive faculty inservice programs need to be developed in Colleges of Education.

PROGRAMS TO MODIFY PEER ACCEPTANCE

Programs to modify attitudes of peers toward handicapped classmates take many forms but may be categorized as representing one of six general types: (1) providing experiences or contacts with handicapped students; (2) providing information about handicapped students; (3) providing both contact and information; (4) often small group nonacademic experiences are organized to facilitate acceptance of handicapped students. (5) team and cooperative learning experiences have been proposed to promote student interactions; and (6) training in social skills has been recently advocated for handicapped students.

Experience or Knowledge

It has been suggested that merely exposing nonhandicapped students to handicapped students in the public school, in and of itself, would result in more positive attitudes toward handicapped individuals. Some studies have supported the relationship. Rapier, Adelson, Carey, & Croke (1972) found 3rd, 4th and 5th graders were more positive toward physically handicapped students after an orthopedically handicapped unit opened on the elementary school's grounds. Sheare (1974) reported junior high school students were more positive toward educable mentally handicapped students if they were in classes (nonacademic) where these students had been integrated. And, Voeltz (1980), who surveyed elementary schools where children had varying degrees of contact with severely handicapped students, found those with most contact expressed the most positive attitudes.

Still other studies have shown that contact does not necessarily result in nonhandicapped students becoming more positive in their attitudes toward nonhandicapped peers. Goodman, Gottlieb, and Harrison (1972) found that educable mentally retarded (EMR) students who were mainstreamed into classes in a nongraded elementary school were rejected more than segregated EMR students. Strauch (1970), however, found that the attitudes of seventh-grade students who had contact with educable mentally retarded students in nonacademic classes did not differ significantly from those of seventh graders in junior high schools where the EMR students were segregated.

Sometimes, however the results have been equivocal. Peterson (1974) tested 5th through 8th graders; on one of the instruments subjects who had no contact with EMR students were more favorable but there were no differences in their attitudes on another instrument.

Contact with handicapped persons can also produce a negative attitudinal shift. Cleland and Chambers (1959) and Sellin and Mulchahay (1965) found taking high school students on a tour of an institution resulted in more negative attitudes. Gottlieb, Cohen, and Goldstein (1974) found in two studies that elementary students who attended schools where they had no contact with retarded students had more positive attitudes than students who were attending schools wherein they had contact with students who were retarded.

The effect of knowledge alone on attitudes has also received considerable attention in literature dealing with attitudinal change. The focus, in this case, is on providing nonhandicapped students with information about the causes, characteristics, and learning problems of handicapped students in order to produce greater levels of acceptance. Similar to the results for the experiential approach, findings for the informational procedure are also inconclusive.

Sometimes information has a positive effect. Gottlieb (1980) reported that showing third through sixth graders a videotape of a mentally retarded student followed by a discussion of the causes and characteristics of mental retardation resulted in more positive attitudes. But in some studies the results have been equivocal. Miller, Armstrong, and Hagan (1981) conducted a 6-week teaching experience. Nonhandicapped third and fifth graders were taught about handicapping conditions. Instruction about the causes, characteristics, and learning problems was coupled with pictures, stories, and simulations. Comparison between the experimental and control group indicated no significant differences, but some positive trends were evidenced. In another experiment (Westervelt & McKinney, 1980), fourth-grade students were shown a film pointing out the similarity between the aspirations and interests of handicapped and nonhandicapped students. Pre- and posttesting indicated that viewing the film had very little effect on the viewers' attitudes, and no effects were evidenced on post posttesting 9 days later.

Experience and Knowledge

Several programs have presented students with a combination of contact experiences and knowledge in order to change their attitudes. These programs are similar to those which have been developed for teachers in that they may contain many different types of activities (representational of contact and knowledge). In the following paragraphs describing several different programs designed to modify peer attitudes, their diversity becomes apparent.

For example, both components of contact and information were included in a program developed by Lazar, Gensley, and Orpet (1971) for changing attitudes of elementary-aged gifted students toward the handicapped. The 4-week program consisted of two major activities. First, students were presented with a unit on creative Americans including those who were handicapped; for example, Thomas A. Edison, hearing impaired; Helen Keller, multiply handicapped; Franklin D. Roosevelt, polio victim. A different model was studied each day with emphasis placed upon achievement, with personal characteristics including handicaps being treated as incidental. Second, guests, including the teacher of a class for mentally retarded children who told the students about her pupils, a family in which the parents were deaf, an epileptic teenager, her epileptic boyfriend, and a legally blind counselor, were invited to the class for weekly discussions. Students evidenced significant positive attitudinal changes on posttesting undertaken on the last day of the program.

In one program, elementary-aged students were exposed to 2½ hour activity sessions. They: (1) observed and experienced the needs and abilities of handicapped people (students queried a deaf junior high school student and her interpreter, received instruction in sign language, the manual alphabet, and engaged in conversation with a severely spastic quadraplegic); (2) engaged in experiences using wheelchairs, prostheses, and other orthopedic appliances; (3) observed, interacted, and arm wrestled with a retarded adolescent; (4) conversed with a blind college student; (5) experienced the use of braille; (6) performed routine games and activities while blindfolded; and (7) watched a film on blind people participating in sports. Brief discussions were held at the end of each activity, children were engaged in creating writing activities about their experiences toward the end of each session, and these activities followed by a summary type discussion. Posttesting one week after the program was completed showed significant positive attitudinal changes (Jones, Sowell, Jones, & Butler, 1981).

A project to modify attitudes of junior and senior high school students included five specific activities: (1) discussion of special education terminology, legislation, barriers, and problems encountered by handicapped persons; (2) preparation of a research report on a specific disability including causes, characteristics, and effects on learning and social adjustment; (3) viewing a film about handicapped children and answering questions about their feelings; (4) participation in 3 or 4 simulation activities to experience a handicap; and (5) a personal interview with a blind student. In this study, the evaluation component required that students assess their own attitude change; 80 percent of the 20 students completing the self-evaluation felt they had become more positive and accepting (Handlers & Austin, 1980).

An experiment (Simpson, Parrish, & Cook, 1976) comparing the effects of information versus information plus experience demonstrated that even when the elements of contact and information are included in a project, the attitudes students have toward handicapped classmates may not change. In this study, the informational component presented to regular class primary-grade students included showing a filmstrip about handicapped students, discussions with professionals in the area of special education, and a visit to a empty special education classroom where another discussion of the special classroom and its enrollees was held. The sessions were held once a week for 4 weeks. Those students in the information plus contact group also spent an additional one hour per week visiting and interacting with students in a self-contained special class for emotionally disturbed children. Posttesting did not demonstrate that significant attitudinal changes occurred in either group.

Small Group Nonacademic Experience

It has been hypothesized that "if the frequency of interaction between two or more persons increases, the degree of their liking for one another will increase, and vice versa" (Homans, 1950, p. 112). Similar hypotheses have been formulated by Allport (1958) and Zajonc (1968). Thus, small group experiences requiring normal and handicapped students to work together have been contrived to increase peer acceptance of the handicapped student. For example, Lilly (1971) required low status students (low-achieving, but not identified as educable mentally retarded) to work with high status students in a film-making project outside of the regular classroom for 20 minutes a week for 5 weeks. Acceptance increased for low status students after the treatment; however, since the gains were not maintained over time, the need for longer treatment was suggested.

In another group project, Ballard, Corman, Gottlieb, & Kaufman (1977) involved educable mentally retarded students and nonhandicapped students in the creation of a multi-media project. Small groups were structured to contain an educable mentally retarded student and 4 or 5 nonhandicapped peers. Teachers attended a 2-day inservice workshop, and a manual was prepared to help them instruct children in small group work. There were four components of the small group project that the authors felt were quite important: (1) the groups were small in order to include sharing and interdependence; (2) "minimally academic manipulative tasks" were used to foster success experiences and decrease "the possibility of frustration and failure leading to misbehavior and subsequent rejection;" (3) the task was structured to encourage division of labor and shared decision making; and (4) the training or project time period was adequate to ensure a maintenance of the effect (these authors provided 40 minutes of training daily for 8 weeks). Results indicated students were more accepting of educable mentally retarded classmates up to 4 weeks after the end of the treatment.

Small group experiences have also been developed to increase the status of handicapped students in their special class. In one study (Chennault, 1967), two low- and two high-status mentally retarded students were identified (using a sociometric scale) and involved in the planning, rehearsal, and presentation of a play. Testing immediately after the presentation showed a significant improvement in the peer acceptance scores for the low–status students. Rucker and Vincenzo (1970) designed a similar program for unpopular EMR students. Again students with the highest and lowest acceptance scores participated in a group project; in this case they met for 2 weeks in 45-minute sessions twice weekly to prepare a class carnival. Posttesting three days after the carnival showed significant gains in peer group acceptance for the low status students; however, posttesting one month later demonstrated this gain was not maintained.

The efficacy of small group procedures to increase handicapped student status has also been demonstrated in programs wherein teachers have been provided with instructions for reorganizing their classes (Barclay, 1967; Schmuck, 1968). Recently Leyser and Gottlieb (1980) reported the success of a program wherein teachers were provided with a 2-hour workshop on how to increase the status of rejected students. A manual containing detailed descriptions of the procedures introduced in the workshop (i.e., methods for grouping students, increasing classroom participation, using peer tutoring and behavioral intervention strategies) was also prepared. Teachers were told the names of rejected students in the classes (identified by a sociometric pretest) and provided with biweekly consulation for 10 weeks. Sociometric data collected at the end of the treatment period showed low status students gained significantly in peer acceptance.

Team and Cooperative Group Learning Approaches

Several specific approaches for conducting small group experiences using learning teams or cooperative instructional groups have been developed primarily as mechanisms for increasing cross racial friendships among students. When these approaches are used, groups of five or six members are formed to include a cross-section of academic ability levels, genders, and racial/ethnic membership.

These approaches include: (1) the Jigsaw Technique; (2) Teams-Games-Tournaments (TGT); (3) Student Teams and Achievement Divisions (STAD); (4) Group-Investigation (G-I); and (5) Cooperative Learning. These approaches are potentially effective methods for increasing interactions among handicapped and nonhandicapped students. They have not, however, usually been tested from this standpoint; thus, except for one approach, they are described briefly. Only the cooperative learning approach has been used more extensively to promote interactions among handicapped students; consequently, it is more thoroughly reviewed.

The Jigsaw Technique (Aronson, Stephan, Sikes, Blaney, & Snapp, 1978) is a method of "required interdependence" among students. Student groups first receive training in how to work as a team. Material to be learned is then divided among members; each student learns part of the information to be mastered and then must present it to the other group members. In the end, the students learn all of the material as a result of an interdependent effort. Mastery is demonstrated on quizzes and tests. Aronson et al. reported that students increase their liking for groupmates as well as other classmates as a result of their participation in jigsaw groups.

Teams-Games-Tournaments (DeVries, Edwards, & Fennessey, 1974) requires students to be grouped into teams. The team members practice or tutor each other on materials the teacher has presented to prepare for game sessions that are part of an ongoing tournament. The tournament regroups team members into groups of students achieving at approximately the same level for competition. Since individual group members compete against individuals from other groups, and points earned by the individuals are earned for their team, the procedure encourages team members to help each other so that the group or team will win points in the tournament. Team scores are published in a weekly class newsletter distributed to all students.

The Student Teams and Achievement Divisions (STAD) (Slavin, 1978a) approach is similar to the TGT approach. Material to be learned is presented by the teacher. This is followed by team practice during which time the students in the group help each other study worksheets containing the information. This session is followed by a quiz; individual scores are converted to a team score; and a class newsletter identifies the teams earning the highest scores. Thus, students cooperate on a team but compete each with each other's teams.

Sharan and Sharan's (1976) small-group investigation (G-I) approach focuses on students learning material as a result of a cooperative group inquiry and discussion. Academically and ethnically heterogeneous groups of students gather, analyze, and interpret information which they then present to their teacher and classmates for evaluation.

Although research has demonstrated the positive effects of the Jigsaw Technique, TGT, STAD, and G-I on student achievement, self-attitudes, peer and cross racial friendships and interaction (Blaney, Stephan, Rosenfield, Aronson, & Sikes, 1977; DeVries & Slavin, 1978; DeVries, Edwards, & Slavin, 1978;

Hansell & Slavin, 1981; Sharan, Hertz-Lazarowitz, & Ackerman, 1980; Slavin, 1978a, 1978b), only a few studies have investigated these approaches in relationship to handicapped students.

Slavin (1977) explored using TGT with students attending a public school designed for children with academic problems and difficulties in "human relationships and/or self-organization." Nineteen 7th, 8th and 9th grade students were assigned to a control group; 20 students were assigned to a social studies TGT class. Classroom observations and sociometric measures were administered at the end of six weeks; results indicated that students in the TGT condition chose more friends and workmates and engaged in significantly higher levels of peer interaction. A 5-month follow-up using the same procedures for data collection indicated that TGT students were still interacting with each other more than control group students even though TGT students were not in the same classes anymore. However, results also showed that some of the interactions were inappropriate and resulted in more off-task behavior. The results of this study suggest that using TGT teams may be a useful procedure meriting further investigation.

Cooperative learning has been described by Johnson & Johnson (1975). When the approach is used: (1) instructional goals for a lesson are stated to the class; (2) appropriately sized groups are formed according to the lesson demands; (3) students are assigned to groups to maximize homogeneity; (4) the classroom is arranged so that group members are in close proximity; (5) materials or tasks are arranged to facilitate interaction; (6) group goals and criteria are established with the understanding that all group members will receive the same grade; (7) student-student interactions are observed; (8) consultation is provided as necessary; and (9) evaluation of group products is criterion referenced. This procedure is examined in greater detail in the following section.

Cooperative vs. Competitive and Individualistic Classroom Instruction

Teachers may structure classrooms in different ways to achieve their instructional goals. Three approaches to structure include a cooperative, competitive, or individualistic style (Deutsch, 1949, 1962).

In the cooperative situation, the goals for individuals in the classroom are linked together so that the student can only obtain his or her individual goal if other students in the group obtain theirs. Students work together and the rewards are given to the group or team. This is in contrast to the competitive situation which rewards an individual for being among the best or highest in the class. Finally, when an individualistic approach is used there is no relationship among the goals of individuals; a student is rewarded for his/her own performance on an assigned task.

Examples of how cooperative (versus competitive or individualistic) instruction may be achieved are found within investigations of the efficacy of the methodologies. Martino and Johnson (1979) used the cooperative and individualistic approach to teach learning disabled and nonhandicapped students to swim. In the cooperative situation, pairs of students were told: (1) they would be helping each other to learn; (2) the goal was for both to learn; (3) to ask each other for help; and (4) that they would be evaluated as a pair. Reinforcement was given to the pair for working together and for their performance. In the individualistic condition, students worked by themselves and were told to: (1) learn each skill; (2) ask the teacher for help if they needed it; (3) ignore other class members; and (4) that they would be evaluated. They were individually praised for performing each skill and for being independent learners. Hypothetically, had a competitive situation been contrived, students would have been told to: (1) work especially hard on learning each skill to be good swimmers; and (2) that they would be graded on their performance and some students would get As but others might only get Bs, Cs and some even Ds and Fs. In otherwords they would be marked on a curve. In this study, twelve males, 6 of whom were learning disabled, were paired with each other. Nine days of instruction for 45 minutes was provided; a 15 minute free-time swim followed instruction during which time observers recorded the interactions among the students. Findings indicated that there were more friendly interactions among nonhandicapped and learning disabled students in the cooperative situation.

Each type of goal structure provides for a different type of interaction among students. Johnson (1980) presented a summary table for the effects of each goal structure on students' interactions with each other, based on previous findings (See Johnson & Johnson, 1975, 1978); this summation appears in Table 6.1. The cooperative structure provides for the greatest amount of interaction; the competitive situation "promotes cautious and defensive student-student interaction"; and, in the individualistic situation there is no interaction (Johnson, 1980, p. 134). Johnson (1980) suggests that cooperative learning results in: (1) feelings of peer acceptance; (2) a greater exchange of information among peers; (3) higher motivation and (4) greater emotional involvement in learning tasks.

Ideally, all three structures would be used in a classroom. Students would experience working together, competition, and learning on their own. However, the competitive and individualistic approaches are more commonly employed (Johnson & Johnson, 1975).

Cooperative Instruction for Handicapped Student Acceptance

Cooperative instruction has been proposed (Johnson & Johnson, 1980) to increase nonhandicapped student acceptance of handicapped students:

> A direct consequence of cooperative experiences is a positive cathexis in which the positive value attached to another person's efforts to help one achieve one's goals become generalized to that person. Thus, students like each other regardless of their individual differences, self esteem increases, and expectations toward reward-

TABLE 6.1
Goal Structures and Interpersonal Processes that Affect Learning

Cooperative	Competitive	Individualistic
High interaction	Low interaction	No interaction
Effective communication	No misleading, or threatening communication	No interaction
Facilitation of other's achievement	Obstruction of other's achievement	No interaction
Peer influence toward achievement	Peer influence against achievement	No interaction
Problem-solving conflict management	Win-lose conflict management	No interaction
High divergent and risk-taking thinking	Low divergent and risk-taking thinking	No interaction
High trust	Low trust	No interaction
High acceptance and support by peers	Low acceptance and support by peers	No interaction
High emotional involvement in and commitment to learning by almost all students	High emotional involvement in and commitment to learning by the few students who have a chance to win	No interaction
High utilization of resources of other students	No utilization of resources of other students	No interaction
Division of labor possible	Division of labor impossible	No interaction
Decreased fear of failure	Increased fear of failure	No interaction

From Johnson (1980). Group processes: Influences of student-student interactions on school outcomes. In. H. H. McMillan (Ed.), *The social psychology of school learning*. New York: Academic Press, p. 134.

ing and enjoyable future interactions between nonhandicapped and handicapped students are built (p. 94).

In contrast to cooperative instruction, competitive or individualistic structures are viewed as promoting rejection by nonhandicapped peers since in competitive situations students are only concerned about outperforming their peers and in the individualistic structure tend to ignore and avoid other students.

Efficacy of Cooperative Instruction

Numerous studies have been undertaken to explore the effects of cooperative versus competitive and individualistic learning (See reviews of Johnson & Johnson, 1974, 1979; Johnson, Maruyama, Johnson, Nelson, & Skon, 1981; Johnson, Johnson, & Maruyama, 1983). Efficacy studies supporting the effect of cooperative instruction on handicapped and nonhandicapped student interactions are a more recent trend and have involved instruction in academic and nonacademic tasks.

Rynders, Johnson, Johnson, & Schmidt (1980) used the cooperative, competitive, and individualistic structures to teach bowling. In this study, 12 trainable mentally retarded students and 18 nonhandicapped junior high school students were randomly assigned to a cooperative, competitive, or individualistic condition. Students bowled for 1 hour per week for 8 weeks and observers recorded the participants verbal interactions. Results indicated that significantly more interactions occurred among handicapped and nonhandicapped students in the cooperative situation. Sociometric ratings assigned to the handicapped students were also higher for this situation, as were the sociometric ratings the handicapped students assigned to their nonhandicapped classmates. Since the mentally retarded students were poor bowlers, the authors pointed out that positive changes in interpersonal attraction can still occur even when a group member's behavior does not facilitate a group goal.

Cooper, Johnson, Johnson, & Wilderson (1980) compared the effects of cooperative, competitive, and individualistic instruction in science, English, and geography. Thirty males and thirty females (19 of whom were black and 12 of whom were indentified by the school system as learning disabled or emotionally disturbed) were randomly assigned to one of the learning situations with stratifying for ethnicity, sex, and achievement level. The students worked together for 3 hours a day for 15 days. Sociometric testing indicated that students in the cooperative situation made more cross ethnic choices and more choices of learning disabled and emotionally disturbed students than students in the competitive or individualistic situation; those in the competitive situation also made more cross ethnic and cross handicapped choices than those in the individualistic situation.

Johnson and Johnson (1981) used cooperative learning with third graders in three classrooms. Of the 21 males and 19 females, 5 males and 3 females had been identified by the school as having severe learning and behavior problems; they were also rejected by their peers. Students participated in an instructional math unit for 25 minutes per day for 16 days in an individualistic or cooperative situation. Results indicated that in the cooperative situation there were significantly more interactions among handicapped and nonhandicapped students both during instructional time as well as during free time sessions. Sociometric testing also showed more nominations among handicapped and nonhandicapped students in the cooperative structure.

Johnson, Johnson, DeWeerdt, Lyons, & Zaidman (1983) recently studied the effects of cooperative learning with mentally retarded students who were in a self-contained classroom. These nine students were randomly assigned to the cooperative or individualistic condition along with 7th–grade nonhandicapped students. In each situation, students worked on a science unit for 10 days for 55 minutes per day. Results indicated there were no significant differences in achievement for the two groups, but significantly more interpersonal attraction and interaction among students in the cooperative situation were evidenced. There were no indications of students rejecting their handicapped peers.

In another study (Johnson & Johnson, 1983) 59 fourth graders, 12 of whom were learning disabled or had severe learning and behavior problems, were assigned to a cooperative, competitive, or individualistic learning situation. The students worked together for 60 minutes a day for 15 days on a social studies unit. The last 10 minutes of each work session was "free time" for the students; they could move around the classroom and engage anyone in play or work activities. Observers recorded interactions during this time period. Results indicated that there was more interaction between the handicapped and nonhandicapped students who were in the cooperative condition. Students in the cooperative group also liked each other more, and felt they provided more help for each other. Findings also suggested that participation in the cooperative group situation promoted higher self-attitudes or self esteem in handicapped and nonhandicapped students. At the same time, nonhandicapped students working with handicapped peers were better able to take the social perspective of handicapped students (the perspective-taking measure designed for this study required students be interviewed and tell a story about a typical school day for a child who had problems learning).

The efficacy of team learning approaches as a mechanism for increasing interactions among handicapped and nonhandicapped peers requires more study. Indeed the cooperative learning situation proposed by Johnson and Johnson (1975) has been tested the most; even in this case, however, because of the different student populations studied and the varied methodologies used to measure social outcomes of increased peer status, interpersonal attraction, and peer interaction, more confirming evidence seems necessary.

It has also been noted that some learners may be more cooperatively, competitively, or individualistically inclined, which may affect the outcomes of team or small group learning (Owens & Barnes, 1982). Similarly, group composition with respect to ability and personality may effect the ensuing interactions among students placed in the team or group situation (Webb, 1982). Differential effects on intra- and interpersonal behaviors of male or female students have also been evidenced (Crockenberg, Bryant, & Wilce, 1976) for cooperative vs. competitive learning environments. Also, training in small-group interaction alone may effect the outcome (Swing & Peterson, 1982). According to Sharan's review (1980), all of the team methods may differentially affect students' attitudes, achievement, and their relationships with racial groups. Consequently, it seems that all of the procedures must be studied more extensively to understand how they might affect handicapped students.

Training in Social Skills

A variety of behavioral procedures and techniques are available to develop, increase, and/or eliminate particular "targeted" student behaviors. These include the use of schedules of reinforcement, punishment (in the form of time out and negative attention), token economy systems, group contingency systems, modeling (live or symbolic), and cognitive behavioral techniques (coaching, self-reinforcement, self-instruction, self-evaluation). These interventions, mediated by teachers as well as peers, have been used to remedy a variety of problem behaviors in handicapped and nonhandicapped populations. Recently, researchers have become interested in using behavioral procedures to teach specific social skills to students.

The concept of "social skills" has been defined in somewhat different ways by various researchers. According to Foster and Ritchey (1979), social skills are "those responses which, within a given situation, prove effective or, in other words, maximize the probability of producing, maintaining or enhancing positive effects for the interactor" (p. 626). Combs and Slaby (1977) define social skill as "the ability to interact with others in a given social context in specific ways that are socially acceptable or valued and at the same time personally beneficial, mutually beneficial, or beneficial primarily to others" (p. 162). These authors include, "skills that are minimally acceptable according to social norms and that are not harmful to others," and "skills that are of primary benefit to others such as altruistic behaviors;" excluded are, "exploitive, deceitful or aggressive 'skills' which may be of individual benefit" (p. 162). Essentially, social skills are situation specific, learned verbal and nonverbal responses that elicit and/or reinforcement. See Van Hasselt, Hensen, Whitehill, & Bellack (1979) for a further discussion of definitions that have appeared in the literature.

The efforts of some researchers have been directed toward developing taxonomies of social skills. Some attempts to delineate skill components have been quite complex; others less so and taking the form of general categories of behavior. A representative list of possible skill components related to peer acceptance has been proposed by La Greca and Mesibov (1979). They break down social behavior into 9 areas: (1) enjoyment of interactions; (2) greeting; (3) joining; (4) inviting; (5) conversation; (6) sharing/cooperation; (7) play skills; (8) complimenting; and (9) appearance and grooming. These skills and their skill components appear in Table 6.2.

There is general agreement among researchers that handicapped students may be deficient in one or more social skills. There have also been numerous studies that have reported on the remediation of social skill deficits. However, most of the research dealing with training in social skills has utilized preschool or nonhandicapped populations (see reviews by Cartledge & Milburn, 1978; Gable, Strain, & Hendrickson, 1979; Gresham, 1981; Strain & Shores, 1977; and Van Hasselt, Hensen, Whitehill, & Bellack, 1979).

When researchers have initiated social skills training programs with handicapped students, most of the time they have worked with students in specialized or isolated settings. For example, Cooke and Apolloni (1976) increased the social interactions among learning disabled students in an experimental classroom. The students were taught behaviors of smiling, sharing, positive physical contacting, and verbal complimenting by trainers using instructions, modeling and praise. Similarly in another study (La Greca & Mesibov, 1981), learning disabled boys participating in a special summer program were taught how to initiate social interactions and communication-conversation skills using modeling, coaching, and behavioral rehearsal. Results indicated an improvement in these skills and increased interactions with normally interacting but learning disabled student groups also attending the program.

There are, however, very few reports about providing social skills training to handicapped students in a mainstreamed situation designed to increase positive interactions with nonhandicapped peers. Since other studies have evidenced the positive effects of training in social skills on the interactions among handicapped

TABLE 6.2
Areas of Interpersonal Functioning and Possible Skill Components

Skill Area	Components
Enjoyment of Interactions	Smile Laughing When to smile (e.g., having a good time, when saying "hello")
Greeting	Look at person Smile Use the person's name Greet nicely (e.g., "Hi," How are you?")

Joining	JOINING SEQUENCE
	Smile
	Look at the person
	Use their name
	Stand near-by
	Greet them
	Ask to join nicely (e.g., "Can I sit with you?")
	Ask a question to enter the conversation
	RESPONDING POSITIVELY WHEN OTHERS JOIN YOU
	Smile
	Acknowledge them nicely (e.ge., "Sure, come on.")
	Offer a reason if turning them down (e.g.,
	    "Sorry, we're in the middle of the game. You
	    can play the next one, though.")
	HANDLING REFUSALS
	Don't get mad
	Leave
	Join other peers or play alone

Inviting	INVITING SEQUENCE
	Initial approach, and greeting may be the same
	    as joining sequence
	Ask the person to do something with you (e.g.,
	    "Would you like to come over after school?")
	Set the date and time
	If person is busy, ask for another time
	RESPONDING POSITIVELY TO INVITATIONS
	Smile, look at person
	Accept nicely (e.g., "Sure!")
	If cannot accept, offer a reason or suggest
	    alternate plan
	HANDLING REFUSALS
	Don't get mad
	Ask for an alternate time/plan
	Leave

continued

TABLE 6.2 (*Continued*)

Skill Area	Components

Conversation	Smile
	Look most of the time, more when listening than talking
	Sit/stand near the person
	Use "normal" voice (e.g., speak clearly, not loud or soft)
	Ask questions
	  More open ended questions
	  Stick to topic of conversation
	  Intersperse questions with information about self (e.g., taking turns in the conversation)
	Talking more
	  Elaborate on responses to questions
	  Volunteer information about self, interests, activities
	Generating topics of conversation
	When someone talks, listen, ask questions

Sharing/Cooperation	Taking turns Following game rules Fairly deciding "who goes first" Offer help when needed Share possessions with others Being a "good winner/good loser" Responding to requests for help

Play Skills	Depends on the game
	  Learning the rules
	  Following rules
	  Practicing game skills

Complimenting	Look at the person Smile Make a positive statement (e.g., "I like the way you helped me, John.") Accepting compliments from others positively (e.g., smile, "Thank you.")
Appearance and Grooming	Hair: clean, neat (combed), acceptable style Face: clean Eyes: acceptable glasses (if applicable) Overall body: clean, smells good, appropriate range of weight for height Clothes: neat, clean, fit well, acceptably stylish

From La Greca and Mesibov (1979). Social skills intervention with learning disabled children: Selecting skills and implementing training. *Journal of Clinical Child Psychology,8,* 234-241.

students in specialized or segregated settings, this avenue of research seems promising. Furthermore, studies using behavioral procedures to eliminate undesirable student behaviors have shown an effect on peer acceptance. For example, in a study conducted in the regular classroom Csapo (1972) had peers model behaviors for students who had been labeled emotionally disturbed by their teachers and referred for special services. Peers also awarded tokens to them for good behaviors. Results showed inappropriate behaviors decreased and appropriate behaviors increased. Interactions were not recorded but peer models who formerly displayed overt criticism exhibited positive behaviors toward these students during and after the treatment.

In another investigation, Drabman, Spitalnik, and Spitalnik (1974) found token economy systems effectively decreased inappropriate behaviors displayed by "disruptive" students in a regular first grade classroom and increased the social status of the students.

Gresham (1981) concluded after a thoughtful review of over 75 research studies that: (1) there is a lack of understanding about which skills need to be selected for training and what the subsequent effect on the relationships between handicapped and nonhandicapped children will be; (2) it is not clear which social skills in which settings affect the social status of handicapped students; (3) evidence regarding the generalization and maintenance of trained social skills is "seriously deficient"; (4) since "children's social interaction might be a two-way street," behavioral procedures such as modeling, coaching, and role playing might also be used with nonhandicapped peers to train them to interact socially with handicapped peers in the regular classroom; and (5) future investigations must determine more clearly which training techniques are more or less successful for which type of handicapping condition.

POTENTIALLY EFFECTIVE PROCEDURES FOR MODIFYING STUDENT ATTITUDES

This section discusses some additional techniques or procedures that may be useful mechanisms for inducing a change in a student's attitudes and interactions. These include: (1) role playing; (2) peer tutoring; (3) bibliotherapy; and (4) game playing.

Role Playing

It is important to distinguish among role taking ability, role taking activity, and role playing. Kitano, Stiehl, and Cole (1978) define role taking as "a covert cognitive process of predicting another person's perspective" (p. 61). Role-taking ability is "the individual's cognitive capacity to anticipate another person's perspective when it differs, or is independent, from one's own" (p. 61). In contrast, role-taking activity "concerns the individual's employment of role-taking ability in a particular situation" (p. 61). A further distinction may be made between cognitive role-taking and affective role-taking. Enright and Lapsley (1980) define cognitive role-taking as "the child's ability to think about what the other is thinking," versus affective role-taking which is "the child's ability to understand another's internal, subjective, or feeling states" (p. 649). Finally, role playing is "the overt enactment of the role attributes (characteristics and behaviors) of another person" (Kitano, Stiehl, & Cole, 1978, p. 61).

Role-taking ability and activity have been described as social skills important for positive peer interactions. It has also been demonstrated that handicapped children may be deficient in these skills, although research on role-taking using handicapped populations is quite limited (see Chapter 4.) Based on their review of the literature, Kitano, Stiehl, and Cole (1978) concluded that further research is also necessary to clarify the ability of the nonhandicapped to take a handicapped person's role, and that there may be a gap between a nonhandicapped student's ability to take a handicapped student's role and their use of that ability or role-taking activity. These authors suggested that role training interventions can be developed in which handicapped students are trained to anticipate the perceptions of others about their actions. At the same time, training nonhandicapped students to perceive the feelings and needs of handicapped classmates may facilitate more positive interactions in the classroom.

Role playing and simulation activities about what it is like to have a handicap have been used fairly extensively as methods for modifying attitudes toward the handicapped held by peers as well as teachers. Frequently, role playing or simulation activities (the terms are used synonymously in the literature to refer to activities in which nonhandicapped individuals act out the part of a handicapped person) are part of a series of activities comprising an attitude modification program (Handlers & Austin, 1980; Jones et al., 1981); but the technique has also been effective when it has been used by itself.

For example, Clore and Jeffrey (1972) used direct and vicarious emotional role playing. One group of college students had to play the role of a person confined to a wheelchair. Subjects were told to imagine that they were victims of an auto accident resulting in paraplegia and were required to take a 25 minute wheelchair trip around campus (outlined to include using elevators, ramps, etc., and visiting the snack bar). Another group of vicarious role players walked 20 feet behind the role players and observed. After returning, participants wrote a 160-word description of their experience, which was later analyzed to determine their affective response to the task, and completed several attitudinal scales. Results indicated significantly more positive attitudes on the immediate posttesting and on a 4-month follow-up measure for both groups.

Role playing isn't always effective, however. In another study, college students in an introductory special education class selected a handicap (blindness, deafness, loss of dominant hand, confinement to a wheelchair), were required to simulate the disability for 8 hours, and to provide a written account of their experiences. No significant attitudinal changes were effected (Wilson & Alcorn, 1969). Similarly, Wilson (1971) found simulations did not modify attitudes toward deafness. Indeed in this experiment, after 2½ hours or simulating deafness while engaged in activities with nonhandicapped individuals, no significant differences were evidenced on a scale designed to measure attitudes toward deafness; but on a scale designed to measure the affective component of attitudes toward deaf persons (a semantic differential) the subjects were less positive than a control group.

Wright (1978) examined the findings for these role playing studies (Clore & Jeffrey, 1972; Wilson, 1971; Wilson & Alcorn, 1969) and expressed concern about the possibility that role playing could actually contribute to or reinforce a participant's stereotype of the handicaps if the experience is not a constructively guided one. From this standpoint, role playing would involve not only exposure to the disability with its inherent losses and difficulties but would also focus on the "possibilities for personal adaptation and change" (p. 181); the experience would be one of problem solving. Wright also recommended "assertive role playing." In this case the disabled and nondisabled participant play out antagonistic roles. For example, Wright suggested a confrontation between a blind person and office manager who refuses to hire him; the blind simulator must respond, argue his competency for the position, and negate the arguments presented by the employer about incompetencies related to the disability. Wright also advocated another form of role playing; in role reversal both participants play each role, and discuss the experience from a helping standpoint.

It seems advisable that future research efforts be directed toward clarifying the effect of constructively guided role playing. Since role playing may help to bridge the gap between role-taking ability and role-taking activity (Kitano, Stiehl, & Cole, 1978), it is particularly important to achieve a greater understanding of how best to conduct the procedure.

Peer Tutoring

Tutoring programs that use students as tutors or teachers for other students actually date back to the first century A.D. The procedure was common practice in one-room schools during the nineteenth and even twentieth centuries, and during the 1960s and 1970s, educators demonstrated a renewed interest in this approach (Allen, 1976; Paolitto, 1976).

Numerous studies have demonstrated the positive effect peer tutoring may have on the academic performance of both tutors and tutees (Bean & Luke, 1972; Erickson & Cromack, 1972; Morgan & Toy, 1970; Sharpley, Irvine, & Sharpley, 1983). Students have also been shown to accrue a variety of psychosocial benefits, such as improved motivation, self-concept, school attitude, and interpersonal skills (Allen & Feldman, 1973; Cloward, 1967; Gartner, Kohler, & Reissman, 1971; Lippitt & Lippitt, 1968).

Although not all the findings are positive, and data on the effects of variables such as age, sex, characteristics of the tutors and tutees, their training, and the training situation, must be more systematically gathered (Devin-Sheehan, Feldman, & Allen, 1976; Paolitto, 1976), peer tutoring seems to be an advantageous procedure for student tutors, tutees, and classroom teachers. (For a review of the literature on peer tutoring see Allen, 1976; Cohen, Kulik & Kulik, 1982; Gartner, Kohler, & Reissman, 1971.)

Recently, peer tutoring has been suggested as a mechanism to facilitate mainstreaming, since handicapped students may in this way receive more individualized help albeit from their peers (Bradfield et al., 1973). When this has been tried, the results have been positive. Mandoli, Mandoli, and McLaughlin (1982) trained the classmate of a learning disabled sixth grader to tutor his peer in spelling; results indicated a positive effect on the tutee's spelling achievement. Another study (McHale, Olley, Marcus, & Simeonsson, 1981) demonstrated that using nonhandicapped peer tutors (aged 6 to 9 years), who visited classrooms of retarded autistic children and coached them in a block-matching task, resulted in positive changes in the autistic students' behavior, including, for example, attending behaviors and increased tolerance for physical contact.

Several studies have demonstrated that handicapped students can also be effective teachers for each other. For example, learning disabled students in special classes (Epstein, 1978) and resource room attendees (Parson & Heward, 1979) successfully tutored their learning disabled peers in word recognition; and primary grade learning disabled students in a private school successfully taught their peers letter recognition (Drass & Jones, 1971).

Other studies have demonstrated that as a result of peer tutoring: aggressive and withdrawn tutors and tutees showed gains in self-concept and behavior (Lazerson, 1980); severely behaviorally disordered adolescents residing in a psychiatric hospital tutored each other and improved in spelling (Stowitschek, Hecimovic, Stowitschek, & Shores, 1982); incarcerated juvenile delinquents successfully taught computational mathematics to incarcerated juvenile delinquents who had been identified as having a learning disability (Kane & Alley, 1980).

The peer tutoring procedure has also been thought to be a helpful mechanism for promoting interactions among handicapped and nonhandicapped students (McCarthy & Stodden, 1979). However, few studies have endeavored to provide empirical support for this notion. Donder and Nietupski (1981) provided 3 hours of training to seventh-grade nonhandicapped volunteers; the goal was for the nonhandicapped tutors to teach age-appropriate playground recreation skills to moderately mentally retarded peers and to facilitate positive peer interactions between retarded and nonhandicapped students. Substantial increases in both were observed. The results of this investigation support tutoring as a mechanism to achieve greater acceptance of the handicapped by nonhandicapped peers.

Clearly, the possible effects of peer tutoring on nonhandicapped acceptance of handicapped students and handicapped students' acceptance of each other (see Chapter 4 for a discussion of prejudice among handicapped students toward each other) can only be speculated. According to the results for other programs that have incorporated experiences and knowledge (which would seemingly be inherent to peer tutoring), positive attitudinal changes could very likely be produced.

Peer tutoring is also a component of team learning approaches; a method which holds promise for increasing peer interactions, peer tutoring seems further supported as a method for changing peer attitudes toward each other. At the same time it must be recognized that since the perceptions of competence and prestige fostered by the tutor role (Bierman & Furman, 1981) could lead to a further devaluation of the handicapped tutee, it seems worthwhile to explore the attitudinal effects of peer tutoring.

Training is undoubtedly an important variable in peer tutoring programs. Because training peers as tutors may be a time consuming effort for the teacher, it should be pointed out that generative programs have been developed. When this procedure is used, peer tutors are trained as a result of their observations of peer tutoring techniques used by other students (see Brown, Fenrick & Klemme, 1971; Starlin, 1971; Thiagarajan, 1973).

Bibliotherapy

Bibliotherapy involves three steps: (1) identification; (2) catharsis; and (3) insight. Readers or listeners identify with the character in the story, and vicariously experience the motivation, conflicts, emotions, and so on of the character, leading to a catharsis. Identification and catharsis lead to insight; when nonhandicapped students listen to or read stories about handicapped children the insights they develop may lead to more positive attitudes and interactions.

Although there are few reports, the use of children's books has been explored as a methodology for persuading students to be more positive toward racial and ethnic groups. For example, Litcher and Johnson (1969) found using multiethnic readers resulted in second-grade students developing more positive attitudes toward black persons. However, in another study (Koeller, 1977), the attitudes of sixth graders were not affected by children's stories about Mexican-Americans.

Similarily, there have not been many reports on the efficacy of using children's literature to modify attitudes toward handicapped persons, and, not unlike the attempts for modifying racial and ethnic attitudes, the results are mixed.

Salend and Moe (1983) compared the effects of reading books about handicapped students to a class versus reading books and combining this listening activity with group discussions, simulations, and explanations about handicapping conditions on the attitudes of fourth, fifth, and sixth graders. Results of the administration of an adjective checklist indicated a significant difference in the attitudes of the students who had been read to and engaged in the accompanying activities. There was no significant effect in the attitudes of the students who had just listened to the stories.

Leung (1980) also used stories combined with discussions in an effort to modify primary grade students' attitudes toward handicapped students. In this investigation of 3 primary-grade classes, each containing two handicapped students, testing indicated that the program resulted in classmates expressing significantly more favorable attitudes toward handicapped peers. However, observational data indicated there was no relationship between the program and the number of social interactions among handicapped and nonhandicapped students in the participating classes. Furthermore, the handicapped students' social status (measured using a sociometric technique) did not improve.

Beardsley (1981) read seven stories about handicapped children to selected third grade classrooms containing mainstreamed handicapped children. One book was read every other day. Attitudinal testing indicated there was no change in the attitudes the nonhandicapped students evidenced toward handicapped classmates. However, as Beardsley pointed out, since the students demonstrated essentially positive attitudes on the pre-testing, perhaps because the instrument was insensitive to the students' attitudes, or because the students hadn't developed any negative attitudes, major attitudinal shifts could not be expected to occur on post-testing.

Bibliotherapy may or may not alter childrens' attitudes. It seems more likely to be effective when it is used in conjunction with discussion including explanations about handicapped persons. One point needs to be made: Leung's findings showed that there were no significant differences in the interactions between handicapped and nonhandicapped students even though there were differences on the attitudinal post-testing. This may also be the case in other studies; but we don't know because student interactions have not commonly been observed before, during, or after the implementation of attitude modification programs. (See Greenbaum, Varas, & Markel, 1980 for a bibliography of stories about handicapped individuals.)

Game Playing

Game-playing activities are a component of team learning approaches and as such have been used to encourage interracial interactions and friendships. As indicated in a preceding section, team learning may also be effective in promoting interactions with handicapped students.

Recently, athletic activities have been advocated to facilitate interactions among handicapped and nonhandicapped students. According to Marlowe (1979), because retarded students are more like the nonhandicapped in the area of motor skills, motor-related activities represent a particularly viable methodology for facilitating interactions between these groups.

In the games analysis procedure developed by Morris (1976), games are structured to take into consideration the individual motor skill differences evidenced by players and to facilitate particular social and/or emotional goals. Morris (1976) used this procedure to increase the social acceptance of an integrated, but socially rejected, 10-year-old mentally retarded student. Classmates involved in the games analysis procedure became familiar with how games could be played in an adapted form which would consider the motoric skill levels of the individual participants. The students played softball, kickball, basketball and volleyball together in their adapted format for 5 weeks. Observational data indicated positive interactions with nonhandicapped peers increased. Sociometric data supported a significant increase in peer status three weeks after the program had ended.

The games analysis procedure was also used by Marlowe (1980) with a gender disturbed 10-year-old who was the least accepted male in the class. After 7 weeks of playing adapted versions of softball, kickball, etc., sociometric testing indicated a significant gain in peer status; a follow-up 8 months later showed this gain was maintained.

A variety of play experiences have been advocated for handicapped and nonhandicapped preschool populations to increase a variety of skills as well as peer interaction. Therefore, it seems play may be a useful procedure for those in elementary school. In one experiment, playing the Bean Bag Game together facilitated interactions among educable mentally retarded children who were integrated into regular classrooms and their nonhandicapped classmates (Aloia, Beaver, & Pettus, 1978).

Another effort, designed to promote positive attitudes toward autistic students, required second and third graders to play with autistic children. The nonhandicapped students were simply told that the autistic children did not know how to play, that they should teach them, and they could engage in any play or game activities they chose. Five daily thirty minute play sessions were conducted. The results of pre- and posttesting indicated that the students were initially positive toward the autistic group and that these positive attitudes were maintained after their experiences. The experience also increased their understanding of autistic children (McHale & Simeonsson, 1980).

One hopes that future game playing experiments with elementary-aged populations will clarify the extent of their usefulness as a mechanism for modifying attitudes and interactions among students. It also may be found that these strategies will be more useful when they are coupled with an informational component. Evidence with preschool students suggests that the type of materials, toys, and activities provided to students can influence social behavior. For example, Quilitch and Risley (1973) categorized social (game of checkers) and isolate toys (Tinker Toys), and found that when children were provided with ''social toys,'' there was a dramatic increase in the number of prosocial interactions. Structured play experiences have been used to increase interactions between handicapped and nonhandicapped preschoolers (Odom, Jenkins, Speltz, & DeKlyen, 1982). Similar experiments with elementary-age handicapped and nonhandicapped students may be a good idea.

Possible Influence of Classroom Organization and Climate

A variety of classroom organizational characteristics have been shown to affect the attitudes and interactions of peers in regular classroom settings. However, the effects of such variables as class size, seating arrangements, etc., have not been explored in relationship to the effect they might have on nonhandicapped peer attitudes toward, and interactions with handicapped students. Understanding the influence of a variety of environmental conditions on student attitudes and interactions must be considered carefully in future research. These variables are briefly reviewed in the following paragraphs. The reader is cautioned that these variables have been assessed in some cases in one or just a few studies and are reported here because of their potential implications. Inadequate replication mitigates against over-interpreting.

Class Size.   The number of students in a classroom may effect the nature and number of interactions that occur among classmates. For example, Hallinan (1979) reported that in larger classes, children form more "best" friendships and that there are fewer isolates or unpopular students than there are in small classes.

Seating Arrangement.   The seat assigned to a student by the classroom teacher may affect how the student is perceived by his classmates. Schwebel and Cherlin (1972) found students assigned seats in the front of the class are more positively perceived by their peers.

Classroom Social Structure.   The characteristics of classmates may effect classroom interactions. Rosenfield, Sheehan, Marcus, & Stephan (1981) examined classroom variables that might be conducive to developing positive interethnic relations. Their findings indicated that group equality in terms of social class and achievement level and the percentage of minority group members present in a group contribute to the number of interactions that will occur among students.

Classroom Organization.   Whether or not a classroom is organized multidimensionally (wherein students work individually on a variety of different tasks and are individually evaluated), or unidimensionally (wherein students are grouped to work on fewer different kinds of tasks) may also affect student perceptions about peers (Rosenholtz & Rosenholtz, 1981; Simpson, 1981). The amount of teacher-directed classroom activity may also influence the positivity of peer interactions (Huston-Stein, Frederick-Cofer, & Susman, 1977). In highly structured classrooms where activities are largely teacher directed, students may be more likely to engage in fewer prosocial behaviors toward peers including, for example, cooperation, helping, and empathy.

Teacher Management Skills.   Styles of classroom management may also be linked to the peer interactions. In classes where teachers have good management skills, students may exhibit less deviant behavior (Borg, Langer, & Wilson, 1975). This may in turn affect peer perceptions of handicapped students, since it appears that the deviant behaviors they exhibit contribute substantially to their rejection by peers (see Chapter 4). Teachers may require training in group processes to facilitate peer interactions (Schmuck, 1968).

Open versus Traditional Schools.   Open schools have been noted to have many positive effects on the social and psychological development of students (Giaconia & Hedges, 1982; Horwitz, 1979). It is not clear how attendance in an open school might affect the status assigned to handicapped students. However, it appears that open classrooms affect the pattern of student friendships such that there are fewer social isolates, and a more even distribution of popularity; on the other hand it appears that students in traditional classes have more friends (Hallinan, 1976). The reader may recall that in a few studies that have attempted to study the effects of open class attendance on the handicapped student status reported in Chapter 4, the results have not been encouraging.

SUMMARY

Several procedures have been described for modifying teacher and student attitudes toward handicapped students. Some potentially efficacious procedures have also been discussed. There are, however, many unanswered questions surrounding the task of attitude modification. For example, future research must be directed toward understanding what types of experience and knowledge should be incorporated into programs for teachers and students. Given a particular classroom situation, which method might prove to be most useful for modifying student attitudes? Which method will work best for teachers? And might different approaches be better to modify attitudes toward some handicaps but not others?

Individual differences in attitudes before treatment must also be considered. For example, if a teacher or student has a positive attitude before being exposed to an attitude modification project, can they be persuaded in a negative direction? The interaction of such variables as age, sex, and attitudinal predisposition deserve further exploration. (The relationships of such factors to attitudes are discussed in Chapter 5.)

It is important to investigate whether attitudinal changes demonstrated at immediate post-testing are maintained over time. Do teachers and students continue to exhibit positivity? Usually post   posttesting has not been undertaken in studies of teachers. When it has been part of student-oriented projects, the results have not been encouraging (Lilly, 1971; Rucker & Vincenzo, 1970; Westervelt & McKinney, 1980). Although Ballard et al. (1977) found that the gains in social status of mentally retarded students who participated in a small group experience were demonstrated (using a sociometric procedure) after 4 weeks, it is important to know if they were maintained for the school year or at least for some significant length of time.

The generalization of positive attitudes toward different exceptionality groups must be questioned. If teachers and students become more accepting of mentally retarded students, will they also be more accepting of learning disabled pupils? Is there a relationship between the severity of a handicap and generalizability? That is, since mental retardation is generally perceived as being more serious than learning disability and is often placed lower on the acceptance hierarchy (see Chapter 4), is it likely that a person who becomes more accepting of mental retardation will also be more positive toward the lesser handicap of learning disability?

Most attitude modification studies have used either an attitudinal scale or a sociometric procedure to demonstrate their effectness. Future research must aim toward clarifying the relationship of expressed positivity on these measures and actual behavioral changes on the part of peers in the classroom. The use of observational data such as are commonly gathered for behavioral interventions and which have been used in efficacy studies for cooperative classroom instruction is suggested. When observational data are recorded, there is also a need to collect maintenance data; follow-up observations must also be undertaken to explore the durability of change effected when behavioral strategies and cooperative classroom procedures have been carried out. Similarly, changes in teacher behaviors must be documented by the collection of observational data.

REFERENCES

Alberto, P. A., Castricone, N. R., & Cohen, S. B. (1978). Mainstreaming: Implications for training regular class teachers. *Education and Training of the Mentally Retarded, 13,* 90–92.

Alexander, C., & Strain, P. S. (1978). A review of educators' attitudes toward handicapped children and the concept of mainstreaming. *Psychology in the Schools, 15,* 390–396.

Allen, V. L. (1976). *Children as teachers: Theory and research on tutoring.* New York: Academic Press.

Allen, V. L., & Feldman, R. S. (1973). Learning through tutoring: Low-achieving children as tutors. *Journal of Experimental Education, 42,* 1–5.

Allport, G. W. (1958). *The nature of prejudice.* New York: Doubleday Anchor Books.

Aloia, G. F., Beaver, R. J., & Pettus, W. F. (1978). Increasing initial interactions among integrated emr students and their nonretarded peers in a game-playing situation. *American Journal of Mental Deficiency, 82,* 573–579.

Anthony, W. A. (1972). Societal rehabilitation: Changing society's attitude toward the physically and mentally disabled. *Rehabilitation Psychology, 19,* 117–126.

Aronson, E., Stephan, C., Sikes, J., Blaney, N., & Snapp, M. (1978). *The jigsaw classroom.* Beverly Hills, CA: Sage Publications.

Austin, D. E., Powell, L. G., & Martin, D. W. (1981). Modifying attitudes towards handicapped individuals in a classroom setting. *The Journal for Special Education, 17,* 135–141.

Ballard, M., Corman, L., Gottlieb, J., & Kaufman, M. J. (1977). Improving the social status of mainstreamed retarded children. *Journal of Educational Psychology, 69,* 605–611.

Barclay, J. R. (1967). Effecting behavior change in the elementary classroom: An exploratory study. *Journal of Counseling Psychology, 14,* 240–247.

Bean, R., & Luke, C. (1972). As a teacher I've been learning. *Journal of Reading, 16,* 128–132.

Beardsley, D. A. (1981/82). Using books to change attitudes toward the handicapped among third graders. *Journal of Experimental Education, 50,* 52–55.

Bierman, K. L., & Furman, W. (1981). Effects of role and assignment rationale on attitudes formed during peer tutoring. *Journal of Educational Psychology, 73,* 33–40.

Blaney, N. T., Stephan, C., Rosenfield, D., Aronson, E., & Sikes, J. (1977). Interdependence in the classroom: A field study. *Journal of Educational Psychology, 69,* 121–128.

Borg, W. R., Langer, P., & Wilson, J. (1975). Teacher classroom management skills and pupil behavior. *Journal of Experimental Education, 44,* 52–58.

Bradfield, R. H., Brown, J., Kaplan, P., Rickert, E., & Stannard, R. (1973). The special child in the regular classroom. *Exceptional Children, 39,* 384–390.

Brooks, B. L., & Bransford, L. A. (1971). Modification of teachers' attitudes toward exceptional children. *Exceptional Children, 38,* 259–260.

Brown, L., Fenrick, N., & Klemme, H. (1971). Trainable pupils learn to teach each other. *Teaching Exceptional Children, 4,* 18–24.

Buttery, T. J. (1978). Affective response to exceptional children by students preparing to be teachers. *Perceptual and Motor Skills, 46,* 288–290.

Buttery, T. J. (1981). Pre-service teachers' affective perceptions on mainstreamed children. *College Student Journal, 15,* 74–78.

Carpenter, R. L., & Robson, D. L. (1979). P. L. 94–142: Perceived knowledge, expectations, and early implementation. *Journal of Special Education, 13,* 307–314.

Cartledge, G., & Milburn, J. F. (1978). The case for teaching social skills in the classroom: A review. *Review of Educational Research, 48,* 133–156.

Chennault, M. (1967). Improving the social acceptance of unpopular educable mentally retarded pupils in special classes. *American Journal of Mental Deficiency, 72,* 455–458.

Cleland, C. C., & Chambers, I. L. (1959). The effect of institutional tours on attitudes of high school seniors. *American Journal of Mental Deficiency, 64,* 124–130.

Clore, G. L., & Jeffrey, K. M. (1972). Emotional role playing, attitude change, and attraction toward a disabled person. *Journal of Personality and Social Psychology, 23,* 105–111.

Cloward, R. D. (1967). Studies in tutoring. *Journal of Experimental Education, 36,* 14–25.

Cohen, P. A., Kulik, J. A., & Kulik, C. C, (1982). Educational outcomes of tutoring: A meta-analysis of findings. *American Educational Research Journal, 19,* 237–248.

Combs, M. L., & Slaby, D. A. (1977). Social skills training with children. In B. B. Lahey & A. E. Kazdin (Eds.), *Advances in Clinical Child Psychology,* (Vol. 1). New York: Plenum Press.

Cooke, T. P., & Apolloni, T. (1976). Developing positive social-emotional behaviors: A study of training and generalization effects. *Journal of Applied Behavior Analysis, 9,* 65–78.

Cooper, L., Johnson, D. W., Johnson, R., & Wilderson, F. (1980). The effects of cooperative, competitive, and individualistic experiences on interpersonal attraction among heterogeneous peers. *The Journal of Social Psychology, 111,* 243–252.

Crockenburg, S. B., Bryant, B. K., & Wilce, L. S. (1976). The effects of cooperatively and competitively structured learning environments on inter- and intra-personal behavior. *Child Development, 47,* 386–396.

Croft, R. G., Stimpson, D. V., Ross, W. L., Bray, R. M., & Breglio, V. J. (1969). Comparison of attitude changes elicited by line and videotape classroom presentations. *Audio Visual Communication Review, 17,* 315–321.

Csapo, M. (1972). Peer models reverse the "one bad apple spoils the barrel theory." *Teaching Exceptional Children, 5,* 20–24.

Dailey, J. L., & Halpin, G. (1981). Modifying undergraduates' attitudes toward the handicapped by videotapes. *Journal of Special Education, 15,* 333–339.

Deutsch, M. (1949). A theory of cooperation and competition. *Human Relations, 2,* 129–152.

Deutsch, M. (1962). Cooperation and trust: Some theoretical notes. In M. Jones (Ed.), *Nebraska symposium on motivation* (Vol. 10). Lincoln, NB: University of Nebraska Press.

Devin-Sheehan, L., Feldman, R. S., & Allen, V. L. (1976). Research on children tutoring children: A critical review. *Review of Educational Research, 46,* 355–385.

DeVries, D. L., Edwards, K. J., & Fennessey, G. M. (1974). *Using teams-games-tournaments (TGT) in the classroom.* Baltimore, MD: Johns Hopkins University, Center for Social Organization of Schools.

DeVries, D. L., Edwards, K. J., & Slavin, R. E. (1978). Biracial learning teams and race relations in the classroom: Four field experiments using teams-games-tournaments. *Journal of Educational Psychology, 70,* 356–362.

DeVries, D. L., & Slavin, R. E. (1978). Teams-games-tournaments (TGT): Review of ten classroom experiments. *Journal of Research and Development in Education, 12,* 28–38.

Donaldson, J., & Martinson, M. C. (1977). Modifying attitudes toward physically disabled persons. *Exceptional Children, 44,* 337–341.

Donder, D., & Nietupski, J. (1981). Nonhandicapped adolescents teaching playground skills to their mentally retarded peers: Toward a less restrictive middle school environment. *Education and Training of the Mentally Retarded, 16,* 270–276.

Drabman, R., Spitalnik, R., & Spitalnik, K. (1974). Sociometric and disruptive behavior as a function of four types of token reinforcement programs. *Journal of Applied Behavior Analysis, 7,* 93–101.

Drass, S. D., & Jones, R. L. (1971). Learning disabled children as behavior modifiers. *Journal of Learning Disabilities, 4,* 16–23.

Efron, R. E., & Efron, H. Y. (1967). Measurement of attitudes toward the retarded and an application with educators. *American Journal of Mental Deficiency, 72,* 100–107.

Enright, R. D., & Lapsley, D. K. (1980). Social role-taking: A review of the constructs, measures, and measurement properties. *Review of Educational Research, 50,* 647–674.

Epstein, L. (1978). The effects of intraclass peer tutoring on the vocabulary development of learning disabled children. *Journal of Learning Disabilities, 11,* 63–66.

Erickson, M. R., & Cromack, T. (1972). Evaulating a tutoring program. *Journal of Experimental Education, 41,* 27–31.

Foster, S. L., & Ritchey, W. L. (1979). Issues in the assessment of social competence in children. *Journal of Applied Behavior Analysis, 12,* 625–638.

Frith, G. H., & Edwards, R. (1981). Misconceptions of regular classroom teachers about physically handicapped students. *Exceptional Children, 48,* 182–184.

Gable, R. A., Strain, P. S., & Hendrickson, J. M. (1979). Strategies for improving the status and social behavior of learning disabled children. *Learning Disability Quarterly, 2,* 33–39.

Gartner, A., Kohler, M., & Reissman, F. (1971). *Children teach children.* New York: Harper.

Giaconia, R. M., & Hedges, L. V. (1982). Identifying features of effective open education. *Review of Educational Research, 52,* 579–602.

Gickling, E. E., & Theobald, J. T. (1975). Mainstreaming: Affect or effect. *Journal of Special Education, 9,* 317–328.

Glass, R. M., & Meckler, R. S. (1972). Preparing elementary teachers to instruct mildly handicapped children in regular classrooms: A summer workshop. *Exceptional Children, 39,* 152–156.

Goodman, H., Gottlieb, J., & Harrison, R. H. (1972). Social acceptance of emrs intergrated into a nongraded school. *American Journal of Mental Deficiency, 76,* 412–417.

Gottlieb, J. (1980). Improving attitudes toward retarded children using group discussion. *Exceptional Children, 47,* 106–111.

Gottlieb, J., Cohen, L., & Goldstein, L. (1974). Social contact and personal adjustment as variables relating to attitudes toward emr children. *Training School Bulletin, 71,* 9–16.

Greenbaum, J., Varas, M., & Markel, G. (1980). Using books about handicapped children. *The Reading Teacher, 33,* 416–419.

Greenwald, A. G., Brock, T. C., & Ostrom, T. M. (Eds.). (1968). *Psychological foundations of attitudes.* New York: Academic Press.

Gresham, F. M. (1981). Social skills training with handicapped children: A review. *Review of Educational Research, 51,* 139–176.

Hallinan, M. T. (1976). Friendship patterns in open and traditional classrooms. *Sociology of Education, 49,* 254–265.

Hallinan, M. T. (1979). Structural effects on children's friendships and cliques. *Social Psychology Quarterly, 42,* 43–54.

Handlers, A., & Austin, K. (1980). Improving attitudes of high school students toward handicapped peers. *Exceptional Children, 47,* 228–229.

Hansell, S., & Slavin, R. E. (1981). Cooperative learning and the structure of interracial friendships. *Sociology of Education, 54,* 98–106.

Harasymiw, S. J., & Horne, M. D. (1976). Teacher attitudes toward handicapped children and regular class integration. *Journal of Special Education, 10,* 393–400.

Higgs, R. W. (1975). Attitude formation—contact or information? *Exceptional Children, 41,* 496–497.

Homans, G. C. (1950). *The human group.* New York: Harcourt, Brace & World.

Horne, M. D. (1983). Elementary classroom teacher attitudes toward mainstreaming. *The Exceptional Child, 30,* 93–98.

Horwitz, R. A. (1979). Psychological effects of the ''open classroom.'' *Review of Educational Research, 49,* 71–86.

Hovland, C. I., & Weiss, W. (1952). The influences of source credibility on communication effectiveness. *Public Opinion Quarterly, 15,* 635–650.

Huston-Stein, A., Friedrich-Cofer, L., & Susman, E. J. (1977). The relation of classroom structure to social behavior, imaginative play, and self-regulation of economically disadvantaged children. *Child Development, 48,* 908–916.

Jaffe, J. (1972). The effects of work conferences on attitudes towards the mentally retarded. *Rehabilitation Counseling Bulletin, 15,* 220–227.

Johnson, A. B., & Cartwright, C. A. (1979). The roles of information and experience in improving teachers' knowledge and attitudes about mainstreaming. *Journal of Special Education, 13,* 453–462.

Johnson, D. W. (1980). Group processes: Influences of student-student interaction on school outcomes. In J. H. McMillan (Ed.), *The social psychology of school learning.* New York: Academic Press.

Johnson, D. W., & Johnson, R. T. (1974). Instructional goal structure: Cooperative, competitive or individualistic. *Review of Educational Research, 44,* 213–240.

Johnson, D. W., & Johnson, R. T. (1975). *Learning together and alone: Cooperation, competition, and individualization.* Englewood Cliffs, NJ: Prentice-Hall.

Johnson, D. W., & Johnson, R. T. (Eds.). (1978). Social interdependence within instruction. *Journal of Research and Development in Education, 12,* (1).

Johnson, D. W., & Johnson, R. T. (1979). Conflict in the classroom: Controversy and learning. *Review of Educational Research, 49,* 51–70.

Johnson, D. W., & Johnson, R. T. (1980). Integrating handicapped students into the mainstream. *Exceptional Children, 47,* 90–98.

Johnson, D. W., Johnson, R. T., & Maruyama, G. (1983). Interdependence and attraction among heterogeneous and homogeneous individuals: A theoretical formulation and meta-analysis of the research. *Review of Educational Research, 53,* 5–54.

Johnson, D. W., Maruyama, G., Johnson, R. T., Nelson, D., & Skon, L. (1981). Effects of cooperative, competitive, and individualistic goal structures on achievement: A meta-analysis. *Psychological Bulletin, 89,* 47–62.

Johnson, R. T., & Johnson, D. W. (1981). Building friendships between handicapped and nonhandicapped students: Effects of cooperative and individualistic instruction. *American Educational Research Journal, 18,* 415–423.

Johnson, R. T., & Johnson, D. W. (1983). Effects of cooperative, competitive and individualistic learning experiences in social development. *Exceptional Children, 49,* 323–329.

Johnson, R. T., Johnson, D. W., DeWeerdt, N., Lyons, V., & Zaidman, B. (1983). Integrating severely adaptively handicapped seventh-grade students into constructive relationships with peers in science class. *American Journal of Mental Deficiency, 87,* 611–618.

Jones, T. W., Sowell, V. M., Jones, J. K., & Butler, L. G. (1981). Changing children's perceptions of handicapped people. *Exceptional Children, 47,* 365–368.

Jordan, J. E., & Proctor, D. I. (1969). Relationships between knowledge of exceptional children, kind and amount of experience with them, and teacher attitudes toward their classroom integration. *Journal of Special Education, 3,* 433–439.

Kane, B. J., & Alley, G. R. (1980). A peer-tutored, instructional management program in computational mathematics for incarcerated, learning disabled juvenile delinquents. *Journal of Learning Disabilities, 13,* 148–151.

Kitano, M. K., Stiehl, J., & Cole, J. T. (1978). Role taking: Implications for special education. *Journal of Special Education, 12,* 59–74.

Koeller, S. (1977). The effect of listening to excerpts from children's stories about Mexican-Americans on the attitudes of sixth graders. *Journal of Educational Research, 70,* 329–334.

Kuhn, J. (1971). A comparison of teachers' attitudes toward blindness and exposure to blind children. *The New Outlook, 65,* 337–340.

La Greca, A. M., & Mesibov, G. B. (1979). Social skills intervention with learning disabled children: Selecting skills and implementing training. *Journal of Clinical Child Psychology, 8,* 234–241.

La Greca, A. M., & Mesibov, G. B. (1981). Facilitating interpersonal functioning with peers in learning disabled children. *Journal of Learning Disabilities, 14,* 197–199, 238.

Larrivee, B. (1981). Effect of inservice training intensity on teachers' attitudes toward mainstreaming. *Exceptional Children, 48,* 34–39.

Lazar, A. L., Gensley, J. T., & Orpet, R. E. (1971). Changing attitudes of young mentally gifted children toward handicapped persons. *Exceptional Children, 37,* 600–602.

Lazerson, D. B. (1980). "I must be good if I can teach!"—Peer tutoring with aggressive and withdrawn children. *Journal of Learning Disabilities, 13,* 43–48.

Leung, E. K. (1980). *Evaluation of a children's literature program designed to facilitate the social integration of handicapped children into regular elementary classrooms.* 1979. *Dissertation Abstracts International, 40,* 4528-A.

Leyser, Y., Abrams, P., & Lipscomb, E. (1982). Modifying attitudes of prospective elementary teachers toward mainstreaming. *Journal for Special Education, 18,* 1–10.

Leyser, Y., & Gottlieb, J. (1980). Improving the social status of rejected pupils. *Exceptional Children, 46,* 459–461.

Lilly, M. S. (1971). Improving social acceptance of low sociometric status, low achieving students. *Exceptional Children, 37,* 341–348.

Lippitt, R., & Lippitt, P. (1968). Cross-age helpers. *Todays Education, 57,* 24–26.

Litcher, J. H., & Johnson, D. W. (1969). Changes in attitudes toward Negroes of white elementary school students after use of multiethnic readers. *Journal of Educational Psychology, 60,* 148–152.

Lombardi, T. P., Meadowcroft, P., & Strasburger, R. (1982). Modifying teacher trainers' attitudes toward mainstreaming. *Exceptional Children, 48,* 544–545.

Mandoli, M., Mandoli, P., & McLaughlin, T. F. (1982). Effects of same-age peer tutoring on the spelling performance of a mainstreamed elementary ld student. *Learning Disability Quarterly, 5,* 185–189.

Marlowe, M. (1979). The games analysis intervention: A procedure to increase the peer acceptance and social adjustment of a retarded child. *Education and Training of the Mentally Retarded, 14,* 262–268.

Marlowe, M. (1980). Games analysis treatment of social isolation in a gender disturbed boy. *Behavioral Disorders, 6,* 41–50.

Martino, L., & Johnson, D. W. (1979). Cooperative and individualistic experiences among disabled and normal children. *The Journal of Social Psychology, 107,* 177–183.

McCarthy, R. M., & Stodden, R. A. (1979). Mainstreaming secondary students: A peer tutoring model. *Teaching Exceptional Children, 11,* 162–163.

McHale, S. M., Olley, J. G., Marcus, L. M., & Simeonsson, R. J. (1981). Nonhandicapped peers as tutors for autistic children. *Exceptional Children, 48,* 263–265.

McHale, S. M., & Simeonsson, R. J. (1980). Effects of interaction on nonhandicapped children's attitudes toward autistic children. *American Journal of Mental Deficiency, 85,* 18–24.

Miller, M., Armstrong, S., & Hagan, M. (1981). Effects of teaching on elementary students' attitudes toward handicaps. *Education and Training of the Mentally Retarded, 16,* 110–113.

Morgan, R. F., & Toy, T. B. (1970). Learning by teaching: A student-to-student compensatory tutoring program in a rural school system and its relevance to the educational cooperative. *Psychological Record, 20,* 159–169.

Morris, G. S. D. (1976). *How to change the games children play.* Minneapolis, MN: Burgess.

Morris, P. S., & McCauley, R. W. (1977). Placement of handicapped children by Canadian mainstream administrators and teachers: A Rucker-Gable survey. Paper presented at the *Annual International Convention of the Council for Exceptional Children,* Atlanta, GA. (ERIC Document Reproduction Service No. ED 139 139)

Naor, M., & Milgram, R. M. (1980). Two preservice strategies for preparing regular class teachers for mainstreaming. *Exceptional Children, 47,* 126–129.

Odom, S. L., Jenkins, J. R., Speltz, M. L., & DeKlyen, M. (1982). Promoting social integration of young children at risk for learning disabilities. *Learning Disability Quarterly, 5,* 379–387.

Orlansky, M. (1979). Active learning and student attitudes toward exceptional children. *Exceptional Children, 46,* 49–52.

Owens, L., & Barnes, J. (1982). The relationships between cooperative, competitive, and individualistic learning preferences and students' perceptions of classroom learning atmosphere. *American Educational Research Journal, 19,* 182–200.

Panda, K. C., & Bartel, N. R. (1972). Teacher perception of exceptional children. *The Journal of Special Education, 6,* 261–266.

Paolitto, P. P. (1976). The effect of cross-age tutoring on adolescence: An inquiry into theoretical assumptions *Review of Educational Research, 46,* 215–237.

Parish, T. S., Eads, G. M., Reece, N. H., & Piscitello, M. A. (1977). Assessment and attempted modification of future teachers' attitudes toward handicapped children. *Perceptual and Motor Skills, 44,* 540–542.

Parson, L. R., & Heward, W. L. (1979). Training peers to tutor: Evaluation of a tutor training package for primary learning disabled students. *Journal of Applied Behavior Analysis, 12,* 309–310.

Peterson, G. F. (1974). Factors related to the attitudes of nonretarded children toward their emr peers. *American Journal of Mental Deficiency, 79,* 412–416.

Quilitch, H. R., & Risley, T. R. (1973). The effects of play materials on social play. *Journal of Applied Behavior Analysis, 6,* 573–578.

Rapier, J., Adelson, R., Carey, R., & Croke, K. (1972). Changes in children's attitudes toward the physically handicapped. *Exceptional Children, 39,* 219–223.

Rosenfield, D., Sheehan, D. S., Marcus, M., & Stephan, W. G. (1981). Classroom structure and prejudice in desegregated schools. *Journal of Educational Psychology, 73,* 17–26.

Rosenholtz, S. J., & Rosenholtz, S. H. (1981). Classroom organization and the perception of ability. *Sociology of Education, 54,* 132–140.

Rucker, C. N., & Vincenzo, F. M. (1970). Maintaining social acceptance gains made by mentally retarded children. *Exceptional Children, 36,* 679–680.

Rynders, J. E., Johnson, R. T., Johnson, D. W., & Schmidt, B. (1980). Producing positive interaction among Down Syndrome and nonhandicapped teenagers through cooperative game structuring. *American Journal of Mental Deficiency, 85,* 268–273.

Salend, S. J., & Moe, L. (1983). Modifying handicapped students' attitudes toward their handicapped peers through children's literature. *Journal for Special Educators, 19,* 22–28.

Saunders, M. K., & Sultana, Q. (1980). Professionals' knowledge of educational due process rights. *Exceptional Children, 46,* 559–561.

Schmuck, R. A. (1968). Helping teachers improve classroom group processes. *Journal of Applied Behavioral Science, 4,* 401–435.

Schwebel, A. I., & Cherlin, D. L. (1972). Physical and social distancing in teacher-pupil relationships. *Journal of Educational Psychology, 63,* 543–550.

Sellin, D., & Mulchahay, R. (1965). The relationship of an institutional tour upon opinions about mental retardation. *American Journal of Mental Deficiency, 70,* 408–412.

Semmel, D. S. (1979). Variables influencing educators' attitudes toward individualized education programs for handicapped children. Paper presented at the American Educational Research Association Annual Meeting, San Francisco.

Sharan, S. (1980). Cooperative learning in small groups: Recent methods and effects on achievement, attitudes and ethnic relations. *Review of Educational Research, 50,* 241–271.

Sharan, S., Hertz-Lazarowitz, R., & Ackerman, Z. (1980). Academic achievement of elementary school children in small-group versus whole-class instruction. *Journal of Experimental Education, 48,* 125–129.

Sharan, S., & Sharan, Y. (1976). *Small-group teaching.* Englewood Cliffs, NJ: Educational Technology Publications.

Sharpley, A. M., Irvine, J. W., & Sharpley, C. F. (1983). An examination of the effectiveness of a cross-age tutoring program in mathematics for elementary school children. *American Educational Research Journal, 20,* 103–111.

Shaw, S. F., & Gillung, T. B. (1975). Efficacy of a college course for regular class teachers of the mildly handicapped. *Mental Retardation, 13,* 3–6.

Sheare, J. B. (1974). Social acceptance of emr adolescents in integrated programs. *American Journal of Mental Deficiency, 78,* 678–682.

Shotel, J. R., Iano, R. P., & McGettigan, J. F. (1972). Teacher attitudes associated with the integration of handicapped children. *Exceptional Children, 38,* 677–683.

Simpson, C. (1981). Classroom structure and the organization of ability. *Sociology of Education, 54,* 120–132.

Simpson, R. L., Parrish, N. E., & Cook, J. J. (1976). Modification of attitudes of regular class children towards the handicapped for the purpose of achieving integration. *Contemporary Educational Psychology, 1,* 46–51.

Slavin, R. E. (1977). A student team approach to teaching adolescents with special emotional and behavioral needs. *Psychology in the Schools, 14,* 77–84.

Slavin, R. (1978a). Student teams and achievement division. *Journal of Research and Development in Education, 12,* 34–49.

Slavin, R. (1978b). Student teams and comparison among equals: Effects on academic performance and student attitudes. *Journal of Educational Psychology, 70,* 532–538.

Stainback, S., & Stainback, W. (1982). Influencing the attitudes of regular class teachers about the education of severely retarded students. *Education and Training of the Mentally Retarded, 17,* 88–92.

Starlin, C. (1971). Peers and precision. *Teaching Exceptional Children, 3*, 129–132, 137–140.

Stowitschek, C. E., Hecimovic, A., Stowitschek, J. J., & Shores, R. E. (1982). Behaviorally disordered adolescents as peer tutors: Immediate and generative effects on instructional performance and spelling achievement. *Behavioral Disorders, 7,* 136–148.

Strain, P. S., & Shores, R. E. (1977). Social interaction development among behaviorally handicapped preschool children: Research and educational implications. *Psychology in the Schools, 14,* 493–502.

Strauch, J. D. (1970). Social contact as a variable in the expressed attitudes of normal adolescents toward emr pupils. *Exceptional Children, 36,* 485–494.

Swing, S. R., & Peterson, P. L. (1982). The relationship of student ability and small group interaction to student achievement. *American Educational Research Journal, 19,* 259–274.

Thiagarajan, S. (1973). Madras system revisited: A new structure for peer tutoring. *Educational Technology, 13,* 10–13.

Vacc, N. A., & Kirst, N. (1977). Emotionally disturbed children and regular classroom teachers. *The Elementary School Journal, 78,* 309–317.

Van Hasselt, V. B., Hensen, M., Whitehill, M. B., & Bellack, A. S. (1979). Social skill assessment and training for children: An evaluative review. *Behavioral Research and Therapy, 17,* 413–437.

Voeltz, L. M. (1980). Children's attitudes toward handicapped peers. *American Journal of Mental Deficiency, 84,* 455–464.

Warren, S. A., Turner, D. R., & Brody, D. S. (1964). Can education students' attitudes toward the retarded be changed? *Mental Retardation, 12,* 235–242.

Webb, N. M. (1982). Group composition, group interaction, and achievement in cooperative small groups. *Journal of Educational Psychology, 74,* 475–484.

Weinsenstein, G. R., & Gall, D. (1978). Adapting teacher education to include mainstreaming: Dean's Grant Projects. *Journal of Teacher Education, 29,* 22–24.

Westervelt, V. D., & McKinney, J. D. (1980). Effects of a film on nonhandicapped children's attitude toward handicapped children. *Exceptional Children, 46,* 294–296.

Wilson, E. D. (1971). A comparison of the effects of disability simulation and observation upon attitudes, anxiety, and behavior manifested toward the deaf. *The Journal of Special Education, 5,* 343–349.

Wilson, E. D., & Alcorn, D. (1969). Disability simulation and development of attitudes toward the exceptional. *The Journal of Special Education, 33,* 303–307.

Wright, B. (1978). The coping framework and attitude change: A guide to constructive role-playing. *Rehabilitation Psychology, 25,* 177–183.

Zajonc, R. B. (1968). Attitudinal effects of mere exposure. *Journal of Personality and Social Psychology Monograph Supplement, 9,* 1–27.

7 Attitudes of Parents and Siblings Toward A Handicapped Family Member

Parents anticipate the birth of a healthy child, and characteristically, they look forward to their child's future achievement in school, success in a profession, marriage, and the birth of grandchildren. Thus, the birth of a handicapped child can have a devastating effect on parents. Even when parents later discover that their school-aged child is handicapped (e.g., diagnosed as having a learning disability or as being mentally retarded), parents may need to undergo stages of recognition wherein they achieve acceptance of the child and make an appropriate reassessment of their expectations.

The purpose of this chapter is to review the research exploring family member attitudes toward a handicapped child. The first part of the chapter discusses parental attitudes; the later section focuses on sibling attitudes. The attitudes of parents and siblings may have a significant effect on the social, emotional, and psychological development of the handicapped child.

PARENTAL ATTITUDES

Numerous writers have documented the feelings of parents when they are informed that their child is handicapped. Initially, parent reactions of blame, guilt, denial, sorrow, grief, mourning, withdrawal, and rejection are evidenced; these feelings may also characterize the response stages that parents progress through as they become more accepting (Bentovim, 1972; Boyd, 1951; Drotar, Baskiewicz, Irwin, Kennell, & Klaus, 1975; Marion, 1981; Olshansky, 1962; Turnbull & Turnbull, 1978). There are differences among authors as to the names and number of the stages, their sequence, and the exact nature of the concerns evidenced by parents (Mori, 1983). It may be concluded, however, that parents initially demonstrate feelings such as grief, shock, and blame; then they reject the diagnosis and may "shop around" looking for a different one before they finally begin to accept their child. Of course not all parents react in the same negative way, and not all parents achieve the same level of acceptance. For example, according to Olshansky (1962), parents of retarded children experience chronic sorrow throughout their lives even though the intensity may vary from time to time, and the sorrow be more or less concealed.

Even when the child demonstrates a more mildly handicapping condition (e.g., learning disability versus blindness), parents exhibit traumatic responses. For example, parents of learning disabled students may be ashamed, embarrassed, confused, and frustrated (Gargiulo & Warniment, 1976; Mori, 1983). Because learning disabled children do not exhibit an apparent disability, parents may demonstrate even more frustrated and rejecting responses (Mori, 1983). Similarly, parents of emotionally disturbed children feel guilty, isolated, stigmatized and frustrated along with feelings of low self-esteem (Marion, 1981).

Definitions of Parental Rejection

Several definitions or descriptions of rejecting parental responses toward handicapped children have appeared in the literature. In an early discussion of parent attitudes toward handicapped children, Gallagher (1956) defined rejection as "the persistent and unrelieved holding of unrealistic negative values of the child to the extent that the whole behavior of the parent towards the child is colored unrealistically by this negative tone" (p. 273–274). According to Gallagher, there were four ways in which parents could express rejection: (1) by having unreasonably low expectations; (2) by setting unreasonably high expectations; (3) by escaping the child by desertion or removal of the child from the home environment, or (4) by using the mechanism of reaction-formation. In reaction-formation the parent defends against the expression of an unacceptable impulse by expressing the opposite feeling. The parent cannot admit to other feelings and believes his or her expression of positivity when indeed he or she feels very negative about his or her child.

Gallagher also distinguished between primary and secondary forms of rejection. In primary rejection the negative attitudes of the parents are the result of, "the basic unchangeable nature of the child" (p. 275). For example, a mother rejects her mentally retarded daughter who will never achieve the professional status she desired for herself. Secondary rejection is the result of the behaviors exhibited by the child; for example, the unusual noises made by a deaf child, or the body movements of a child with cerebral palsy. Unfortunately, as Gallagher noted, it is difficult to distinguish between primary and secondary rejection.

Consequently, professionals should assume that parents are evidencing secondary rejection and attempt to modify the behaviors of the child; if parental negativity persists even though many behavior problems have been brought under some form of control, primary rejection may be indicated.

According to Bryant (1971), the three parental attitudes most frequently observed by professionals in a clinical setting are: (1) acceptance; (2) rejection; and (3) compensation. Bryant's observation of parental compensation is similar to the reaction-formation response of parents discussed by Gallagher. Bryant describes the compensating parent as one who is trying to replace negative or rejecting attitudes with positivity or acceptance. As illustrated in Table 7.1, the compensation may be the result of various combinations of acceptance and rejection, with end products that may be harmful to the handicapped child.

"Parentalplegia" is a term proposed (Murray & Cornell, 1981) to describe a cyclical process wherein parents fail to adjust to having a handicapped child, respond inappropriately and possibly exacerbate their child's physiological impairment. Over-protection, rejection, and "unrealistic prodding" are the most common types of parentalplegia. According to MacKeith (1973), parental rejection of a handicapped child may take the form of: (1) "cold rejection" and unfeeling response; (2) "rationalized rejection" wherein parents consider placing the child in an institutional situation because the placement can provide the specialized care the child needs; (3) "dutiful caring" without any warmth; or (4) "lavish care" wherein the parents overcompensate for their rejecting attitude.

Parents cannot, however, be condemned for having negative attitudes toward their handicapped child. As Gallagher (1956) pointed out:

Total positive acceptance of a handicapped child or any child in the absence of any negative attitudes is something this writer has never seen and does not anticipate seeing in the near future (p. 294).

TABLE 7.1
Combinatorial Responses of Compensating Parents

Acceptance		Rejection		Compensation
love	+	indifference	=	possessiveness
empathy	+	selfishness	=	sympathy
forgiveness	+	fault finding	=	overpermissiveness
gentleness	+	cruelty	=	smothering
caution	+	carelessness	=	suspicion
activity	+	apathy	=	overactivity

Reprinted by special permission of The Professional Press, copyright by the Professional Press. From Bryant (1971), Parent-child relationships: Their effect on rehabilitation. *Journal of Learning Disabilities, 4*, 325-329.

Parental Rejection

Parents may reject their handicapped child. The literature evidences the negative attitudes parents may have toward mentally retarded (Worchel & Worchel, 1961), cerebral palsied (Miller, 1958), and cerebral palsied, retarded children (Thurston, (1960). For instance, Thorne and Andrews (1946) showed that institutionalized mentally retarded children, regardless of their level of retardation, were, over time, progressively ignored and eventually forgotten about by their parents. Grebler (1951) indicated that negative parental attitudes were associated with demanding, neglecting, and punishing behaviors toward the retarded child. Another study (Peck & Stephens, 1960) showed that the negative attitudes parents expressed toward their retarded child on a rating scale were related to the amount of rejecting behaviors professionals observed during home visits.

Some studies have shown that even the less severely handicapped child may be rejected. A study by Hilliard and Roth (1969) found that mothers of achievers had more accepting attitudes toward their children than did mothers of under-achievers. Gerber's (1976) results showed that parents of learning disordered children were less accepting of their children than were the parents of emotionally disturbed children, who in turn were less accepting of their offspring than were parents of normal children. Gerber's findings also showed discrepancies in the perceptions of mothers and fathers of handicapped children; parents of the handicapped tended to be polarized in their attitudes with one parent evidencing more acceptance than the other. In another study, Wetter (1972) found that parents of learning disordered children were more rejecting and overindulging than were parents of normal children; but there was no difference in overprotection. The results did not reveal any differences in the perceptions mothers and fathers of normal and learning disabled children had of their child's adjustment but did demonstrate parents of learning disordered children evidenced more disagreements about their child's overall adjustment than parents of nonhandicapped children.

Investigations of parental attitudes afford evidence for the possibility that parents of mildly, moderately, and severely handicapped students may have a negative regard for their children.

Parental Attitudes: Investigations Using PARI

Numerous investigations of parental attitudes have been conducted using the Parental Attitudes Research Instrument (PARI) (Schaefer & Bell, 1958). PARI consists of 23 scales related to attitudinal factors of authoritarian control (suppressive, punitive attitudes), hostility-rejection (attitudes of strictness, hostility toward family members) and democracy (sharing, equalitarianism). See Chapter 3 for a further discussion of this instrument.

Some studies have not shown any differences in the attitudes of mothers of schizophrenics (Zuckerman, Barrett, & Bragiel, 1960; Zuckerman, Oltean, & Monashkin, 1958); however, when Klebanoff (1959) administered the PARI to mothers of hospitalized schizophrenic, brain-damaged, and mentally retarded children and a group of mothers of nonhandicapped children, results showed the mothers of the handicapped children tended to have "more generally pathological over-all attitudes with little specificity." When Tolor and Rafferty (1963) administered PARI to mothers of disturbed hospitalized patients and to mothers of nonhandicapped high school students, the former group had significantly more authoritarian-controlling attitudes. Cook (1963a) found mothers of blind and severely handicapped children had over-protective attitudes; mothers of the deaf and organically impaired children had over-indulgent attitudes; and mothers of Down's syndrome and cerebral palsied children showed punitive attitudes. Results also showed that more authoritarian attitudes characterized mothers of severely versus mildly mentally handicapped children.

Ricci (1970) found that mothers of retarded children were more rejecting than mothers of emotionally disturbed children; mothers of normal children were least rejecting. Further, mothers of normal children were most authoritarian; mothers of emotionally disturbed children the least authoritarian. Moll and Darley (1960) showed mothers of speech-delayed children had more negative attitudes toward encouraging verbalizations than did mothers of articulatory impaired or nonhandicapped children; mothers of articulatory-impaired children also had stronger attitudes about "breaking a child's will" (a subtest on PARI related to the authoritarian-control factor) and were more disapproving of children's activities. A comparison of mothers of children with reading disabilities and mothers of nonreading disabled children showed that the former had stricter and more controlling attitudes; discouraged verbalization, comradeship and sharing; suppressed sexual interests; and were more unhappy in their marriage (Goldman & Barclay, 1974). Somewhat similarly, Humphries and Bauman (1980) showed that mothers of learning disabled students were more authoritarian and controlling but less hostile and rejecting that were mothers of normal children.

It seems that findings of investigations using the PARI provide additional evidence that parents of handicapped children may express negative feelings toward their children.

Mother-Child Verbal and Nonverbal Interactions

Some studies have examined the verbal and nonverbal interactions between mothers and their handicapped children. Marshall, Hegrenes, and Goldstein (1973), for example, studied retarded and nondisabled preschool mother-child pairs. The verbal behaviors of "manding" (including demanding, commanding, requesting, asking), "tact" (naming, labeling, describing), "intraverbal responses" (under the control of verbal stimuli), and "echoic" responses (repetition of a response) were observed. Results for the children showed significant differences for all four verbal behaviors; mands, tact, and intraverbals occurred more with the nonretarded children; echoics occurred more frequently with retarded children. But the frequencies of the tacts, intraverbals, and echoics were not different for the mothers; however, mothers of retarded children manded with much greater frequency.

Kogan and Tyler (1973) compared the verbal and nonverbal communication patterns among nonhandicapped, physically handicapped, and mentally retarded mother-child pairs. The behaviors examined included ratings on control (giving an order), assertiveness (restraining the child), affect (warm, friendly statements, or physical expressions of feeling), and involvement (the extent to which a member of a pair focused their attention on the other). Results showed that mothers of physically handicapped students evidenced more behaviors related to control and affect than comparison mothers; they were not different from mothers of mentally retarded children.

In another study (Doleys, Cartelli & Doster, 1976) behavioral observations of the verbal behaviors of mother-child pairs of nonhandicapped children, noncompliant children, and learning disabled children showed that mothers of learning disabled children dispensed more rewards (verbal attention to the child) and asked more questions than mothers of nonhandicapped and noncompliant children. There were no significant differences for command behaviors or criticisms, but mothers of learning disabled students tended to engage in these behaviors more often.

Observations of the interactions between handicapped children and their mothers suggest that their communication patterns may be different, sometimes qualitatively inadequate, lacking in reinforcement, or overly directed toward structuring of the child and his environment. The differential patterns of communication a mother and her handicapped child may have an attitudinal basis. Sheare and Kastenbaum (1966) observed mother-child interactions with severely cerebral palsied children. Findings indicated that parents can be taught how to interact with their child, but that the success of this type of program depended upon the mother's attitude toward the child.

Parental Expectations for School Achievement: Learning Disabilities

Several studies have focused on the expectations mothers have for their learning disabled child's school achievement. Findings by Chapman and Boersma (1979) indicated that, compared to mothers of normal children, mothers of learning disabled students demonstrated more negative reactions to their children's school achievement behaviors, reported more negative interactions with their children, and had lower expectations for future school performance. The latter finding was also reported by Hiebert, Wong, and Hunter (1982).

In an investigation by Bryan, Pearl, Zimmerman, & Matthews (1982), when ratings of mothers of nondisabled students were compared to mothers of learning disabled students, the latter more often expected that their children would perform poorly in school, and assigned them significantly lower rankings in their ability to express themselves, pay attention, follow directions, and get along with others. Both groups of mothers attributed their children's performance to internal characteristics of the child. Somewhat similarly, Boersma and Chapman (1982) found that parents of learning disabled students, as compared to parents of normally achieving students, expected their children to perform lower in reading, spelling, language arts, and social studies; but there were no differences for math or science. Parents of learning disabled and hyperactive boys also had lower expectations than did parents of nondisabled students (Ackerman, Elardo, & Dykman, 1979).

Pearl and Bryan (1982) explored the attributions of mothers as to the causes of their children's successes and failures. Results indicated that the mothers of learning disabled children thought that ability was less of a reason for their children's success and that a lack of ability was more of a reason for their failures than did mothers of nondisabled children. Mothers of learning disabled children attributed their children's success more to luck.

Studies of parental expectations for a learning disabled child generally suggest that parents of the learning disabled have lowered expectations for them and are likely to ascribe their successes more to luck than to effort or ability. It may be that parental expectations contribute to their child's performance; therefore, parental aspirations, not only for learning disabled children but for other handicapped children as well, merit further inquiry. So far research on what parents expect of their handicapped children has been focused on expectations for future performance or performance over a long term. These studies are discussed in the next section.

Parental Expectations for Future Achievement

Parents of handicapped children may display unrealistic attitudes about what their handicapped children are capable of achieving. Zuk (1959a) studied parental and professional ratings of mentally retarded children and concluded that parents showed a positive bias (''autistic distortion'') in the ratings of their handicapped children when the child was relatively normal in motor functioning. However, when the child was also motorically handicapped, parents were more realistic. Zuk interpreted the findings from a Freudian perspective: when a motor handicap was not evidenced . . . ''unconscious, (i.e., nonverbalized) desires for normalcy could be reinforced by their perception of relatively normal motor functioning despite the lag in learning ability.''

Most of the studies have supported a parental tendency to overestimate the future growth and development of their handicapped child. For example, Boles

(1959) reported that mothers of cerebral palsied children tended to over-rate their children's capacity. In this study approximately 75 percent of the children had below average intelligence, but about 50 percent of the parents felt their children would ultimately finish college and assume professional standing. At the same time, parents were not unrealistic in their appraisals of current functioning.

Similarly, Jensen and Kogan (1962) found that mothers and fathers over-estimated their retarded children's potential; those most over-rated were the younger and more severely retarded children. However, Barclay and Vought (1964) indicated that regardless of the degree of handicap or age of the child, mothers of retarded cerebral palsied children overestimated their potential for future achievement. Mothers of deaf children have also been shown to be unrealistic about future employment expectations (Freeman, Malkin, & Hastings, 1975). Tew, Payne, Laurence, & Rawnsley (1974) studied the reactions parents of spina bifida and normal children had to intelligence test results for their children. The findings indicated that parents of spina bifida children distorted the results; when they were interviewed between one and four months later they saw their children as having higher IQs. But in another study (Shulman & Stern, 1959), parents made accurate assessments of the mental ages of their retarded children. Long and Moore (1979) compared the expectations parents have for an epileptic child versus their expectations for nonhandicapped siblings. Results showed that (compared to siblings) parents expected epileptic children to have more emotional problems, be "more unpredictable" and "highly strung."

It seems that regardless of the type or degree of handicap, parents may hold to unrealistic expectations for a handicapped child.

Differences in the Attitudes of Mothers and Fathers

Some studies have demonstrated that there are differences between fathers and mothers in their reactions toward having a handicapped child. As compared to mothers, the fathers in Tallman's (1965) study: (1) had more difficulty coping; (2) were more concerned about the stigma of having a retarded child; and (3) reacted differently depending on the sex of the child. Fathers evidenced either extreme involvement with or complete withdrawal from their sons whereas they evidenced a limited, routine involvement with their daughters. Gumz and Gubrium (1972) found that, for mothers, having a retarded child was more of an emotional crisis than it was for fathers. Fathers were more concerned about the future achievements of the retarded child, but mothers evidenced more concern about the child's social relationships. Cummings (1976) reported that fathers of chronically ill and mentally retarded children demonstrated a diminished sense of competence as parents and more readily admitted to the "psychic pain" they were experiencing than did mothers. Literature reviews also have indicated differences between the attitudes of parents and have suggested the consequences of these differences. According to Price-Bonham and Addison (1978), there may be differences in mothers' and fathers' reactions to a mentally retarded child, in their emotional reactions, concerns, and patterns of acceptance. Lamb (1983) concluded that the fathers are likely to react negatively to their mentally retarded children and that their rejecting and withdrawing behaviors will result in mothers bearing more of the "burden," which, in turn, may adversely affect their marriages. Lamb also pointed out that there is a scarcity of studies about how fathers react to a handicapped child and underscored the need for further investigations in this area.

Clearly it seems that future research must be directed toward a better understanding of the differential reactions of mothers and fathers toward various handicapping conditions. Most studies have focused on parental reactions to a retarded child, and it is not clear how parents may differ in their reactions to children with other handicapping conditions.

Factors Influencing Parental Attitudes

Several factors have been shown to be related to the attitudes parents have toward their handicapped children. These include: (1) severity of the handicap; (2) social acceptability of the handicap; (3) socioeconomic status of the family; (4) sex; (5) age of the handicapped child; and (6) religiosity.

Severity of the Handicap. The severity of the child's handicap influences parental attitudes (Mori, 1983). However, it cannot be assumed that less severely handicapped children will necessarily be more accepted by parents. A differential effect for different handicaps appears to exist; and in addition to severity, acceptance appears to depend upon interaction of a number of variables (e.g., socioeconomic status, social acceptability of the handicap, sex of the child, and the age of onset). According to Mori (1983), parents differentially respond to different types of handicaps. For example, parents of learning disabled children may have a difficult time accepting the diagnosis and redefining the expectations they have for their child because the child displays many appropriate behaviors; whereas parents of blind children may exhibit overprotection, and those of the physically impaired will not be able to accept the fact of their having produced a deformed child.

Social Acceptability of the Handicap. As indicated in Chapter 4, different types of handicaps are regarded more or less positively by societal members; as Mori (1983) asserted the attitudes of parents of handicapped children are influenced by the attitudes of societal members. Indeed it also must be recognized that prior to the experience of having a handicapped child, parents very likely had internalized societal beliefs about different handicapping conditions; now they may be faced with overcoming their belief system.

Socioeconomic Status. The socioeconomic status of parents has also been shown to affect parent attitudes. Although there is some evidence that low socioeconomic status parents may be more rejecting (Holt, 1958a), most researchers have concluded that high socioeconomic status parents evidence greater difficulty in accepting their handicapped child (Downey, 1963; Meadow & Meadow, 1971). Marion (1981) and Mori (1983) suggested that the attitudes of high socioeconomic parents are the result of the higher achievement expectations these parents have for their children; when the child is handicapped, the parents experience greater disappointment because their child cannot "measure up." On the other hand, lower socioeconomic status families may suffer more adverse effects because they do not have the financial resources to gain assistance in caring for the child (Gallagher, Beckman, & Cross, 1983).

Sex of the Child. The sex of the handicapped child may also affect parental attitudes. Farber (1959) reported that in lower class families, having a mentally retarded boy had a more acute effect on marriages than did having a retarded girl; but the sex of the child was not related to marital integration in middle class families. The results for lower class families were presumed to be related to the parents having higher career expectations for males. Meadow and Meadow (1971) suggested that having a handicapped firstborn son is more distressing to parents than having a firstborn handicapped daughter, or later-born handicapped son. Spiker (1982) studied mothers of retarded children involved in an early intervention program; results showed that the mothers had more difficulty in their interactions with young males with Down's syndrome than with females. These studies suggest that having a handicapped male child may be more catastrophic for parents; but since the research is limited, the question is still left open.

Age of the Child. There is some indication that parents may be more rejecting of older handicapped children. Parents have more difficulty accepting a diagnosis of a handicapping condition when the child is older (Mori, 1983). This has been found to be true for deaf children (Neuhaus, 1969) and cerebral palsied children (Boles, 1959). Boles provided a rather thought-provoking summary of maternal attitudes which also seems to have implications for the effect of mainstreaming on parents:

> The finding that mothers of older children were more rejecting of their children than mothers of younger children may be related to the fact that in our culture the child is often overevaluated, overprotected, or may be the primary object of the mother's affections, and consequently, subject to many ambivalent feelings from the mother as natural growth processes of the child tend to disrupt the relationship.
>
> In the case of the handicapped child, the initial phase tends to be prolonged until the age of five or six, or school age. School age marks the beginning of a particularly difficult period for the parents of a handicapped child. Whether the child goes

to school or not, at this time comparisons of achievements between the handicapped and normal child become unavoidable, and painful for these parents. The mother of a cerebral palsied child, in contact with mothers of nonhandicapped children, with each additional year becomes more acutely aware of her child's differences—physically, intellectually, and socially—from the normal child, and by extension, of her own difference from the neighborhood social group of mothers of normal children. Her feelings of difference extend to an ability even to share in their expressed criticisms or disappointments in their children, for she may feel that her feelings of criticism and disappointment lie at a deeper and different level. As an example, one parent bitterly commented in response to an item in the questionnaire concerned with children's lying, "I wouldn't care if he lied to me, if he could only talk." Comparisons during this period tend to force the mother of a cerebral palsied child into a more realistic evaluation of her child. Facing the reality of the child's handicapped condition may be particularly difficult for the mother who may have spent years in over-caring for the child, denying herself and her family many satisfactions, and living with the hope that either her efforts, her prayers, or a medical miracle would suddenly change the situation. In this case, the reactions of discouragement, disillusionment, and self-blame may be particularly strong at this time, with equally strong feelings of hostility and rejection towards the child as the cause of her frustration and trouble. Thus, the finding that mothers of both nonhandicapped and cerebral palsied children were more rejecting of older children may be based on a similar dynamic root—the mother's disappointment in the child. Further, the findings that rejection of the child is not significantly greater among mothers of cerebral palsied children than among mothers of nonhandicapped children may be interpreted that the degree of disappointment experienced by the mother is related to the mother's own subjective values and expectations, rather than to any objective measure of the degree of imperfection in the child. This finding suggests an area for further research (pp. 209–210).

Religiosity.   Religion may be a factor in the attitudes parents have toward their handicapped child. For example, Boles (1959) found there were differences in Catholic, Jewish, and Protestant mothers of cerebral palsied children. Although religion did not differentiate among the groups in terms of rejection, Protestant mothers were significantly less anxious than Catholic and Jewish mothers. However, according to Zuk (1959b), guilt is an important religious concept and Catholic doctrine absolves parents from personal guilt because the doctrine is specific about handicapped children being a special gift from God. Therefore it is not surprising that Zuk (1959b) and Zuk, Miller, Bartram, & Kling (1961) found that Catholic mothers were more accepting of their retarded child than were Protestant mothers.

Gallagher, Beckman, & Cross (1983) reviewed a number of factors related to stress in families of handicapped children. These included the characteristics of the handicapped child; parental characteristics of socioeconomic status, intelligence, verbal skills, personality characteristics; amount of interpersonal, familial, friend, and professional support; and participation in training. These authors concluded that considerable research is necessary before we can understand the contribution and relative potency of parent, child, and social variables as they relate to the stressful reactions parents of handicapped children evidence.

Effects of a Handicapped Child on Parents

A more thorough understanding of the attitudes parents have toward a handicapped child may be achieved by recognizing how pervasive an effect the child may have on the parents. The presence of a handicapped child in the family can have profound consequences for the marital satisfaction of parents; parents may decide not to have any more children and will also be faced with a number of practical problems. Finally, parents may be plagued by a feeling that they are different because they have a handicapped child. Indeed they may feel that they themselves, as well as their child, are stigmatized by community members.

Marital Problems

Having a handicapped child may adversely effect the marital relationship. Interview studies have found that tension and stress result from parents arguing and worrying about their mentally retarded child (Farber, 1959; Schonnell & Watts, 1956). Similarly, parents of a psychotic child have been reported to argue about how to handle the child, and to blame each other for the situation. These behaviors lead to marital discord (Marcus, 1977). Indeed there are high rates of divorce in families with a mentally retarded child (Price-Bonham & Addison, 1978) and with a school-aged child with meningomyelocele (Kolin, Scherzer, New, & Garfield, 1971). But parents who had been married at least 5 years seemed better able to cope with having a handicapped child (Kolin et al., 1971). Also, on a positive note, a marriage may be strengthened by the experience of having a handicapped child, at least when the child is learning disabled (Gargiulo & Warniment, 1976).

Comparisons of marital status between parents of handicapped and nonhandicapped children suggest that the problems indicated by parents of handicapped children may not be entirely unique to their status. For example, Martin (1975) studied mothers of children with spina bifida, juvenile diabetes, and healthy children. Results showed that there were no significant differences in divorce rates among the 3 groups. Similarly, DeMyer (1979) did not find significant differences in marital happiness ratings for parents of autistic and normal children. However, there were more very happy marriages among parents of normal children and more very unhappy marriages among the parents of autistic children. In another study (Freeman, Malkin, & Hastings, 1975), the rates of divorce and separation in Canadian families with deaf children did not differ from comparison families.

On the other hand, several studies of British populations have shown that families with retarded (Gath, 1977) and spina bifida (Richards & McIntosh, 1973; Tew, Laurence, Payne, & Rawnsley, 1977) children experience varying degrees of marital problems. Lonsdale (1978) noted problems in the marital relationship of parents who had children with a variety of handicapping conditions. But in another study, Freeston (1971) found the majority of parents of spina bifida children did not feel their marriage had been adversely affected and some even felt their relationship had been strengthened. Similarly, marital problems have been noted in relationship to having a child with cerebral palsy, limb deficiency, and spina bifida among Australian parents (McAndrew, 1976). Differences in British, Australian, and American society preclude specific comparisons; however, the cross-cultural data support the potentially negative effect of a handicapped child on a marital relationship. At the same time, there is some limited evidence that having a handicapped child can bring parents closer together.

Clearly there is a need for further research to explain the nature of the effect a handicapped child may have on parents. As Murphy (1979a) indicated, "We do not know what effect an impaired child has on the relationship of the father and mother as husband and wife" (p. 270).

Family Limitation

The experience of having a handicapped child may result in parents deciding not to have any more children. Holt (1958b) found that parents of retarded children did not want to have any more children and that their decision seemed to be a direct result of having a handicapped child. When Price-Bonham and Addison (1978) reviewed the data on parents with a mentally retarded child, they also concluded that the experience contributed to decisions to limit family size. Parents of deaf children also try to limit further issue (Freeman, Malkin, & Hastings, 1975). Of the 116 parents McAndrew (1976) interviewed, half of the parents of children with spina bifida, a quarter of the parents of children with spina bifida, a quarter of the parents of cerebral palsied children, and a fifth of those with a child who had a limb deficiency did not wish to have any more children. Cook (1963b) reported that families who had a cerebral palsied child used family limitations as a coping strategy. However, whether a family decided not to have any more children was related to the severity of their child's handicap and the mother's age; limitation was used less if the child's handicap was mild or the mother was under 30 years old.

Practical Problems

Parenting even a moderately handicapped child presents many practical problems that may influence parental attitudes and reactions. These include problems related to (1) relationships with extended family members; (2) socialization; (3) parental health; and (4) expenses.

Relationships with Extended Family Members.   Farber (1959) reported that mothers supported and assisted their daughters in the management of a retarded child. Mothers-in-law were more likely to blame their son's wife for the child and sometimes implied that the retarded child was a punishment for something the mother had done. Freeman, Malkin, and Hastings (1975) found parents of deaf and hearing impaired children reported that about a third of their relatives were helpful, but another third reacted with denial and blame; some encouraged further diagnosis and using faith healers. In another study (McAndrew, 1976), parents reported the grandparents had difficulty accepting their spina bifida, limb deficient, or cerebral palsied grandchildren. Marcus (1977) found that comments made to parents of psychotic children by relatives contributed to parental feelings of guilt and inadequacy.

Socialization.   Numerous studies have documented the restrictions having a handicapped child places on the social life of parents. They engage in far fewer leisure time activities together and interact socially less with friends (DeMyer, 1979; Lloyd-Bostock, 1976; Lonsdale, 1978; McAllister, Butler, & Lei, 1973; McAndrew, 1976; Schonell & Watts, 1956).

Parental Health.   Having a handicapped child has affected the emotional health of some parents (Farber, 1960). McAndrew (1976) found 17 of 65 mothers of spina bifida, cerebral palsied, or limb deficient children had had psychiatric treatment. The physical exhaustion parents experience caring for a retarded child has been documented by Holt (1958b). Similarly, Marcus (1977) reported on the physical and emotional exhaustion displayed by parents of psychotic children.

Expenses.   Families have often reported the additional expenses associated with having a handicapped child. Although some have reported a money shortage (DeMyer, 1979; Gumz & Gubrium, 1972), the handicapped child has not always caused a financial hardship. Nevertheless funds have had to be diverted toward meeting the expenses of additional laundry, modifying the home structurally to accommodate the child, repairing damages done by the child, and so forth (Gumz & Gubrium, 1972; Lloyd-Bostock, 1976; McAndrew, 1976).

Stigma

Goffman (1963) uses the term ''stigma,'' which refers to an attribute that is ''discrediting'' or ''undesired'' to describe the inferior status society assigns disabled individuals. It may also be that parents of handicapped children are assigned an inferior status or discredited by societal members because they have a child with a handicap. Goffman (1963) asserted that in order to overcome this image, the stigmatized person may strive to present an image that is positive and controlled. According to Goffman:

> . . . the stigmatized individual is likely to feel that he is 'on,' having to be self-conscious and calculating about the impression he is making, to a degree and in areas of conduct which he assumes others are not (p. 14).

Reports from parents suggest that they may experience a feeling of devaluation or stigma by societal members. Marcus (1977) reported on parents of psychotic children:

> . . . great efforts are made to include the child in most social activities, such as eating at restaurants, shopping, visiting friends, etc.; but these can only succeed with careful preparation and contingency planning. For all families, dealing with the public means confronting ignorance or callousness, having to explain inexplicable behavior, suppressing anger or shame, and eventually developing a 'thick skin,' a sense of humor, or a casual indifference.

Parents have reported feeling isolated and stigmatized by their neighbors (Freeman et al., 1975; Holt, 1958b); and, community member reactions such as pity, staring, and pointing, have made some parents feel like outcasts (McAndrew, 1976; Stone, 1948). Watson and Midlarsky (1979) compared the attitudes of mothers of nonhandicapped and mentally retarded children and found there was a significant difference in the mothers' perceptions of community attitudes; most of the members of retarded children indicated that the community members had negative attitudes; but mothers of nonhandicapped children perceived community members as being positive. According to MacKeith (1973), parental attitudes toward their handicapped child may be influenced by the attitudes of societal members. Consequently, it is important to achieve an understanding of the perceptions handicapped parents have of themselves in society.

FAMILY EFFECTS ON A HANDICAPPED CHILD

A handicapped child can have an influence on his/her family. However, family members can also have an important impact on the social, psychological, and emotional adjustment of the handicapped child. According to Ausubel, Balthazar, Rosenthal, Blackman, Schpoont, and Welkowitz (1954), a child's feelings about himself are related to the amount of acceptance or rejection the parent evidences toward the child. Indeed, Hurley (1967) demonstrated a relationship between parental malevolence and children's intelligence.

Unfortunately there have not been many investigations of the effects parental attitudes have on handicapped children. Fotheringham and Creal (1974) maintained in a literature review that the handicapped child's home environment will influence the achievements of the handicapped child. In a very early study, Witmer (1933) showed that parental attitudes and behavior toward their handicapped child affected the outcome of treatment delivered to children by a child guidance clinic. In another study (Peck & Stephens, 1960), results indicated that the attitudes parents expressed toward their mentally retarded child were related to the child's interest in learning and ability to relate to other adults in the environment.

When Neuhaus (1969) studied deaf children aged 3 to 19 and their parents, results showed that there was a relationship between the deaf child's emotional adjustment and parental attitudes. In another study, Large (1982) interviewed eight blind men and women ranging in age from 20 to 65 years. There were significant common experiences reported by the blind subjects; they were unanimous in their expression that there was at least one family member whom they felt had a very strong influence on their adjustment to being blind. Lairy and Harrison-Covello (1973) reviewed the literature on children's adjustment to blindness and their own data and concluded that "it is the inadequate attitude of the environment, and primarily the family, which is responsible for the failure to adapt to blindness" (p. 15).

Davis (1975) attributed poor adjustment of physically disabled children to poor parental attitudes. Furthermore, Davis asserted that in planning for the evaluation and treatment of a child with a chronic illness or disability, parents and siblings be evaluated. Clinicians should:

1. Identify significant positive and negative premorbid psychodynamics in parents and siblings.
2. Identify presence of any common psychopathogens in parental attitudes toward the child's specific disability.
3. Plan initial education and supportive measures to include both parents and all children (p. 1041).

There is considerable evidence supporting the effect parents have on their child's development, including, for example, their sex-role and moral development, achievement, and psychological adjustment. However, for the most part these data have been gathered using nonhandicapped populations. Clearly, it is justifiable to presume the generalizability of such findings to handicapped populations. At the same time, it is evident that parents of handicapped children may be characterized by different feelings or attitudes toward their child. Consequently, it becomes important to develop a better understanding of the relationship between parental attitudes and the development of handicapped children.

MODIFYING PARENT ATTITUDES

Professionals can help parents of handicapped children to achieve a more positive attitude toward, and consequently a better relationship with, their handicapped child. And the attitudes and interactions a handicapped child experiences in the home environment may significantly impact upon his/her future growth and development.

Gallagher (1956) summed up what professionals can expect of parents of handicapped children:

> We can hope that parents will accept the child's handicap, even though they don't like it. We can expect that parents will want the child to perform at the level of social and intellectual ability that the child is capable of (and the professional worker has the responsibility of providing this information to the parents). Finally, we can expect that aspirations of parents for their child's future are in line with all that is known about the child's potential skills and abilities. We should expect that these parents will harbor feelings of resentment toward other parents who have had the good fortune to have healthy children and that they will occasionally become downcast and discouraged over the special problems that have sometimes seemed to set them apart from other parents (p. 294).

There are several approaches for helping parents of handicapped children achieve acceptance of their child. Among the major strategies are: (1) individual counseling; (2) group counseling; (3) family therapy; and (4) bibliotherapy. Involving parents in the education of their handicapped child, primarily by teaching them how to use behavioral management techniques to modify their child's behavior, has been increasingly advocated and may also contribute to an attitudinal change.

Individual Counseling.   The best approach to use with some parents of handicapped children may be individual counseling. According to Laborde and Seligman (1983), the individual counseling process may consist of three components: (1) educative counseling to explain the nature, prognosis, and impact of the handicap on the child and family members as well as legislated rights and services available; (2) facilitative counseling to support and assist parents in dealing with their thoughts and feelings about the child, including, for example, guilt, shame, rejection, and helplessness; and (3) personal advocacy counseling wherein parents are helped to become advocates for obtaining support and services for their child.

Group Counseling.   Parents of handicapped children may feel stigmatized by community group members. Even relatives and friends may not be supportive. But participation in a parent group meeting, talking, and sharing experiences with other parents who have a handicapped child is, as Meyerson (1983) pointed out, a supportive experience. Finding out that they are "not alone" is a potent force. According to Meyerson, parent groups usually have one of the following orientations: (1) an informational or educational focus wherein parents learn about their child's handicap and how to help; (2) a counseling or therapeutic focus wherein the emphasis is not the child but the parents and their feelings and attitudes; or (3) a combination of educational and therapeutic orientation. Parent groups usually meet weekly for approximately 2 hours over a 10-week period. The groups are usually sponsored by agencies or educational institutions.

An early report (Popp, Ingram, & Jordan, 1954) describes the development of a course for parents of retarded children. Class topics that emerged out of discussions with the parents included the causes and characteristics of mental retardation, the emotional needs of the retarded child, the relationship of the retarded child to family members and the community in general, and how parents could meet their child's needs. Among the changes observed in parents were a reduction in their feelings of guilt, shame, etc. about their child, and a more accepting attitude.

Bricklin (1970) reported on counseling groups for parents of learning disabled children. Initial sessions focused of the causes and characteristics of learning disabilities; later sessions focused on parents' feelings and reactions toward their child's behavior. Parents demonstrated an increased understanding of their child's behavior and learned to recognize and accept their feelings about the child. Some parents, realizing that many of their problems with their children stemmed from deeper needs, sought individual psychotherapy.

Family Therapy.   Meyerson (1983) suggested that family therapy is widely accepted because the approach considers the impact of the handicapped child on the entire family. Via the family therapy approach as described by Meyerson, the family initially receives information about the child's handicap, (e.g., nature, prognosis, services) and is given help in dealing with their feelings toward the handicapped child. When the family has gained a reasonable degree of acceptance of the handicapped child, the sessions are directed toward improving communication among family members, assisting members in becoming aware of their own family's particular dynamics (alliances, controlling members), and helping members to develop emotional coping skills (e.g., planning time for social activities, meeting the needs of the marital relationship). Weekly sessions over 10 to 20 weeks characterize family therapy. Meyerson (1983) compared family and group therapy and pointed out some of the advantages and disadvantages of each methodology. In parent group therapy, parents have an opportunity for information and feedback from other parents, not just the counselor or group leader; parents also have an opportunity to observe the coping behaviors (positive and negative) of other parents of handicapped children that may help them to make appropriate changes in their own behavior. On the other hand, some parents may feel uncomfortable about expressing their feelings in a group situation, making family therapy a more desireable option. Also, since family therapy includes the parents, handicapped child, and siblings, and allows the therapist to make first-hand observations about the patterns of interactions among family members, this approach may be more helpful. Meyerson proposed that parents of handicapped children should have an opportunity to benefit from both the group experience initially and family therapy on an adjunctive basis.

Bibliotherapy. Mullins (1983) described the use of bibliotherapy with parents of handicapped children. Basically, when this procedure is used, parents read books selected by the counselor, and are given an opportunity to discuss the reading with the counselor. Mullins cited the procedure as described by Holland (1969), which consists of four stages. In the "identification/affiliation stage, the parent sees others in the book in a situation similar to their own; for example, a mother of a mentally retarded child would read a book about a parent of a mentally retarded child and the problems he or she encountered. In the second stage, "projection of self," the reader identifies with the character(s) in the text. An "emotional catharsis" or "emotional purging" occurs as the reader vicariously experiences the feelings, emotions, and motivations of the character, which facilitates the reader's ability to gain "intellectual insight and new personal integration" with respect to their own situation. (See Mullins for a discussion of criteria for selecting books for parents and a bibliography of texts for parents).

Behavioral Strategies. The use of behavioral strategies to modify handicapped as well as nonhandicapped child behaviors has received increasing support. A review of 70 studies on parent training in behavior modification (O'Dell, 1974) credited Pumroy with making the first effort to train parents to use behavioral principles in 1965. O'Dell concluded the approach showed great promise for helping parents change their child's behavior at home, but at the same time pointed out the need for methodological improvements. There is now evidence that parents can work cooperatively with teachers and function as change agents using behavioral strategies to modify their child's school behaviors (Atkeson & Forehand, 1979; Barth, 1979). Indeed Bernal and North (1978) located and reviewed thirty training manuals designed to teach parents and professionals how to use behavioral strategies with handicapped and nonhandicapped children. While it has been suggested that school psychologists can play a significant role in training parents to use behavioral strategies (Simpson & Poplin, 1981), there is some evidence that parents can succeed with the procedure just by reading a manual (Heifetz, 1977). Parents have also been shown to be effective teachers of other parents (Jenkins, Stephens, & Sternberg, 1980; Hall & Nelson, 1981), and spouses have been demonstrated to be able teachers of each other (Adubato, Adams, & Budd, 1981).

Most studies using a behavioral strategy with parents have not investigated the effects parent involvement has on parental attitudes. However, it seems likely that as parents begin to experience some control over their child's behavior, they will begin to feel more positive toward their child. Future research must be directed toward understanding potential attitudinal outcomes related to parental involvement.

PARENTS AND THE MAINSTREAMING LEGISLATION

Mainstreaming legislation calls for the placement of handicapped children, traditionally assigned to special classes, closer to the mainstream to the maximum extent possible. Public Law 94-142 also gives parents of handicapped children a right to be involved in the educational process. In essence, according to this legislation, parents: (1) are entitled to a free and appropriate education for their child; (2) must consent to the evaluation of their handicapped child, receive an explanation of the results, and may request an outside or independent evaluation; (3) have access to all educational records; and (4) can request a due process hearing if they disagree with the evaluation and/or placement procedures proposed by school personnel.

Parent Attitudes Toward Mainstreaming

Numerous studies of professional attitudes toward mainstreaming have been undertaken (See Chapter 4). However, parents have seldom been queried; although, in the opinion of teachers, parents of nonhandicapped children were considered opposed to mainstreaming handicapped students, and parents of handicapped students were favorable toward the concept (Horne, 1983).

Descriptive research suggests that some parents of handicapped children are positive about mainstreaming, but this is not always the case. This is evident in the responses of parents documented by Paul and Bekman-Bell (1981). For example:

> Mrs. H.
> Kent is so young that my outlook is limited. I am slowly but surely making opinions about mainstreaming. It seems that about the time I set my views, something changes and I have to reassess my view.
>
> There is a law to be passed in our state that is frightening. It is a law of definitions of how the school people can legally modify the behavior of our kids. They are going from one extreme to another. They range from physical handling, to confinement, etc., to extremes most of us would call child abuse. They call it "betterment" of our children's actions.
>
> We should never allow our children to be affected by such a law, but because the retarded are such a minority it will probably be passed unnoticed by the masses (pp. 148–149).

Mrs. D.

Sara was mainstreamed before we heard the word; therefore I wish the same for all other children. I believe very strongly that normal children benefit when they get to know the handicapped children. I think the general public also benefits when there is more awareness of handicapping conditions and the personhood of those whose bodies or minds are less than whole (p. 149).

Mlynek, Hannah, and Hamlin (1982) surveyed parents who were members of organizations concerned with emotional disturbance, mental retardation, and learning disabilities. Responses to statements about handicapped children (e.g., "Handicapped children will learn how to cope with the real world better if they are in a regular school setting") showed that the three groups of parents responded differently. Only the parents of learning disabled students felt that mainstreaming would result in classmates having more positive attitudes toward handicapped students and would help handicapped students "learn how to cope with the real world better." The parents of learning disabled children also indicated they thought that: regular classroom teachers had time to work with handicapped children, mainstreaming was a "practical" solution, and that special classes were not an effective educational approach. Parents of learning disabled and emotionally disturbed students agreed that regular classroom placements would reduce the likelihood of their child being perceived as "different" and that their children would "enjoy" being with nonhandicapped students; these responses were significantly different from parents of retarded children. All three groups of parents responded differently to ratings about how happy they felt handicapped children would be in the regular classroom; parents of learning disabled were the most positive, next parents of emotionally disturbed, and parents of mentally retarded children were the least optimistic.

Abramson, Willson, Yoshida, and Hagerty (1983), who queried parents of mainstreamed learning disabled students, found that some parents supported the approach; others did not. Parents differ in their perceptions of the social and academic benefits of the procedure, but they may not have been clear about the goals of mainstreaming.

Boles (1959) discussed the relationship of a child's age to parental attitudes and illustrated how school attendance might affect the feelings of parents of handicapped children. Based on the analysis of the literature on the attitudes of parents of preschool handicapped children, Turnbull and Blacher-Dixon (1980) concluded: (1) when a handicapped child is mainstreamed, the differences between the handicapped child and nonhandicapped peers become more apparent and may serve as a constant reminder to the parent that their child is different. This may, in turn, negatively affect the attitudes the parent has toward the disabled child; (2) parents of handicapped children may feel they are stigmatized or undesirably different from other parents because they have a handicapped child, and consequently may perceive themselves as being rejected by parents of children who are not handicapped whether or not their perception is accurate; (3) it is difficult for parents of handicapped children to identify with parents of nonhandicapped children since they may not have the same interests and concerns as parents of nonhandicapped children; (4) parents of mainstreamed children may have to assume more responsibility for helping the teacher become more understanding of their child's behavior, and consequent social and educational needs (in contrast to a special class program wherein trained staff are familiar with the characteristics and needs of handicapped children); and, (5) mainstreamed, as opposed to special, programs may not provide support services which meet the special needs of the parent of a handicapped child.

Further research is necessary to understand how parents of children with different handicapping conditions feel about mainstreaming and what its ramifications might be for parents. An apt appraisal of the situation was presented by Turnbull and Blacher-Dixon (1980) who stated, ". . . in order to understand the effects of mainstreaming on handicapped children, the effects on parents must be studied as well" (p. 25). These authors suggested future research must be directed toward: (1) understanding how parents feel about normalization and mainstreaming; (2) the relationship between parental values and placement; (3) understanding whether or not it is the parents' or child's interests that must be served when professionals and parents disagree as to the most appropriate setting for the child; (4) what should be the nature of orientation programs for preparing parents for mainstreaming; and, (5) what is the relationship between parents' attitudes toward mainstreaming and a child's success in school.

Parental Involvement in Mainstreaming

The IEP (Individualized Educational Program) is an outgrowth of the evaluation process that documents the proposed placement procedures for the handicapped child. An IEP conference, which is mandated by P.L. 94-142, presents information about the child's evaluation and allows parents and professionals an opportunity to discuss the educational program most appropriate for the child. Thus, the IEP meeting theoretically facilitates meaningful involvement of parents in the mainstreaming process. According to the Federal Register (1981):

> The IEP meeting serves as a communication vehicle between parents and school personnel, and enables them as equal participants to jointly decide what the child's needs are, what services will be provided to meet those needs, and what the anticipated outcomes will be (p. 5462).

Unfortunately, there is some evidence suggesting that the IEP conference procedures are really not fulfilling the goal of increased parent involvement; nor do the conferences always evidence professional awareness of the importance of these meetings. Parents do not seem to be contributors in IEP meetings. For example, Gilliam and Coleman (1981) found that parents were rated low by other participants in their actual contributions (ranked 10th out of a group of 12 team members) and influence (ranked 8th out of a group of 10 team members) at the IEP meetings. The most influential were (from most to least) special education teachers, psychologists, directors, and supervisors of special education. At the same time Soffer (1982) showed that parents want greater participation in decisions about their child. Soffer found parents of retarded students were dissatisfied about their participation in decisions about when their child's next evaluation would occur and how their child's progress would be evaluated.

But it also appears that parents who participate in IEP meetings are not informed about their rights and may not understand decisions related to their child's eligibility for special education, placement, program goals, or review dates (Hoff, Fenton, Yoshida, & Kaufman, 1978).

Goldstein, Strickland, Turnbull, and Curry (1980) observed 14 IEP conferences, 11 of which involved students who were being considered for special education placement for the first time; the students were classified as mildly mentally retarded or learning disabled. During the meetings (mean length 36 minutes) resource teachers talked about twice as much as other participants. Topics, ranked in order of the frequency they were discussed, and the total percent of times a topic was cited were: curriculum goals and objectives (20%), behavior (14%), performance (13%), miscellaneous conference procedures (signing papers, explaining forms) (12%), evaluation (11%), personal/family 7%), instructional materials (5%), placement (4%), special services (4%), rights and responsibilities (2%), individual responsibilities (2%), health (1%), future contacts (1%), and future plans (0%). Clearly, the focus of the meetings was on curriculum, behavior, and performance; but topics that are seemingly very important to parents, such as placement, nature of special services, parental rights, and responsibilities, and future contacts with school personnel and plans were hardly addressed. Yet parents expressed a high degree of satisfaction with the meetings. The latter finding may reflect the parents': (1) lack of understanding of the IEP conference's purpose; (2) relief because the conference was not just another meeting to hear about how much of a problem their child was; (3) gratitude for the extra help their child would be getting; or, (4) previous experience of poor communication with school personnel.

It is alarming to think that professionals may not be very positive about parental participation in educational planning. Yet, one survey (Yoshida, Fenton, Kaufman, & Maxwell, 1978) of the attitudes of educational planning team members toward parental participation in IEP meetings indicated that of 24 potential parent activities (e.g., suggest students subject matter needs, resolve conflicts of opinion, interpret information), only two were regarded as appropriate for participating parents by more than 50 percent of the members. These were presenting and gathering relevant information. The authors concluded that planning team members do not expect parents to be active participants in the decision making about their child's program.

Attendance records of some parents and professionals are also alarming. Scanion, Arick, and Phelps (1981) surveyed the attendance of parents and teachers of retarded, disturbed, deaf, blind, physically handicapped and learning disabled children at IEP conferences. Results indicated a significant difference in attendance and showed that many professionals did not attend IEP conferences on their clients. Mothers of emotionally disturbed children attended 77.7 percent of the time while all others attended 99 percent of the meetings. However, teachers of emotionally disturbed children attended meetings only 55 percent of the time, those of physically handicapped children only 57 percent of the time, teachers of learning disabled students only 60 percent of the time, and teachers of mentally retarded students 20 percent of the time. Teachers of deaf or blind children were present about 80 percent of the time, and teachers of physically handicapped students attended 64.3 percent of the time.

It seems that future research must be directed toward understanding what is happening at IEP conferences and why. The literature suggests that parents may need some assistance in how to participate. At the same time, professionals must also improve their awareness of the need to be active listeners, and facilitate broader topical discussions. Clearly professionals need to learn to respond to topics which may be differentially important to parents. Professionals must also develop more positive attitudes toward parental participation and become more conscientious about their responsibility to attend and participate in IEP meetings.

Another concern is the interactions professionals have with parents outside of the IEP conference (Stearns, 1981). Training designed to help professionals understand the attitudes of parents of handicapped children and to communicate effectively with parents seems essential. Sawyer and Sawyer (1981) demonstrated that a microcounseling approach (which included viewing parent-teacher videotapes, role playing, and discussion) assisted classroom teachers of handicapped children to respond appropriately to difficult questions (concerning their child's future) or situations (responding to the parents overprotective behavior) posed by parents of handicapped children during initial contacts.

Turnbull and Leonard (1981) reviewed the literature on parent involvement and suggested that school psychologists should facilitate parents' active participation at IEP meetings. School psychologists could also assume the role of a parent trainer and provide parents of handicapped children with information about their legal rights so that parents would function more effectively as advocates for their child. Furthermore, school psychologists and other professionals may themselves need to recognize that they must become more effective in their interactions with parents. According to Turnbull and Leonard this might be accomplished by examining the competencies parents and professionals need, and then selecting a training strategy (i.e., individual or group meetings).

THE HANDICAPPED CHILD: EFFECTS ON SIBLINGS

Most studies of families with handicapped children have focused on parent-child relationships. Even more often, the focus has been on the relationship between the mother and her handicapped child. But the effect of a handicapped child may be even greater for siblings than for parents (Banta, 1979). The research in this area, however, is very limited. Pfouts (1976) referred to the sibling relationship as "a forgotten dimension." In Pfouts's opinion, the scarcity of research on sibling relationships is the result of two factors. First, a belief by researchers in the potency of the parent-child relationship which results in a tendency to overlook the importance of sibling relationships. Second, the complex nature of the necessary research designs (factors of sex, birth order, spacing of siblings may influence sibling relationships and therefore must be considered individually and in interaction) is discouraging.

This section initially considers: (1) sibling attitudes toward handicapped brothers and sisters; (2) the emotional and behavioral effects of having a handicapped sibling; (3) factors that may contribute to emotional and behavioral effects; (4) the effects having a handicapped sibling may have on life goals; and (5) the concerns that nonhandicapped siblings may evidence. A final section addresses the effect normal siblings have on their handicapped brother or sister.

Sibling Attitudes

More often than not, classmates reject their handicapped peers (see Chapter 4). What happens when a handicapped person is a family member—a brother or sister? Some studies have reported that nonhandicapped siblings are not necessarily positive about having a handicapped brother or sister and experience a variety of feelings including a negative reaction. But other studies have demonstrated accepting attitudes.

Families interviewed by Holt (1958b) reported that siblings of retarded children resented the attention given to the handicapped child; they were also ashamed and embarrassed. In another study, McAndrew's (1976) interviews with parents of children with spina bifida reported frequent fighting, bossing, teasing, jealousy, and embarrassment on the part of nonhandicapped siblings. However, Lloyd-Bostock (1976) found parents reported that their nonhandicapped children were very positive, loving, and accepting toward their mentally handicapped sibling.

Adolescent sisters and brothers who were interviewed understood the diagnosis of mental retardation and reported they were accepting of their handicapped sibling. They all helped out at home in some way, but did not feel burdened (Graliker, Fishler, & Koch, 1962). A similar positive attitude was revealed by adults' recollections of their experiences as siblings of a retarded brother or sister (Cleveland & Miller, 1977).

Interviews with siblings, however, have also demonstrated negative reactions. Klein (1972a, 1972b) interviewed college-aged siblings of children who had a congenital defect, were retarded, or were brain injured. The brothers and sisters discussed childhood recollections of: being teased, having to protect or defend their disabled sibling, feeling embarrassed, and resenting the differential treatment accorded their handicapped sibling by parents. Similar feelings of resentment toward retarded siblings were voiced by some college students interviewed by Grossman (1972).

Seligman (1983) pointed out that siblings are more likely to evidence feelings of anger and resentment toward a handicapped sibling than they would toward a nonhandicapped brother or sister. Whether feelings are openly expressed or internalized depends on a number of factors:

1. The extent to which the sibling is held responsible for a handicapped brother or sister.
2. The extent to which a handicapped sibling takes advantage of (manipulates) a normal brother or sister.
3. The extent to which the handicapped sibling restricts one's social life or is considered a source of embarrassment.
4. The extent to which a handicapped sibling requires time and attention from the parents.
5. The extent to which the family's financial resources are drained by services for the handicapped child.
6. The number of siblings.
7. The sex of siblings.
8. The overall accommodation parents have made to their special circumstances (p. 164).

Siblings of handicapped children may be embarrassed by their handicapped sibling. They may be worried about the reactions of their friends and classmates. Feelings of shame, resentment, and embarrassment may contribute to guilt feelings (Marion, 1981; Mori, 1983; Seligman, 1983).

It appears that one of the best predictors of sibling attitudes are the attitudes expressed by parents. Honest and open communication among family members about a child's handicap, including its nature and characteristics, facilitates the development of positive attitudes and healthy adjustment on the part of the nonhandicapped children in the family (Grossman, 1972; Marion, 1981; Mori, 1983). Einstein and Moss (1967) stated that, "... the family climate and parents' overt and covert messages about sibling roles decisively condition the interrelationship between siblings" (p. 549).

Emotional and Behavioral Effects

Davis (1975) hypothesized that siblings of handicapped children are "usually affected psychologically by a family member's disability, either directly or indirectly by the disability, and by the degree of paternal deprivation, anxiety, and successful coping" (p. 1040). However, there have not been very many empirical investigations documenting the possible emotional and behavioral effects of a handicapped sibling on nonhandicapped brothers and sisters.

In some studies, parents have been asked to assess how nonhandicapped brothers and sisters are affected. McAndrew (1976) found that over twenty-five percent of 51 parents of spina bifida, cerebral palsied, and limb deficient children reported that one of their other children was experiencing emotional or behavioral problems that they felt were in some way attributable to having a handicapped sibling. In another study, Lonsdale (1978) interviewed parents of children with a variety of handicaps. Parents reported that of their 116 nonhandicapped children, 9 percent evidenced behavior disorders, 13 percent had disturbed relationships with their peers, and 13 percent had disturbed relationships with their handicapped sibling.

The findings of other studies in which parents and teachers have reported on the behaviors of siblings of handicapped students and matched controls are not consistent. For example, Gath (1972) studied elementary-school-aged siblings of Down's Syndrome children, siblings of children who had a surgically treated cleft lip or palate, and a control group. The hypothesis that there would be more emotional and behavioral problems evidenced by the siblings of the retarded students was not supported by results of parent and classroom teachers' reports. However in another study, Gath (1973) examined school-aged siblings of Down's Syndrome children and a control group. Behavioral ratings by teachers and parents showed that females but not males demonstrated more deviant behaviors as compared to the control group. Among the common symptoms were difficulty with peer relationships, restlessness, disobediance, misery, and temper tantrums. A further examination of the data (Gath, 1974) just compared the siblings of the Down's Syndrome children. Results showed that brothers of handicapped children also demonstrated deviant behavior. Older females appeared to be more at risk, perhaps because of more responsibility.

Tew and Laurence (1973) studied 59 children with spina bifida, their 44 siblings, and a matched control group of nonhandicapped children. Teacher ratings of social adjustment indicated the incidence of maladjustment was four times greater in siblings of spina bifida, regardless of whether the handicapped sibling was at home or attended a residential school.

In another study (Breslau, Weitzman, & Messenger, 1981), mothers of handicapped (cystic fibrosis, cerebral palsy, myelodysplasia, and multiple handicaps) children were interviewed and siblings administered a psychiatric inventory; when the results were compared to a random sample, siblings scored higher on some scales (mentation problems, fighting, and delinquency) but not others, suggesting that siblings of handicapped children may not demonstrate higher overall rates of psychological disorder but may demonstrate disturbances in specific areas.

San Martino and Newman (1974) contended that siblings of retarded children are emotionally at risk for several reasons, but the primary factor is guilt. They provided the following analysis:

> Parental guilt based on fantasies about the meaning of having a retarded child, unconscious and intolerable, is often projected onto the normal sibling who is then held responsible for the trouble. Parental superegos indict the sibling who is perceived as angry and destructive. Anger at the retardate, which further intensifies parental guilt, is displaced onto the scapegoated sibling whose own conflicts over aggression are intensified. Via the mechanism of introjection and identification the normal child in some cases takes on some of the characteristics of the retarded sibling; this identity both serves a defensive purpose to ward off anxiety and guilt and leads adaptively to parental acceptance. In other cases the guilt may lead to overcompliance, nonlearning, or a masochistic search for punishment. The guilt-ridden sibling may further project his own guilt and take on a blaming and attacking attitude toward others including therapists (pp. 168–169).

According to San Martino and Newman (1974) early intervention programs must be provided for siblings to prevent the development of emotional problems.

Guilt, it seems, may affect siblings throughout their lives. Samuels and Chase (1979) interviewed adult siblings (aged 24 to 46 years) of schizophrenics (aged 21 to 50 years). Extensive case histories for the 14 siblings were prepared. Although the siblings themselves were well adjusted, guilt was a predominating feature in their lives. The healthy sisters and brothers felt guilty about their "wellness." They also expressed the guilt they felt over their indifference and hostility during childhood and adolescence.

Factors Contributing to Emotional and Behavioral Effects

There are several factors in addition to parent attitudes that may contribute to the effect a handicapped sibling has on the adjustment of nonhandicapped brothers and sisters. These include (1) socioeconomic status; (2) gender; (3) age and sex; and (4) severity of handicap.

Socioeconomic Status.   The financial status of the family will affect the amount of stress experienced by siblings. Siblings in higher socioeconomic status families are more likely to be better adjusted. This is primarily because financially secure parents are more able to purchase caretaking services, rather than relying on help from siblings (Farber, 1960; Gath, 1974; Grossman, 1972).

Gender.   A sibling's adjustment may be more influenced by a same-sex handicapped sibling (Grossman, 1972). Also, Samuels and Chase (1979) found guilt was more evident among same-sexed siblings.

Age and Sex.   It is not clear whether older or younger nonhandicapped siblings are more adversely affected. Several studies have demonstrated that older females are more likely to assume more responsibility for caring for their younger handicapped siblings (Cleveland & Miller, 1977; Schwirian, 1977). However, the effect these caretaking demands have on adjustment are not clear. Samuels and Chase (1979) contended that the lives of younger siblings are more seriously disrupted, but Breslau, Weitzman and Messinger (1981) reported that younger male siblings and older female siblings were more psychologically affected by having a handicapped sibling. It is not clear why younger males but not younger females are more influenced. But one report (Gath, 1974) demonstrated that family size and birth order may mediate the psychological effect of a handicapped sibling on females; for males socioeconomic status and family size may be important.

Severity of Handicap.   It is not clear whether nonhandicapped siblings are more adversely effected when their brother or sister is more or less severely handicapped. Although a relationship to severity has been evidenced in siblings of mentally retarded children (Grossman, 1972), another study of the psychological adjustment of siblings of children with cystic fibrosis, cerebral palsy, myelodysplasia, and multiple handicaps did not support the influence of the nature of the child's handicap.

Research on the effects handicapped children have on nonhandicapped siblings is exceedingly scarce. As Seligman (1983), who reviewed the extant literature, stated, "Perhaps most limiting in terms of making useful and conclusive statements about this population is the remarkably small number of reported studies" (p. 155).

Effect on Life Goals

Having a handicapped sibling may influence the life goals of nonhandicapped brothers and sisters. Cleveland and Miller (1977) found that the majority of interviewed adults reported that their life commitments were not effected by having a retarded sibling. However, there was some indication that oldest female siblings, who were frequently responsible for helping to care for the retarded child, were more likely to choose "helping" careers because of this caretaking experience. Farber (1963) found that siblings who interacted more with their handicapped brothers and sisters ranked life goals having to do with making a contribution to a worthwhile cause and to mankind higher than did siblings who interacted with less frequency. High-frequency interactors also downgraded goals having to do with personal relationships. According to Farber, these results suggest that "... the sustained interaction with the retarded sibling comes to be regarded as a duty by the normal siblings. In the performance of this duty, the normal sibling internalizes welfare norms and turns his life career towards the improvement of mankind or at least toward the achievement of goals which will require much dedication and sacrifice" (p. 98). Samuels and Chase (1979) also noted that all but 2 of the 14 siblings of schizophrenics had chosen careers within the helping professions (psychology, psychiatry, social work, occupational therapy, special education). They hypothesized that the siblings become helpers in order to compensate for feelings of guilt and helplessness; but Samuels and Chase also cautioned that this interpretation could be overly superficial. An examination of the styles of professional involvement indicated a direct relationship to styles of family involvement. For example, siblings who demonstrated objectivity about their handicapped sibling were in positions requiring objectivity about clients. Those who had been very involved with their handicapped sibling were in positions of involvement, such as teaching special education.

Sibling Concerns

According to Murphy (1979b), siblings of handicapped children share similar concerns related to the relationships existing among family members as well as with individuals outside the family group. Murphy pointed out that there are also a number of more general questions needing to be addressed by professionals. Among these concerns are: Concerns having to do with family relationships:

1. How do I deal with my parents?
2. How do I share my real feelings with my parents?
3. What do my parents really expect of me?
4. How do my parents feel about my handicapped brother/sister?
5. How do I wish my parents would behave?
6. What are the points of agreement/disagreement between my parents and me?
7. What are similarities and differences between my siblings and myself in family interactions (p. 356)?

Concerns about relationships outside the family:

1. How do I deal with my friends?
2. How do I explain the handicap and what it means to them? Help them to understand?
3. How does my handicapped sibling affect my social life?

4. What do you say to people when they say unwise or unpleasant things about your handicapped sibling?
5. How do we handle our feelings when our friends show off their brothers and sisters—talk about their accomplishments?
6. What effect will this have on my relationships with the opposite sex—now or later and will my chances of marriage be lessened?
7. Should I get married? What will my own children be like? (p. 356)

Other concerns of siblings of handicapped children:

1. What can I do to help?
2. How do I deal with various feelings—good and bad—I have about my handicapped sibling?
3. Why do they behave the way they do?
4. How much can we expect of them?
5. Do they understand such issues as right from wrong? Good and bad?
6. Will they improve?
7. What eventually will become of them?
8. Do they really know what their problem is and can they ever accept it?
9. What are their hopes for the future?
10. What is our responsibility toward our handicapped sibling in the event our parents die (pp. 356–375)?

Murphy (1979b) reported that there will be some differences, of course, among siblings in their reactions; however, sibling support groups are important for, "catharsis, support, insight concerning relationships with family members and others, and techniques for managing various situations" (p. 358).

Schrieber and Feeley (1965) reported on support groups they established for adolescent siblings of retarded children. In their program, brothers and siters of retarded siblings met for 1½ hours biweekly for 8 months. In the first session the voluntary nature of the group was underscored; the purpose of the meeting was established as an opportunity for siblings to share their problems and concerns in order to help each other. Over the course of the meetings, siblings talked about such topics as explaining a retarded sibling to their peers; the effect having a retarded sibling might have on their own marital expectations; dealing with parents who had not discussed the problems of mental retardation in the family and its implications; their responsibility for their retarded sibling in the eventuality of parental demise; and parental attitudes and expectations. The authors concluded that although the sessions did not always result in a change or modification in basic attitudes, siblings did come to realize that others had similar problems and that it was "okay" to feel the way they did. Siblings developed an ability to express themselves, became more realistic about their situation, and were better prepared to cope with being the sibling of a retarded child. Kaplan and Fox (1968) described their efforts to develop a "preventive-therapeutic" experience for adolescent siblings of retarded children. A pilot effort indicated some of the difficulties that had to be overcome in designing the experience; primary problems were eliciting parental cooperation, and helping group leaders learn to cope with the anxiety siblings had about talking about their retarded brothers and sisters. Combining volunteer activities at a center for retarded children with group discussions served as a stepping stone toward overcoming the siblings' reluctance to discuss mental retardation. As the meetings progressed, participants became increasingly more comfortable about sharing their problems. Among the major concerns raised by participants were worries about their own normality; how their siblings felt about being retarded; how to respond to the behaviors their sibling demonstrated; what to do about the negative reactions of community members including neighbors, classmates and friends; and how to talk to their parents about mental retardation. The later concern apparently evoked an anxious response on the part of the siblings and parents akin to discussions about sex.

EFFECT OF NORMAL SIBLINGS ON A HANDICAPPED BROTHER OR SISTER

Much of the research which has been done on sibling relationships has focused on the effect handicapped siblings have on their brothers and sisters, but, in turn, brothers and sisters may also have an effect on their handicapped sibling. Unfortunately there are very few reports about what these effects might be.

Handicapped siblings can learn a great deal as a result of modeling their nonhandicapped brothers and sisters (Lavine, 1977). However, most of the documentation available has to do with the efficacy of training siblings as helpers or therapists to help in the home management of their handicapped sibling. For example, Weinrott (1974) trained older brothers and sisters to use behavior modification to increase the positive behaviors of their handicapped sibling. In another study (Lavigueur, 1976), siblings functioned as co-therapists with parents in a behavioral management program designed to decrease the disruptive behaviors of a sibling. Future research must be directed toward understanding not only what effects normal siblings can have on handicapped siblings, but must also include a focus on how training the nonhandicapped sibling as helpers may alleviate some of the stresses noted in families of handicapped children. Furthermore, such involvement may help to diminish some of the concerns nonhandicapped siblings have expressed.

Another major question has to do with the feelings nonhandicapped siblings engender in their handicapped brothers and sisters by virtue of their normality. This may well be the least researched topic in the area of sibling studies. One of the few investigations in this area was undertaken by Pfouts (1976), who compared the interactions of pairs of brothers with different personality and IQ test scores. Results indicated that when brothers differed in personality or intellectual ability, the low scorer demonstrated hostile feelings toward his more able brother; whereas the more intellectually able, well adjusted brother was ambivalent toward his less endowed sibling. Pfouts concluded that ". . . although the problems of the less adequate child do not cause his sibs to feel personally threatened and hostile toward him, the insidious comparisons he must endure give rise to feelings of low self-esteem and resentment of the more able children in the family" (p. 203). Einstein and Moss (1967) identified several dimensions of sibling relationships. Siblings may (1) develop a very close and caring or distant and indifferent relationship; (2) choose to model each other to try to be different; (3) depend upon each other or strive for independence; (4) support each other or be critical; (5) demonstrate jealousy (more likely toward younger siblings) or rivalry (more likely toward older siblings); (6) feel more or less superior or inferior toward each other; (7) support or devalue each other; (8) share in doing things together, dividing resources or refuse to share; (9) experience a reduction of sexual tensions as a result of observation and experimentation with each other; and (1) form alliances against parents, peers, or outsiders to defend themselves. Einstein and Moss pointed out that these areas of attitude and behavior should be observed and described by family counselors because of their importance in understanding the dynamics of the family. It is the author's suggestion that these factors be explored from the perspective of the handicapped as well as the nonhandicapped child.

SUMMARY

The experience of having a handicapped child can be devastating for parents. Negative parental responses have been documented for the mildly, as well as moderately, and severely, disabled; but it would not be accurate to characterize parents of the handicapped as rejecting of their child. Parents are not uniformly affected, and their attitudes may vary according to the severity of their child's handicap, the social acceptability of the handicap, and their socioeconomic status; the sex and age of the child may also influence parental attitudes. Some parents' attitudes are influenced by their religious beliefs as well.

At the same time professionals should be aware of the many potential problems associated with having a handicapped child. Not only can marriages dissolve as a result of the tension that may develop in a family, but parents must learn how to cope with different kinds of day-to-day hardships that may be imposed on them as a result of parenting a handicapped child. Among these are possible isolation from extended family members, friends, and community members; parents may become physically exhausted as a result of meeting the needs of their handicapped child and might find taking a vacation impossible not only because of financial hardships related to meeting the needs of the handicapped child; but they might also find it difficult to find someone to care for the child.

Professional counseling for parents of handicapped children may be necessary to help them learn to accept their child and deal positively with their child's individual needs.

Mainstreaming is a new approach for educating children who are handicapped. Parents may need professional guidance to understand this legislation; furthermore, they may need guidance to take advantage of the opportunity the legislation affords them for becoming involved with their child's educational experience. Parents may also need to learn how to relate to professionals, and, in turn professionals to parents.

Siblings of handicapped children may be an "at risk" population. Possibly the nonhandicapped child's feelings of negativity toward a handicapped sibling may contribute to guilt, which may result in emotional or behavioral problems. Unfortunately the social, emotional, and psychological status of siblings of handicapped individuals has been somewhat neglected by researchers as well as clinicians.

Extant research on handicapped children and their families has focused primarily on parental attitudes, and usually the mother's attitudes toward their handicapped child have been studied. A second area of emphasis in the literature has been to investigate the effects the handicapped child has on parents. Questions that have not been answered include information about: attitudes fathers have toward parenting a handicapped child; the feelings the handicapped child has about his/her relationship with family members; and, the effect family variables such as family size, sibling birth order, child gender, age, socioeconomic status, and severity of a child's handicap have on the attitudes of family members. Urgently needed is a better understanding of handicapped and nonhandicapped sibling interactions. Finally, it is important that therapeutic programs be designed for siblings of handicapped children to respond to their concerns related to having a handicapped sister or brother.

REFERENCES

Abramson, M., Willson, V., Yoshida, R. K., & Hagerty, G. (1983). Parents' perceptions of their learning disabled child's educational performance. *Learning Disability Quarterly 6*, 184–194.

Ackerman, P. T., Elardo, P. T., & Dykman, R. A. (1979). A psychosocial study of hyperactive and learning-disabled boys. *Journal of Abnormal Child Psychology, 7*, 91–99.

Adubato, S. A., Adams, M. K., & Budd, K. S. (1981). Teaching a parent to train a spouse in child management techniques. *Journal of Applied Behavior Analysis, 14*, 193–205.

Atkeson, B. M., & Forehand, R. (1979). Home-based reinforcement programs designed to modify classroom behavior: A review and methodological evaluation. *Psychological Bulletin, 86*, 1298–1308.

Ausubel, D. P., Balthazar, E. E., Rosenthal, I., Blackman, L. S., Schpoont, S. H., & Welkowitz, J.

(1954). Perceived parent attitudes as determinants of children's ego structure. *Child Development, 25,* 173–183.

Banta, E. M. (1979). Siblings of deaf-blind children. *Volta Review, 81,* 363–369.

Barclay, A., & Vought, G. (1964). Material estimates of future achievement in cerebral palsied children. *American Journal of Mental Deficiency, 69,* 62–65.

Barth, R. (1979). Home-based reinforcement of school behavior: A review and analysis. *Review of Educational Research, 49,* 436–458.

Bentovim, A. (1972). Emotional disturbances of handicapped pre-school children and their families—attitudes to the child. *British Medical Journal, 3,* 579–581.

Bernal, M. E., & North, J. A. (1978). A survey of parent training manuals. *Journal of Applied Behavior Analysis, 11,* 533–544.

Boersma, F. J., & Chapman, J. W. (1982). Teachers' and mothers' academic achievement expectations for learning disabled children. *Journal of School Psychology, 20,* 216–221.

Boles, G. (1959). Personality factors in mothers of cerebral palsied children. *Genetic Psychology Monograph, 59,* 159–218.

Boyd, D. (1951). The three stages in the growth of a parent of a mentally retarded child. *American Journal of Mental Deficiency, 55,* 608–611.

Breslau, N., Weitzman, M., & Messenger, K. (1981). Psychologic functioning of siblings of disabled children. *Pediatrics, 67,* 344–353.

Bricklin, P. M. (1970). Counseling parents of children with learning disabilities. *Reading Teacher, 23,* 333–338.

Bryan, T., Pearl, R., Zimmerman, D., & Matthews, F. (1982). Mothers' evaluations of their learning-disabled children. *Journal of Special Education, 16,* 149–159.

Bryant, J. E. (1971). Parent-child relationships: Their effect on rehabilitation. *Journal of Learning Disabilities, 4,* 325–329.

Chapman, J. W., & Boersma, F. J. (1979). Learning disabilities, locus of control, and mother attitudes. *Journal of Educational Psychology, 71,* 250–258.

Cleveland, D. W., & Miller, N. (1977). Attitudes and life commitments of older siblings of mentally retarded adults: An exploratory study. *Mental Retardation, 15,* 38–41.

Cook, J. J. (1963a). Dimensional analysis of child-rearing attitudes of parents of handicapped children. *American Journal of Mental Deficiency, 68,* 354–361.

Cook, J. J. (1963b). Family limitation subsequent to the birth of a cerebral palsied child. *Cerebral Palsy Review, 24,* 8–9.

Cummings, S. T. (1976). The impact of the child's deficiency on the father: A study of fathers of mentally retarded and of chronically ill children. *American Journal of Orthopsychiatry, 46,* 246–255.

Davis, R. E. (1975). Family of physically disabled child. *New York State Journal of Medicine, 75,* 1039–1041.

DeMyer, M. K. (1979). *Parents and Children in Autism.* New York: Wiley.

Doleys, D. M., Cartelli, L. M., & Doster, J. (1976). Comparison of patterns of mother-child interactions. *Journal of Learning Disabilities, 9,* 371–376.

Downey, K. J. (1963). Parental interest in the institutionalized severely mentally retarded child. *Social Problems, 11,* 186–193.

Drotar, D., Baskiewicz, A., Irwin, N., Kennell, J., & Klaus, M. (1975). The adaptation of parents to the birth of an infant with a congenital malformation: A hypothetical model. *Pediatrics, 56,* 710–717.

Einstein, G., & Moss, M. S. (1967). Some thoughts on sibling relationships. *Social Casework, 48,* 549–555.

Farber, B. (1959). Effects of a severely mentally retarded child on family integration. *Monographs of the Society for Research in Child Development, 24,* No. 2. Serial No. 71.

Farber, B. (1960). Perceptions of crisis and related variables in the impact of a retarded child on the mother. *Journal of Health and Human Behavior, 1,* 108–118.

Farber, B. (1963). Interaction with retarded siblings and life goals of children. *Marriage and Family Living, 25,* 96–98.

Federal Register, January 19, 1981. Washington, D.C.: U.S. Government Printing House.

Fotheringham, J. B., & Creal, D. (1974). Handicapped children and handicapped families. *International Review of Education, 20,* 355–373.

Freeman, R. D., Malkin, S. F., & Hastings, J. O. (1975). Psychosocial problems of deaf children and their families: A comparative study. *American Annals of the Deaf, 120,* 391–405.

Freeston, B. M. (1971). An enquiry into the effect of a spina bifida child upon family life. *Developmental Medicine and Child Neurology, 13,* 456–461.

Gallagher, J. J. (1956). Rejecting parents. *Exceptional Children, 22,* 273–276, 294.

Gallagher, J. J., Beckman, P., & Cross, A. H. (1983). Families of handicapped children: Sources of stress and its amelioration. *Exceptional Children, 50,* 10–19.

Gargiulo, R. M., & Warniment, J. (1976). A parents' perspective of learning disabilities. *Academic Therapy, 9,* 473–480.

Gath, A. (1972). The mental health of siblings of congenitally abnormal children. *Journal of Child Psychology and Psychiatry, 13,* 211–218.

Gath, A. (1973). The school-age siblings of mongol children. *British Journal of Psychiatry, 123,* 161–167.

Gath, A. (1974). Sibling reactions to mental handicap: A comparison of the brothers and sisters of mongol children. *Journal of Child Psychology and Psychiatry, 15,* 187–198.

Gath, A. (1977). The impact of an abnormal child upon the parents. *British Journal of Psychiatry, 130,* 405–410.

Gerber, G. L. (1976). Conflicts in values and attitudes between parents of symptomatic and normal children. *Psychological Reports, 38,* 91–98.

Gilliam, J. E., & Coleman, M. C. (1981). Who influences IEP committee decisions? *Exceptional Children, 47,* 642–644.

Goffman, E. (1963). *Stigma.* Englewood Cliffs, NJ: Prentice-Hall.

Goldman, M., & Barclay, A. (1974). Influence of maternal attitudes on children with reading disabilities. *Perceptual and Motor Skills, 38,* 303–307.

Goldstein, S., Strickland, B., Turnbull, A. P., & Curry, L. (1980). An observational analysis of the IEP conference. *Exceptional Children, 46,* 278–286.

Graliker, B. V., Fishler, K., & Koch, R. (1962). Teenage reaction to a mentally retarded sibling. *American Journal of Mental Deficiency, 66,* 838–843.

Grebler, A. M. (1951). Parental attitudes toward mentally retarded children. *American Journal of Mental Deficiency, 56,* 475–483.

Grossman, F. K. (1972). *Brothers and sisters of retarded children.* Syracuse, NY: Syracuse University Press.

Gumz, E. J., & Gubrium, J. F. (1972). Comparative parental perceptions of a mentally retarded child. *American Journal of Mental Deficiency, 77,* 175–180.

Hall, M. C., & Nelson, D. J. (1981). Responsive parenting: One approach for teaching single parents parenting skills. *School Psychology Review, 10,* 45–53.

Heifetz, L. J. (1977). Behavioral training for parents of retarded children: Alternative formats based on instrumental manuals. *American Journal of Mental Deficiency, 82,* 194–203.

Hiebert, B., Wong, B., & Hunter, M. (1982). Affective influences on learning disabled adolescents. *Learning Disability Quarterly, 5,* 334–343.

Hilliard, T., & Roth, R. M. (1969). Maternal attitudes and the non-achievement syndrome. *Personnel and Guidance Journal 47,* 424–428.

Hoff, M. K., Fenton, K. S., Yoshida, R. K., & Kaufman, M. J. (1978). Notice and consent: The school's responsibility to inform parents. *The Journal of School Psychology, 16,* 265–273.

Holland, N. (1969). *The dynamics of literary response.* New York: Oxford Press.

Holt, K. S. (1958a). The home care of severely retarded children. *Pediatrics, 22,* 744–755.

Holt, K. S. (1958b). The influence of a retarded child on family limitation. *Journal of Mental Deficiency, 2,* 28–36.

Horne, M. D. (1983). Elementary classroom teacher attitudes toward mainstreaming. *The Exceptional Child, 30,* 93–98.

Humphries, T. W., & Bauman, E. (1980). Maternal child rearing attitudes associated with learning disabilities. *Journal of Learning Disabilities, 13,* 459–462.

Hurley, J. R. (1967). Parental malevolence and children's intelligence. *Journal of Consulting Psychology, 31,* 199–204.

Jenkins, S., Stephens, B., & Sternberg, L. (1980). The use of parents as parent trainers of handicapped children. *Education and Training of the Mentally Retarded, 15,* 256–263.

Jensen, G. D., & Kogan, K. L. (1962). Parental estimates of the future achievement of children with cerebral palsy. *Journal of Mental Deficiency Research, 6,* 56–64.

Kaplan, F., & Fox, E. (1968). Siblings of a retardate: An adolescent group experience. *Community Mental Health, 4,* 499–508.

Klebanoff, L. B. (1959). Parents of schizophrenic children. *American Journal of Orthopsychiatry, 29,* 445–454.

Klein, S. D. (1972a). Brother to sister, sister to brother: Interview with siblings of disabled children, Part I. *Exceptional Parent, 2,* 10–15.

Klein, S. D. (1972b). Brother to sister, sister to brother: Interview with siblings of disabled children, Part 2. *Exceptional Parent, 3,* 24–27.

Kogan, K. L., & Tyler, N. (1973). Mother-child interaction in young physically handicapped children. *American Journal of Mental Deficiency, 77,* 492–497.

Kolin, I. S., Scherzer, A. L., New, B., & Garfield, M. (1971). Studies of the school-age child with meningomyelocele: Social and emotional adaptation. *The Journal of Pediatrics, 78,* 1013–1019.

Laborde, P. R., & Seligman, M. (1983). Individual counseling with parents of handicapped children: Rationale and strategies. In M. Seligman (Ed.), *The family with a handicapped child: Understanding and treatment.* New York: Grune & Stratton.

Lairy, G. C., & Harrison-Covello, A. (1973). The blind child and his parents: Congenital visual defect and the repercussion of family attitudes on the early development of the child. *American Foundation for the Blind Research Bulletin,* Number 25, 1–17.

Lamb, M. E. (1983). Fathers of exceptional children. In M. Seligman (Ed.), *The family with a handicapped child: Understanding and treatment.* New York: Grune & Stratton.

Large, T. (1982). The effects of attitudes upon the blind: A reexamination. *Journal of Rehabilitation, 48,* 33–34, 45.

Lavigueur, H. (1976). The use of siblings as an adjunct to the behavioral treatment of children in the home with parents as therapists. *Behavior Therapy, 7,* 602–613.

Lavine, M. B. (1977). An exploratory study of the sibships of blind children. *Journal of Visual Impairment and Blindness, 71,* 102–107.

Lloyd- Bostock, S. (1976). Parents' experiences of official help and guidance in caring for a mentally handicapped child. *Child: Care, Health and Development, 2,* 325–338.

Long, O. G., & Moore, J. R. (1979). Parental expectations for their epileptic children. *Journal of Child Psychology and Psychiatry, 20,* 299–311.

Lonsdale, G. (1978). Family life with a handicapped child: The parents speak. *Child: Care Health and Development, 4,* 99–120.

MacKeith, R. (1973). The feelings and behaviour of parents of handicapped children. *Developmental Medicine and Child Neurology, 15,* 524–527.

Marcus, L. M. (1977). Patterns of coping in families of psychotic children. *American Journal of Orthopsychiatry, 47,* 388–399.

Marion, R. L. (1981). *Educators, parents, and exceptional children.* Rockville, MD: Aspen Systems Corp.

Marshall, N. R., Hegrenes, J. R., & Goldstein, S. (1973). Verbal interactions: Mothers and their retarded children vs. mothers and their nonretarded children. *American Journal of Mental Deficiency, 77,* 415–419.

Martin, P. (1975). Marital breakdown in families of patients with spina bifida cystica. *Developmental Medicine and Child Neurology, 17,* 757–764.

McAllister, R. J., Butler, E. W., & Lei, T. J. (1973). Patterns of social interaction among families of behaviorally retarded children. *Journal of Marriage and the Family, 35,* 93–100.

McAndrew, I. (1976). Children with a handicap and their families. *Child: Care, Health and Development, 2,* 213–237.

Meadow, K. P., & Meadow, L. (1971). Changing role perceptions for parents of handicapped children. *Exceptional Children, 38,* 21–27.

Meyerson, R. C. (1983). Family and parent group therapy. In M. Seligman (Ed.), *The family with a handicapped child: Understanding and treatment.* New York: Grune & Stratton.

Miller, E. A. (1958). Cerebral palsied children and their parents. *Exceptional Children, 24,* 298–302.

Mlynek, S., Hannah, M. E., & Hamlin, M. A. (1982). Mainstreaming: Parental perceptions. *Psychology in the Schools, 19,* 354–359.

Moll, K. L., & Darley, F. L. (1960). Attitudes of mothers of articulatory impaired and speech-retarded children. *Journal of Speech and Hearing Disorders, 25,* 377–384.

Mori, A. A. (1983). *Families of children with special needs: Early intervention techniques for the practitioner.* Rockville, MD: Aspen Systems Corp.

Mullins, J. B. (1983). The uses of bibliotherapy in counseling families confronted with handicaps. In M. Seligman (Ed.), *The family with a handicapped child: Understanding and treatment.* New York: Grune & Stratton.

Murphy, A. T. (1979a). The families of handicapped children: Context for disability. *Volta Review, 81,* 265–278.

Murphy, A. T. (1979b). Members of the family: Sisters, and brothers of handicapped children. *Volta Review, 81,* 352–362.

Murray, J. N., & Cornell, C. J. (1981). Parentalplegia. *Psychology in the Schools, 18,* 201–207.

Neuhaus, M. (1969). Parental attitudes and the emotional adjustment of deaf children. *Exceptional Children, 35,* 721–727.

O'Dell, S. (1974). Training parents in behavior modification: A review. *Psychological Bulletin, 81,* 418–433.

Olshansky, S. (1962). Chronic sorrow: A response to having a mentally defective child. *Social Casework, 43,* 190–193.

Paul, J. L., & Beckman-Bell, P. (1981). Parent perspectives. In J. L. Paul (Ed.), *Understanding and working with parents of children with special needs.* New York: Holt, Rinehart and Winston.

Pearl, R., & Bryan, T. (1982). Mothers' attributions for their learning disabled child's successes and failures. *Learning Disability Quarterly, 5,* 53–57.

Peck, J. R., & Stephens, W. B. (1960). A study of the relationship between the attitudes and behaviors of parents and that of their mentally defective child. *American Journal of Mental Deficiency, 64,* 839–844.

Pfouts, J. H. (1976). The sibling relationship: A forgotten dimension. *Social Work, 21,* 200–204.

Popp, C. E., Ingram, V., & Jordan, P. H. (1954). Helping parents understand their mentally handicapped child. *American Journal of Mental Deficiency, 58,* 530–534.

Price-Bonham, S., & Addison, S. (1978). Families and mentally retarded children: Emphasis on the father. *The Family Coordinator, 3,* 221–230.

Pumroy, D. K. September 1965. *A new approach to treating parent-child problems.* Paper presented at the meeting of the American Psychological Association, Chicago, IL.

Ricci, C. S. (1970). Analysis of child-rearing attitudes of mothers of retarded, emotionally disturbed, and normal children. *American Journal of Mental Deficiency, 74,* 756–761.

Richards, I. D., & McIntosh, H. T. (1973). Spina bifida survivors and their parents: A study of problems and services. *Developmental Medicine and Child Neurology, 15,* 292–304.

Samuels, L., & Chase, L. (1979). The well siblings of schizophrenics.*American Journal of Family Therapy, 7,* 24–35.

San Martino, M., & Newman, M. B. (1974). Siblings of retarded children: A population at risk. *Child Psychiatry and Human Development, 4,* 168–177.

Sawyer, H. W., & Sawyer, S. H. (1981). A teacher-parent communication training approach. *Exceptional Children, 47,* 305–306.

Scanlon, C. A., Arick, J., & Phelps, N. (1981). Participation in the development of the IEP: Parents' perspective. *Exceptional Children, 47,* 373–374.

Schaefer, E. S., & Bell, R. Q. (1958). Development of a parental attitude research instrument. *Child Development, 27,* 339–361.

Schonell, F. J., & Watts, B. H. (1956). A first survey of the effects of a subnormal child on the family unit. *American Journal of Mental Deficiency, 61,* 210–219.

Schreiber, M., & Feeley, M. (1965). Siblings of the retarded: A guided group experience. *Children, 12,* 221–225.

Schwirian, P. M. (1976). Effects of the presence of a hearing-impaired preschool child in the family on the behavior patterns of older "normal siblings." *American Annals of the Deaf, 121,* 373–380.

Seligman, M. (1983). Siblings of handicapped persons. In M. Seligman (Ed.), *The family with a handicapped child: Understanding and treatment.* New York: Grune & Stratton.

Sheare, E., & Kastenbaum, R. (1966). Mother-child interaction in cerebral palsy: Environmental and psychosocial obstacles to cognitive development. *Genetic Psychology Monographs, 73,* 255–335.

Shulman, J. L., & Stern, S. (1959). Parents' estimate of the intelligence of retarded children. *American Journal of Mental Deficiency, 63,* 696–698.

Simpson, R. L., & Poplin, M. S. (1981). Parents as agents of change. *School Psychology Review, 10,* 15–25.

Soffer, R. M. (1982). IEP decisions in which parents desire greater participation. *Education and Training of the Mentally Retarded, 17,* 67–70.

Spiker, D. (1982). Parent involvement in early intervention activities with their children with Down's Syndrome. *Education and Training of the Mentally Retarded, 17,* 24–29.

Stearns, S. E. (1981). Understanding the psychological adjustment of physically handicapped children in the classroom. *Children Today, 10,* 12–15.

Stone, M. M. (1948). Parental attitudes to retardation. *American Journal of Mental Deficiency, 53,* 363–372.

Tallman, I. (1965). Spousal role differentiation and the socialization of severely retarded children. *Journal of Marriage and the Family, 27,* 37–42.

Tew, B., & Laurence, K. M. (1973). Mothers, brothers and sisters of patients with spina bifida. *Developmental Medicine and Child Neurology, 15,* 69–76.

Tew, B. J., Laurence, K. M., Payne, H., & Rawnsley, K. (1977). Marital stability following the birth of a child with spina bifida. *British Journal of Psychiatry, 131,* 79–82.

Tew, B., Payne, H., Laurence, K. M., & Rawnsley, K. (1974). Psychological testing: Reactions of parents of physically handicapped and normal children. *Developmental Medicine and Child Neurology, 16,* 501–506.

Thorne, F. C., & Andrews, J. S. (1946). Unworthy parental attitudes toward mental defectives. *American Journal of Mental Deficiency, 3,* 411–418.

Thurston, J. R. (1960). Attitudes and emotional reactions of parents of institutionalized cerebral palsied, retarded patients. *American Journal of Mental Deficiency, 65,* 227–235.

Tolor, A., & Rafferty, W. (1963). The attitudes of mothers of hospitalized patients. *Journal of Nervous Mental Disorder, 136,* 76–81.

Turnbull, A. P., & Blacher-Dixon, J. (1980). Preschool mainstreaming: Impact on parents. In J. J. Gallagher (Ed.), *New directions for exceptional children*, pp. 25–46. San Francisco: Jossey-Bass.

Turnbull, A. P., & Leonard, J. (1981). Parent involvement in special education: Emerging advocacy roles. *School Psychology Review, 10*, 37–44.

Turnbull, A. P., & Turnbull, H. R. (1978). *Parents speak out: Views from the other side of the two-way mirror*. Columbus, Ohio: Charles E. Merrill.

Watson, R. L., & Midlarsky, E. (1979). Reactions of mothers with mentally retarded children: A social perspective. *Psychological Reports, 45*, 309–310.

Weinrott, M. R. (1974). A training program in behavior modification for siblings of the retarded. *American Journal of Orthopsychiatry, 44*, 362–375.

Wetter, J. (1972). Parent attitudes toward learning disability. *Exceptional Children, 38*, 490–491.

Witmer, H. L. (1933). Parental behavior as an index to the probably outcome of treatment in a child guidance clinic. *American Journal of Orthopsychiatry, 3*, 431–444.

Worchel, T. L., & Worchel, P. (1961). The parental concept of the mentally retarded child. *American Journal of Mental Deficiency, 65*, 782–788.

Yoshida, R. K., Fenton, K. S., Kaufman, M. J., & Maxwell, J. P. (1978). Parental involvement in the special education pupil planning process: The school's perspective. *Exceptional Children, 44*, 531–533.

Zuckerman, M., Barrett, B. H., & Bragiel, R. M. (1960). The parental attitudes of parents of child guidance cases: I. Comparisons with normals, investigations of socioeconomic and family constellation factors, and relations to parents' reactions to the clinics. *Child Development, 31*, 401–417.

Zuckerman, M., Oltean, M., & Monashkin, I. (1958). The parental attitudes of mothers of schizophrenics. *Journal of Consulting Psychology, 22*, 307–310.

Zuk, G. H. (1959a). Autistic disorders in parents of retarded children. *Journal of Consulting Psychology, 23*, 171–175.

Zuk, G. H. (1959b). The religious factor and role of guilt in parental acceptance of the retarded child. *American Journal of Mental Deficiency, 64*, 139–147.

Zuk, G. H., Miller, R. L., Bartram, J. B., & Kling, F. (1961). Maternal acceptance of retarded children: A questionnaire study of attitudes and religious background. *Child Development, 32*, 525–540.

8

Suggestions for Future Research

This chapter proposes some directions for future research related to professional, peer, and parental attitudes toward handicapped individuals and to the self-attitudes of handicapped persons. It also discusses mainstreaming, the importance of attitudes to the success or failure of placing handicapped students in regular classroom settings, and the possible effects of mainstreaming on nonhandicapped students.

Each section is followed by a set of research questions. It is not suggested that these questions can be answered as a result of any short term effort. Nor does their placement imply that questions raised in one section are not related to, or interactive with, questions related to other subtopics. The listings are hardly exhaustive. It is hoped that these questions will stimulate researchers and practitioners to work toward solutions—and to generate more research questions.

PROFESSIONAL ATTITUDES

There is considerable evidence that handicapped students are likely to experience attitudes of rejection from professionals in the school environment. As a beginning toward constructive intervention, two major areas for research and development can be identified: (1) teacher training in the affective domain; and (2) skill-related competencies. Each is discussed in the following paragraphs.

Affective Education for Professionals

It is unreasonable to expect professionals to experience positive feelings toward all their clients. But this does not preclude attempts to assist them in learning to deal with their feelings and emotions toward handicapped students. The data suggest the potential value of requiring affective training experiences. Unfortunately, such experiences are not routinely associated with either pre- or inservice programs. Despite its desirability, however, it is not clear what forms such endeavors should take.

Professionals also need to be assured by "authorities" or those responsible for their training that holding negative attitudes toward handicapped individuals does not discredit their professionalism. Rather, they need to understand that such negative attitudes are a societal reality, and that no one is immune from prejudice. As members of a majority group, they are socialized to a belief system for which they are not solely responsible. The important thing is that they can and should attempt to overcome many of their negative feelings. Similarly, those responsible for training professionals must also confront their own biases.

But is it idealistic to expect that professionals can become equally positive toward different disability groups? Can training make them as "comfortable" working with, for instance, blind and deaf persons as they are about interacting with physically handicapped individuals? Such questions are not usually raised in the literature. This is an untenable stance. It seems far more realistic to expect that professionals: (1) can be made aware of their attitudes toward different disability groups; (2) can be assisted in decreasing their social distance toward different disability groups (i.e. become more willing to test, teach, or interact with clients with different disabilities); and (3) can learn to monitor their interactions with disability groups, particularly those disability group members toward whom they experience increased feelings of rejection or negativity. It is also important for classroom teachers to understand that their own attitudes toward certain students may be responsible for, or at least contribute to, the status assigned handicapped students by peers.

Some Research Questions

Future research should seek to answer questions related to the development and maintenance of attitudes, as well as questions related to attitude modification. These research questions should include:

—Do negative professional attitudes fulfill any function? If so, which functions?

—What types of client behaviors and/or characteristics arouse the most negative attitudes, and how do these relate to professional characteristics such as their age, sex, and education?

—What psychological characteristics of professionals are related to their attitudes toward handicapped persons? How strong are the relationships?

—Is it possible to develop a psychological profiling procedure for determining the degree to which individuals differ in the modifiability of their attitudes toward handicapped individuals?

—What should be the content and format of affective education programs designed to help professionals overcome negative, fearful, or hostile attitudes toward persons with a handicap?

—What kinds of programs best help professionals develop an awareness of the negative behaviors they may be evidencing toward clients with differing handicaps.

—What is the feasibility of a mainstreaming procedure whereby teacher preferences toward disability groups are evaluated, and handicapped students are then placed with teachers who prefer working with the particular type of handicapped child.

Skill Related Competencies

A significant problem associated with "mainstreaming" is the lack of professional preparation in knowing how to deal with the needs of handicapped students. Indeed, negative attitudes may arise from the frustration of not having the necessary skills to work with children who have various kinds of disabilities. Thus, attitudinal changes may be promoted by providing professionals with needed skills. Crisci (1981), who reviewed the literature on the competencies needed by regular classroom teachers and special educators to work with handicapped students, concluded that: (1) preservice teacher education programs should be modified to prepare educators to work with handicapped students; (2) there is a considerable degree of similarity in the areas in which special and regular educators require training; (3) there is still much confusion about the relative importance of competencies; and (4) there are many problems associated with the methodology for service delivery and evaluation procedures. Other school personnel also need to learn more about working with mainstreamed handicapped students. School psychologists exhibit needs similar to those of teachers (Franzoni & Jones, 1981; Sullivan & McDaniel, 1982), and school administrators need training in the financial aspects of the mainstreaming legislation as well as in understanding the characteristics and needs of handicapped students (Crisci, 1981).

Inservice programs have been successful in helping teachers to be more effective managers of the behaviors manifested by emotionally disturbed and learning disabled mainstreamed children (Borg & Ascione, 1982). Presumably, the teachers can also become more effective in working with other handicapped groups when they are provided with training. However, just as there are many questions about the nature of preservice education, there is also a great deal of debate about the content, format, goals, and objectives of inservice education (Anderson, Fredericks, Baldwin, Dalke, & McDonnell, 1978; Johnson, 1981; Powers, 1983; Redden & Blackhurst, 1978).

Many of the competencies listed as being important for pre- and inservice education programs focus on skills related to assessment, behavior management, and teaching procedures for academic areas. Training in the attitudinal area is often overlooked (Zemanek & Lehrer, 1977). Yet professionals need skills related to attitude assessment, and they need to know what procedures might increase positive interactions among handicapped and nonhandicapped students.

Some Research Questions

Future research should comprehensively examine and clarify the professional skills essential for meeting the needs of handicapped students in the mainstream:

—Are there certain skills that are absolutely essential? Are some skills more important than others?

—Are some skills essential for working with all types of handicapped students or do the needed skills differ with the childrens' handicap?

—What skills are more or less important for different professionals (e.g., regular classroom teacher, special educator, school psychologist)?

—How can the competencies for working with handicapped students by different school professionals be structured to be more complimentary?

—How can pre- and inservice programs best be structured and delivered?

PEER ATTITUDES

The research clearly suggests that attitudes of nonhandicapped students toward handicapped classmates are a major stumbling block to successful mainstreaming. But it may be very difficult to increase the social status of handicapped children even though there are a variety of potentially effective methodologies for doing so (see Chapter 4). As Bonney (1971) pointed out:

1. The response of the members of a group toward any one individual in it are heavily determined by the expressed attitudes of high prestige members (or the significant others). This is a well established principle in sociometrics and social psychology.

2. The evaluation of anyone's ability performance in a group is very much affected by how this individual is regarded as a person. Interpersonal assessments color all other judgments.

3. Socialization is a two-edged sword—it cuts both positively and negatively. The more all the members of a group respond to each other, the greater the probability of stimulating both positive and negative attitudes toward particular individuals. John French demonstrated as early as 1941 that cohesive groups, as contrasted with loosely organized ones, are characterized not only by more we-feeling and interdependence but also by more frustrations and interpersonal aggressions. In otherwords, the more some low pupils interacted with the rest of their

classmates the more they aroused toward themselves both positive and negative evaluations. To know some people better is to dislike them more.

4. The worth of any contribution to a group is never determined on a specific basis but always in reference to the contributions of others. In Gestalt terms, the quality of a figure is strongly affected by the ground on which it occurs.

5. How the performance of any individual is perceived is heavily predetermined by a generalized perception of how this person is expected to perform. Much data from the psychology of perception supports this statement (p. 363).

Thus when a low status student performed in class or in some way contributed to the group Bonney found:

. . . he frequently had everything going against him. Pupils of high prestige would sometimes ignore or obviously reject his contribution, his poor personal acceptability throughout his group cast a negative halo over his efforts, sometimes he behaved in such ways that his greater visibility worked against him, quite often what he had to offer was below the quality-standard of his class, and he performed against a social atmosphere of derogating expectations (p. 363).

Bonney concluded that intensive efforts over a long period of time are necessary to change peer attitudes toward each other.

Bonney's conclusions reflected the classroom social status of nonhandicapped children; the low-social-status students had normal intelligence tests scores but were performing poorly on academic tasks. Handicapped children may not only demonstrate lower achievement but also may behave in a less socially acceptable manner. Furthermore, they may evidence a visible physical difference. Consequently, their status may be particularly difficult to alter. The difficulty of modifying peer attitudes toward handicapped students is compounded since: (1) even very young students demonstrate negative attitudes toward those with a handicap; (2) schools are a societal institution wherein students are socialized to the values of society; and (3) affective education is not assigned a high priority by classroom teachers. It is recommended that affective goals become an integral part of the curriculum and receive no less emphasis than cognitive goals. There is a marked need for classroom interventions stressing the awareness and acceptance of interpersonal differences.

Some Research Questions

There are many questions surrounding the issue of peer attitudes. Since many handicapped children are currently being educated in regular classrooms where they are likely to be experiencing attitudes of peer rejection, it is imperative that research be directed toward clarifying how to improve the social status of handicapped students within their regular classrooms:

—How can nonhandicapped classmates best be prepared to accept and interact with a handicapped student being mainstreamed into their class?

—How can the implementation of interventions stressing the awareness and acceptance of interpersonal differences be encouraged in classrooms?

—How can peer attitudes best be changed?

1. What kinds of social interactions among classroom groups best facilitate the development of positive attitudes?
2. How can the classroom physical setting be altered to facilitate positive attitudes and interactions among handicapped and nonhandicapped students?
3. What kinds of materials, activities, and apparatus might best stimulate positive classroom interactions among handicapped and nonhandicapped students?

—Which attitude change procedures are most effective for which nonhandicapped students?

—What should the duration be for attitude modification projects?

—Do attitudinal changes last over time?

Early Attitude Intervention

Preschool programs provide a good opportunity to foster positive attitudes toward handicapped persons because it is likely that attitudes toward handicapped individuals are most maleable during the formative stages. As noted in Chapter 5, the research generally indicates that by the time they finish kindergarten, students are beginning to show definite preferences for interacting with nonhandicapped peers. Consequently, experiences for preschool children should be designed to underscore a recognition and respect for individual differences among children. Furthermore, it seems that preschool programs should incorporate instructional procedures that would teach children about handicaps.

Some Research Questions

—What should be the nature of programs designed to develop positive attitudes toward handicapped persons among preschool children?

—What are the longitudinal effects of preschool attitude modification programs?

ASSISTANCE FOR PARENTS AND SIBLINGS

Educators and other professionals such as school psychologists, administrators, and speech pathologists must become more skilled in working with the parents of handicapped children. They must be able to give information to parents about their child's handicap and be able to help them understand and take advantage of the rights provided by Public Law 94-142. These professionals must also be cognizant of the problems created by having a handicapped child in the family. They must understand that no one is prepared to parent a handicapped child and that parents may express a range of feelings toward their child. Therefore professionals should be knowledgeable about ways in which they can assist parents in achieving an accepting attitude toward their child.

Professionals in public schools are not always aware of the numerous state and local human service agencies that provide support services to families of handicapped children. They need to become aware of these services and be able to assist families in gaining access to appropriate services.

In Chapter 7, siblings of the handicapped were referred to as an emotionally "at risk" population. Who takes responsibility for helping these children? Special services such as counseling groups for siblings of handicapped children are not a common practice in public school systems; perhaps they should be.

Some Research Questions

Among the many research questions related to parent and sibling attitudes toward a handicapped family member are those concerning the need for providing support services:

—What modifications should be made in professional training programs to help professionals respond more effectively to the needs of parents and siblings of handicapped students?

—What kinds of special programs and/or services should public school systems provide for parents and siblings of handicapped students?

ATTITUDES OF HANDICAPPED STUDENTS TOWARD THEMSELVES

Like other children, those with a handicap need to experience success. In their case, however, repeated failure experiences and/or being physically or emotionally different from their peers may make it even more important that the handicapped child have a positive school experience. This goal will not be easy to achieve because handicapped students may be distressed and discouraged by the low status position assigned them by their classmates. They also may be deeply hurt by their teacher's negative response to them and by their devaluation by parents and siblings. Such feelings may, in turn, reinforce their low self-esteem, and a vicious cycle is set in motion. Indeed, handicapped children may "give up" on themselves and become resigned to chronic failure from an intellectual, social as well as emotional standpoint.

To a considerable extent, research dealing with the attitudes of handicapped students has been confined to an appraisal of their self-concepts and to comparisons of the effects of regular- versus special-class placements on the self-attitudes of students with a handicap. Directions for future research should include an effort to learn how handicapped students feel about their educational experience and social interactions and what concerns they have related to their handicaps.

Some Research Questions

Numerous studies have explored the attitudes of the nonhandicapped toward handicapped persons; but there seems to be a dearth of research on the attitudes handicapped individuals possess toward themselves, professionals, peers, and family members:

—What kinds of preparatory experiences would be most profitable for the handicapped student about to be mainstreamed?

—What are the attitudes of handicapped students toward their educational placements?

—What is the relationship between the nature of the child's disability and his preference toward educational placements?

—What are the perceptions of handicapped students concerning their interactions with peers, professionals, parents, and community members? How do these perceptions relate to the nature of their disability?

—Are there particular concerns expressed by a given type of handicapped student?

—What procedures are effective in helping handicapped students cope with attitudes of rejection expressed toward them?

Training Students to Train Teachers

Some researchers, who have focused on the utility of behavioral methodologies, have demonstrated that students may be trained to use procedures to obtain positive attention and reinforcement from their teachers (Cantor & Gelfand, 1977; Polristock & Greer, 1977; Sherman & Cornier, 1974). One study (Morgan, Young, & Goldstein, 1983) dealt with behaviorally disordered students who were enrolled in special classes because of their aggressive and disruptive behavior and their inability to interact with teachers or peers. They were trained to modify the behaviors of the teachers in whose classes they were mainstreamed for part of the school day. Although the students were not able to modify the amount of praise and approval they received from regular-classroom teachers, they were able to increase the amount of help they received. Future research needs to be directed toward an examination of training methodologies that handicapped students might use to elicit more positive reactions from and interactions with teachers. The research to date is promising but still at an early stage.

Some Research Questions

Research needs to be directed toward identifying procedures whereby handicapped students may play a more active role in determining the nature of their interactions with nonhandicapped persons:

—What strategies might be used by those with a handicap to enhance their interactions with peers, family, and community members?

—Can students with different types of handicaps be taught strategies which will influence the attitudes of nonhandicapped persons toward them?

EVALUATING MAINSTREAMING

It has been approximately 10 years since legislation mandated the education of handicapped students in the least restrictive environment. Over this time period, varied investigations related to the efficacy of the mandate have been initiated. For example, some researchers have concentrated on studying the intellectual, social, or emotional outcomes for handicapped students. Others have been interested in the development or efficacy of different types of special education service delivery models. Although there is no conclusive evidence about the efficacy of mainstreaming, comprehensive reviews of the literature on mainstreaming effects suggest that handicapped children have profited in many ways from educational experiences in the regular classroom, but that a major problem is the negative attitudes nonhandicapped students demonstrate toward their handicapped classmates (Leinhardt & Pallay, 1982; Madden & Slavin, 1983). It seems that the success of mainstreaming may be in jeopardy unless the issue of attitudes is confronted. The development of programs to foster positive attitudes toward handicapped students on the part of professionals and peers must become a highly regarded pursuit.

Mainstreaming and the Nonhandicapped Student

To a great extent, investigations of the effects of mainstreaming on nonhandicapped students have been limited to the attitudinal component (e.g., the results of providing information and/or contact with handicapped persons). But we may have yet to discover other ways in which nonhandicapped students are influenced by interactions with handicapped students.

For example, Kennedy and Thurman (1982) conducted an experiment on student helping behaviors and found that nonhandicapped students were more likely to help handicapped peers than nonhandicapped peers. Kennedy & Thurman suggested that teachers need to monitor classroom helping behaviors so that dependent relationships (the handicapped upon the nonhandicapped) do not develop. On the other hand, it is possible that prosocial behaviors such as sharing, comforting, helping, and sympathizing among nonhandicapped children may be fostered as a result of interactions with handicapped students.

Another experiment (Luftig, 1983) found that viewing attempts to recall items by students who were labeled as "mentally retarded" and "nonretarded" affected the estimates students made of their own memory ability. After watching the "nonretarded student," the viewers made lower estimates of their ability; when they viewed "retarded" students, they increased their estimates. These findings suggest that nonhandicapped average or "slower learners" in the regular classroom might feel more confident about themselves and their abilities when they observe handicapped children. In turn, these positive self-assessments may contribute to more positive classroom performance.

Some Research Questions

Nonhandicapped students may profit from exposure to handicapped students in many as yet, unexplored ways:

—In what ways might nonhandicapped students profit from contact with handicapped students in these classes?

—What are the potential intellectual, social, or emotional outcomes for nonhandicapped students who are educated in classrooms with handicapped students?

SUMMARY

There are many unanswered questions important to understanding professional, peer, and parent attitudes toward the handicapped. We also do not know a great deal about the attitudes of the handicapped student. One hopes that research in the area of attitudes toward the handicapped will continue to gain momemtum and, in the process, also become more sophisticated.

REFERENCES

Anderson, R., Fredericks, H. D. B., Baldwin, V. L., Dalke, B., & McDonnell, J. J. (1978). A data based inservice training model for public school systems. *Education and Training of the Mentally Retarded, 13,* 224–228.

Bonney, M. E. (1971). Assessment of efforts to aid socially isolated elementary school pupils. *Journal of Educational Research, 64,* 359–364.

Borg, W. R., & Ascione, F. R. (1982). Classroom management in elementary mainstreaming classrooms. *Journal of Educational Psychology, 74,* 85–95.

Cantor, N. L., & Gelfand, D. M. (1977). Effects of responsiveness and sex of children on adults' behavior. *Child Development, 48,* 232–238.

Crisci, P. E. (1981). Competencies for mainstreaming: Problems and issues. *Education and Training of the Mentally Retarded, 16,* 175–182.

Franzoni, J. B., & Jones, R. W. (1981). Implications for school psychologists: The challenge of Public Law 94-142. *Professional Psychology, 12,* 356–362.

Johnson, A. B., (1981). Teacher's attitudes toward mainstreaming: Implications for inservice training and program modifications in early childhood. *Child Care Quarterly, 10,* 137–147.

Kennedy, A. B., & Thurman, S. K. (1982). Inclinations of nonhandicapped children to help their handicapped peers. *Journal of Special Education, 16,* 319–327.

Leinhardt, G., & Pallay, A. (1982). Restrictive educational settings: Exile or haven? *Review of Educational Research, 52,* 557–578.

Luftig, R. L. (1983). Effects of peer labeling on the metamnemonic estimates of mentally retarded and nonretarded children. *American Journal of Mental Deficiency, 87,* 522–527.

Madden, N. A., & Slavin, R. E. (1983). Mainstreaming students with mild handicaps: Academic and social outcomes. *Review of Educational Research, 53,* 519–569.

Morgan, D., Young, R., & Goldstein, S. (1983). Teaching behaviorally disordered students to increase teacher attention and praise in mainstreamed classrooms. *Behavioral Disorders, 8,* 265–273.

Polristock, S. R., & Greer, R. D. (1977). Remediation of mutually aversive interactions between a problem student and four teachers by training the student in reinforcement techniques. *Journal of Applied Behavior Analysis, 10,* 707–716.

Powers, D. A. (1983). Mainstreaming and the inservice education of teachers. *Exceptional Children, 49,* 432–439.

Redden, M. R., & Blackhurst, A. E. (1978). Mainstreaming competency specifications for elementary teachers. *Exceptional Children, 44,* 615–617.

Sherman, T. M., & Cornier, W. H. (1974). An investigation of the influence of student behavior on teacher behavior. *Journal of Applied Behavior Analysis, 7,* 11–21.

Sullivan, P. D., & McDaniel, E. A. (1982). Survey of special education coursework in school psychology training programs. *Exceptional Children, 48,* 541–543.

Zemanek, D. H., & Lehrer, B. E. (1977). The role of university departments of special education in mainstreaming. *Exceptional Children, 43,* 377–379.

Author Index

Subject Index

A

Academic Competence, 81–82
Achievement
  and expectations, 109–112
  and teacher attitudes, 122–124
  and peer attitudes, 81, 137
Activities Index, 54
Adjective Checklist, 37
Adjective checklist technique, 37–39
Adjustment
  and social status, 21
  of handicapped, 21
  of peers, 144–145
Affective education for professionals, 234
Age
  and parent attitudes, 203
  and sibling attitudes, 222
  of peers and attitudes, 143–144
  of teacher and attitudes, 133–134
Athletic ability
  and peer attitudes, 142
Attitude change
  of parents, 210–213
  of professionals, 156–163
  of peers, 163–185
  of siblings, 224–225
Attitude measurement, 26–54
  adjective checklists, 37–39
  behavioral observations, 45–46

interviews, 44
paired comparisons, 35
physiological reactions, 49–50
projective methods, 46–47
Q-sort technique, 32–35
questionnaires, 47–49
scales, 26–32, 50–54
semantic differential technique, 35–37
sociometric procedures, 39–44
some commonly used measures, 50–54
Attitude scales, 26–32
  Likert-type, 27–28
  Equal-appearing interval scales, 28–29
  Guttman scales, 31
  Rank order scales, 31–32
  Picture ranking procedures, 32
Attitude stability, 22–23, 185–186, 237–238
Attitude theories
  behavioral theories, 5
  cognitive dissonance theory, 8–11
  consistency theories, 7–8
  functional theory, 11–12
  information integration theory, 12
  Yale perspective, 6–7
Attitude Toward Disabled Persons Scale, 50–51
Attitudes
  and behavior, 3
  and mainstreaming, 19–20, 89–98
  and P. L. 94—142, 15–17